Applied English Phonology

Applied English Phonology

Mehmet Yavaş

Blackwell
Publishing

© 2006 by Mehmet Yavaş

BLACKWELL PUBLISHING
350 Main Street, Malden, MA 02148-5020, USA
9600 Garsington Road, Oxford OX4 2DQ, UK
550 Swanston Street, Carlton, Victoria 3053, Australia

First published 2006 by Blackwell Publishing Ltd

7   2010

Library of Congress Cataloging-in-Publication Data

Yavas, Mehmet
    Applied English phonology / Mehmet Yavaş.
        p. cm.
    Includes bibliographical references and index.
    ISBN: 978-1-4051-0871-3 (hardcover : alk. paper
    ISBN: 978-1-4051-0872-0 (pbk : alk. paper)   1. English language—Study and teaching—Foreign speakers.   2. English language — Phonology.   I. Title.

    PE1128.A2Y38 2005
    428′.0071 — dc22

                                                                                              2005010993

A catalogue record for this title is available from the British Library.

Set in 10/12.5 Palatino
by Graphicraft Ltd, Hong Kong
Printed and bound in Singapore
by C.O.S. Printers Pte Ltd

The publisher's policy is to use permanent paper from mills that operate a sustainable forestry policy, and which has been manufactured from pulp processed using acid-free and elementary chlorine-free practices. Furthermore, the publisher ensures that the text paper and cover board used have met acceptable environmental accreditation standards.

For further information on
Blackwell Publishing, visit our website:
www.blackwellpublishing.com

Contents

Preface

It has been widely recognized that professionals working in the field of remediation (teaching/therapy) of sound patterns need to have a good understanding of phonology in order to evaluate the productions of their clients (students/patients), which differ from the norm in a systematic fashion. The aim of this book is to provide material on the sound patterns of American English that is usable by students and professionals in the field of phonological remediation.

During my career, I have had several opportunities to work with individuals from applied fields such as TESOL and Communication Sciences and Disorders. My constant message to them has been that the more linguistic knowledge (phonology in this particular case) they have, the better remediators they can become. This has been based on the well-established principle that any attempt at remediation requires a detailed phonological profile of the client, and the ability to do this can only be gained via good familiarity with the normative sound patterns.

To provide a needed source for the applied fields, one needs to decide carefully the degree of sophistication of the material coming from a technical field such as linguistics. On the one hand, one wants to account for the patterns accurately with no distortions; on the other, one would like to make the material comprehensible and useful to practitioners in remediation. I aimed to strike such a balance with this book, and the greatest help I received in this respect has come from my several years of experience with students from applied fields.

I would like to thank my students who helped me by asking questions and making comments that made me think and rethink about the issues and answers and their relevance to the applied fields. I am also indebted to the reviewers for their comments on the earlier draft; these comments are deeply appreciated. I would like to thank my copy-editor Pandora Kerr Frost for her expert work on my typescript. Finally, sincere thanks are due to Emily Finlan for her assistance in preparing the manuscript and to Sarah Coleman and Ada Brunstein of Blackwell Publishing, who were extremely helpful at every stage of the completion of this text.

M.Y.

Note to the Instructor

The material presented in this book has been, partially or in its entirety, used effectively on different occasions. Instructors who work with a specific student body and/or certain time constraints often have to make adjustments in the inclusion or exclusion of the material found in the texts. There are three chapters that might deserve some comments in this respect. Firstly, chapter 8 ('Structural Factors in Second Language Phonology') may appear to be relevant only to the field of language teaching. However, the increasing participation of individuals from the field of Communication Disorders with respect to issues such as 'bilingual phonology' and 'accent reduction', makes this chapter very relevant to this field too. Secondly, to have a chapter on spectrographic analysis (chapter 5) may appear rather uncommon in a book like this, and it may be skipped depending on time constraints. The experience I have, however, has been very encouraging with respect to its inclusion. Students have repeatedly stated that it has added a valuable new dimension to their understanding of issues. Finally, chapter 9 ('Spelling and Pronunciation') may be of concern. I find the inclusion of this chapter useful, as it enhances the understanding of matches and mismatches between spelling and phonological patterns. As such, it may be read right after chapter 2, relating it to the discussion of Phonemics.

Finally, a few words in relation to the phonetic transcription are in order. I have put passages for phonetic transcription at the end of the chapters with the central theme of history and varieties of the English language. I am aware of the fact that these are not sufficient, and that students need more opportunities to feel comfortable with transcription. However, I did not want to inflate the number of pages in the sections on exercises, because the materials in this text can be, and indeed have always been, used very effectively together with a transcription workbook.

Phonetics

1.1 Introduction

Our aim in this book is to study the sound patterns of English. The understanding of phonological patterns cannot be done without the raw material, phonetics. In order to be able to come up with reliable phonological descriptions, we need to have accurate phonetic data. Thus, students and professionals who deal with the patterns of spoken language in various groups of speakers (linguists, speech therapists, language teachers) need a basic knowledge of phonetics.

Phonetics, which may be described as the study of the sounds of human language, can be approached from three different perspectives. *Articulatory phonetics* deals with the physiological mechanisms of speech production. *Acoustic phonetics* studies the physical properties of sound waves in the message. *Auditory phonetics* is concerned with the perception of speech by the hearer. The coverage in this book will be limited to the first two of these approaches. The exclusion of auditory phonetics is basically due to the practical concerns of the primary readership as well as the little information available about the workings of the brain and speech perception. In this chapter, we will look at the basics of speech production. Acoustic properties, in a limited form of spectrographic analysis, will be the subject of chapter 5.

1.2 Phonetic Transcription

Because we are constantly involved with reading and writing in our daily lives, we tend to be influenced by the orthography when making judgments about the sounds of words. After all, from kindergarten on, the written language has been an integral part of our lives. Thus, it is very common to think that the number of orthographic letters in a word is an accurate reflection of the number of sounds. Indeed, this is the case for many words. If we look at the words pan, form, print, and spirit, for example, we can see the match in the number of letters (graphemes) and the sounds: three, four, five, and six, respectively. However, this match in number of graphemes and sounds is violated in so many other words. For example, both _though_ and _choose_ have six graphemes but only three sounds. _Awesome_ has seven graphemes and four sounds, while _knowledge_ has nine graphemes and five sounds. This list of non-matches can easily be extended to thousands of other words. These violations, which may be due to 'silent letters' or a sound being represented by a combination of letters, are not the only problem with respect to the inadequacies of orthography in its ability to represent the spoken language. Problems exist even if the number of letters and sounds match. We can outline the discrepancies that exist between the spelling and sounds in the following.

(a) _Same sound is represented by different letters._ In words such as _each, bleed, either, achieve, scene, busy_, we have the same vowel sound represented by different letters, which are underlined. This is not unique to vowels and can be verified with consonants, as in _shop, ocean, machine, sure, conscience, mission, nation_.

(b) _Same letter may represent different sounds._ The letter _a_ in words such as _gate, any, father, above, tall_ stands for different sounds. To give an example of a consonantal letter for the same phenomenon, we can look at the letter _s_, which stands for different sounds in each of the following: _sugar, vision, sale, resume_.

(c) _One sound is represented by a combination of letters._ The underlined portions in each of the following words represent a single sound: _thin, rough, attempt, pharmacy_.

(d) _A single letter may represent more than one sound._ This can be seen in the _x_ of _exit_, the _u_ of _union_, and the _h_ of _human_.

One or more of the above are responsible for the discrepancies between spelling and sounds, and may result in multiple homophones such as _rite, right, write_, and _wright_. The lack of consistent relationships between letters and sounds is quite expected if we consider that the alphabet English uses tries to cope with more than forty sounds with its limited twenty-six letters. Since letters can only tell about spelling and cannot be used as reliable tools for pronunciation, the first rule in studying phonetics and phonology is to _ignore spelling_ and _focus only on the sounds_ of utterances.

   To avoid the ambiguities created by the regular orthography and achieve a system that can represent sounds unambiguously, professionals who deal with language (linguists, speech therapists, language teachers, etc.) use a phonetic alphabet that is guided by the principle of a consistent one-to-one relationship between each phonetic symbol and the sound it represents. Over time, several phonetic alphabets have been devised. Probably, the most widespread is the one known as the _International Phonetic Alphabet_ (IPA), which was developed in 1888, and has been revised since then. One may encounter some modifications of some symbols in books written by American scholars. In this book, we will basically follow the IPA usage while pointing out common alternatives that are frequently found in the literature. First, we will present the symbols that are relevant for American English (see table 1.1) and later in the chapter

Table 1.1 English consonant and vowel symbols with key words

Phonetic symbol	Word positions		
	Initial	Medial	Final
Consonants			
p	*p*ack	su*p*er	ma*p*
b	*b*ed	ru*bb*er	ro*b*
t	*t*ea	a*tt*ack	grea*t*
d	*d*ate	a*d*ore	goo*d*
k	*c*atch	pi*ck*ing	loo*k*
g	*g*ate	do*gg*y	ba*g*
f	*f*at	co*ff*ee	loa*f*
v	*v*ery	mo*v*ing	do*v*e
θ	*th*in	ru*th*less	dea*th*
ð	*th*ey	mo*th*er	brea*th*e
s	*s*ad	si*s*ter	bu*s*
z	*z*oom	rai*s*in	bu*zz*
ʃ (š)	*sh*ine	ma*ch*ine	ca*sh*
ʒ (ž)	—	vi*s*ion	massa*g*e
h	*h*ead	be*h*ind	—
tʃ (č)	*ch*air	tea*ch*er	whi*ch*
dʒ (ǰ)	*j*ump	lar*g*er	hu*g*e
m	*m*ail	re*m*ind	roo*m*
n	*n*est	te*n*or	bea*n*
ŋ	—	a*ng*er	ki*ng*
j (y)	*y*ard	be*y*ond	so*y*
w	*w*ay	re*w*ind	lo*w*
ɹ (r, ɻ)	*r*ain	bo*r*ing	fou*r*
l	*l*ight	bu*ll*et	mai*l*
Vowels and diphthongs			
i (ij, iy)	*ea*se	f*ee*t	b*ee*
ɪ	*i*t	s*i*t	—
e (ej, ei, ey)	*ei*ght	b*a*ke	s*ay*
ɛ	*e*dge	r*e*d	—
æ	*a*nger	n*a*p	—
ʌ	*o*ven	lo*v*e	—
ə	*a*bove	oft*e*n	Tamp*a*
ɑ	*a*rch	f*a*ther	sp*a*
ɔ	*a*ll	h*a*ll	s*aw*
o (ow, oʊ)	*o*at	g*o*at	b*ow*
ʊ	—	b*oo*k	—
u (uw)	*oo*ze	l*oo*se	tw*o*
aɪ (aj, ay)	*i*ce	s*i*de	b*uy*
ɔɪ (ɔj, ɔy, oɪ, oj, oy)	*oi*l	v*oi*ce	b*oy*
aʊ (au, aw)	*ou*t	s*ou*nd	h*ow*

we will add some non-English sounds that are found in languages that our readership is likely to come in contact with. The dialectal variations, since they are examined in detail in chapters 3 and 4, will not be dealt with here.

The following should be pointed out to clarify some points about table 1. Firstly, certain positions that are left blank for certain sounds indicate the unavailability of vocabulary items in the language. Secondly, the table does not contain the symbol [ʍ] (or [hw], [w̥]), which may be found in some other books to indicate the voiceless version of the labio-velar glide. This is used to distinguish between pairs such as <u>witch</u> and <u>which</u>, or <u>Wales</u> and <u>whales</u>. Some speakers make a distinction by employing the voiceless glide for the second members in these pairs; others pronounce these words homophonously. Here, we follow the latter pattern. Finally, there is considerable overlap between final /j/ and the ending portion of /i/, /e/, /aɪ/, and /ɔɪ/ on the one hand, and between final /w/ and /o/, /u/, and /aʊ/ on the other. The alternative symbols cited make these relationships rather clear, and this point will be taken up in chapter 4.

1.3 Description and Articulation of Sounds of English

1.3.1 The vocal tract

Our examination of how sounds are made will begin with the vocal organs. The air we use in sound production comes from the lungs, proceeds through the larynx where the vocal cords are situated, and then it is shaped into specific sounds at the vocal tract. In sound production, it is generally the case that the articulators from the lower surface of the vocal tract (lower articulators, i.e. the lower lip, the lower teeth, and the tongue) move toward those that form the upper surface (upper articulators, i.e. the upper lip, the upper teeth, the upper surface of the mouth, and the pharyngeal wall). Figure 1.1 shows the vocal tract.

Starting from the outer extreme, we have the lips and the teeth. In the upper surface, behind the upper teeth, there is a bumpy area (alveolar ridge), which is followed by a larger bony area (hard palate). Further back is a flaccid area, the 'soft palate' (or 'velum') which is unsupported by bone. The soft palate is a movable organ, which opens and closes the velopharyngeal passage (the passage that links the pharynx to the nasal cavity). Finally, at the back, the velum narrows to a long, thin pointed structure that is called the 'uvula'.

In the lower part of the mouth, after the lower lip and the teeth, lies the tongue. The 'tip' (or 'apex') of the tongue is the foremost part. Just behind the tip is the small surface called the 'blade' (or 'lamina'). The so-called 'front' part of the tongue is the area between tip/blade and the center. The hindmost part of the horizontal surface of the tongue is called the 'back' (or 'dorsum'). At the end of the tongue, we have the 'root', which is the vertical surface against the pharyngeal wall. Finally, we have the 'epiglottis', which is a leaf-shaped cartilage that sticks up and back from the larynx.

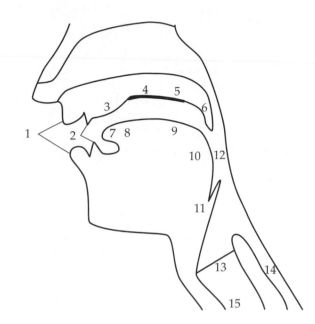

1 Lips
2 Teeth
3 Alveolar ridge
4 Hard palate
5 Soft palate (velum)
6 Uvula
7 Tip of the tongue
8 Front of the tongue
9 Back of the tongue
10 Root of the tongue
11 Epiglottis
12 Pharynx
13 Larynx
14 Esophagus
15 Trachea

Figure 1.1 The vocal tract

1.3.2 Voicing

The larynx, which sits on top of the trachea, is composed of cartilages held together by ligaments. It houses the vocal cords, which lie horizontally just behind the Adam's apple (see figure 1.2). The space between the vocal cords, which is known as the 'glottis', assumes different configurations for sounds known as 'voiced' and 'voiceless'. When the cords are apart (open), the air passes freely through the glottis. Sounds made with such a configuration of the glottis are called 'voiceless' (see figure 1.3).

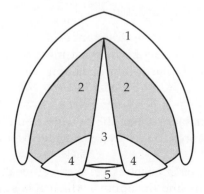

1 Thyroid cartilage
2 Vocal cords
3 Glottis
4 Arytenoid cartilages
5 Cricoid cartilage

Figure 1.2 View of larynx, looking down

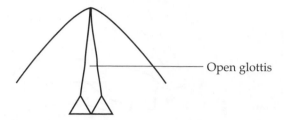

Figure 1.3 Configuration for voiceless sounds

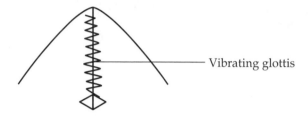

Figure 1.4 Configuration for voiced sounds

If, on the other hand, the vocal cords are brought together, the air passing through creates vibration, and the resulting sounds are 'voiced' (see figure 1.4). It is important to point out that the cord vibration is not a muscular action. When the cords are brought close to one another, the passing air creates a suction effect (Bernoulli principle), and the cords are brought together. As soon as the cords are together, there is no suction effect and the cords move apart. As soon as they are apart the suction is reinitiated, and the cycle repeats itself.

One can easily feel the difference between certain voiced and voiceless sounds. If you pronounce the initial sounds of the word pairs 'sip'–'zip' and 'cheap'–'jeep' and place your index finger on your Adam's apple or place your index fingers in both ears, you could feel the buzz created by the voicing of /z/ and /dʒ/; this effect will not be present in their voiceless counterparts /s/ and /tʃ/.

1.3.3 Places of articulation

The place of articulation of a consonant is the description of where the consonantal obstruction occurs in the vocal tract by the placement of the tongue or by lip configurations. Below are the places of articulation relevant for the consonants of English.

- **Bilabial:** In the production of bilabial sounds the two lips come together. The initial consonants of the words pay, bay, and may exemplify the English bilabials /p, b, m/.
- **Labiodental:** Labiodental sounds of English, /f, v/ (e.g. feel, veal), involve a constriction between the lower lip and the upper teeth. Bilabials and labiodentals together are called 'labials'.

- **Interdental:** /θ/ and /ð/ sounds of English (e.g. thin, that) are made by placing the tip or blade of the tongue between the upper and lower front teeth. For some speakers, the tongue tip/blade just barely touches behind the upper teeth (thus, the term 'dental' used instead in some manuals).
- **Alveolar:** When the active articulator, the tongue tip or blade, goes against the alveolar ridge, we have an alveolar sound. The initial consonants of the words tip, dip, sip, zip, nip, lip exemplify the English alveolars /t, d, s, z, n, l/ respectively.
- **Palato-alveolar:** In the production of palato-alveolar sounds of English, /ʃ, ʒ, tʃ, dʒ/ (exemplified by the final consonants of fish, garage, rich, ridge, respectively), the blade of the tongue moves towards the back of the alveolar ridge (approximates in the case of /ʃ, ʒ/ and touches in the case of /tʃ, dʒ/).
- **Retroflex:** Retroflex sounds are made by curling the tip of the tongue up and back towards the back of the alveolar ridge. The only retroflex in American English is the r-sound (/ɹ/). Although both in retroflex sounds and in palato-alveolars the constriction is at the back of the alveolar ridge, these two groups are not identical; the former is 'apical' (with the tip of the tongue), and the latter is said to be 'laminal' (with the blade of the tongue. It should also be noted that not all speakers use the retroflex r-sound; many speakers have a 'bunched' r-sound by raising the blade of the tongue with the tip turned down.
- **Palatal:** /j/, as in yes, is the only palatal sound of English, which is made with the front of the tongue articulating against the hard palate.
- **Velar:** In the production of English velars, /k, g, ŋ/, exemplified by the final sounds of back, bag, sing, respectively, the back of the tongue articulates against the velum (soft palate).
- **Glottal:** These are sounds formed at the glottis, which include /h/ (e.g. home), and the glottal stop /ʔ/.
- **Labio-velar:** The sound /w/ (e.g. we) is the only consonant that has two places of articulation. In the production of this sound, the lips are rounded (thus, 'labial'), while at the same time the back of the tongue is raised toward the velum (thus, 'velar'). As a result, we place the symbol both in bilabial and velar places and call the sound 'labio-velar'.

1.3.4 Manners of articulation

The manner of articulation of a sound is the degree and the kind of obstruction of a consonant in the vocal tract. For example, if we compare the first sounds of the words tip and sip, we realize that the airflow is obstructed in the same area (alveolar), and in both sounds, /t/ and /s/, the configuration of the vocal cords is the same (voiceless). The difference between the two sounds lies in the type of obstruction of the airflow. While in /t/ we stop the air completely before the release, we simply obstruct (not stop) the airflow with a narrowing created by the articulators in /s/.

- **Stop:** A stop consonant involves a complete closure of the articulators and thus total blockage of airflow. The stops found in English are /p, b, t, d, k, g/.
- **Fricative:** A fricative is a sound that is made with a small opening between the articulators, allowing the air to escape with audible friction. In English /f, v, θ, ð, s, z, ʃ, ʒ, h/ are the fricative sounds. The common denominator of fricatives is partial airflow with a friction noise. Some manuals, adhering strictly to the requirement of turbulent airstream, do not consider /h/ as a fricative. A subgroup of fricatives (alveolars and palato-alveolars), which are more intense and have greater amounts of acoustic energy at higher frequencies, are known as 'sibilants'.
- **Affricate:** In a stop sound, the release of the closure is quick and abrupt; however, in sounds where the closure release is gradual, it creates friction. Such sounds are called affricates. In other words, affricates start like stops (complete closure), and end like fricatives. Both affricates of English, /tʃ, dʒ/, are produced in palato-alveolar place of articulation. The symbols used for these sounds reveal the combination of stops /t/, /d/ with the fricatives /ʃ/, /ʒ/, respectively. An important point to remember is their one-unit (inseparable) status. Unlike consonant clusters (e.g. /sk/, /pl/), which are made up of two separable phonological units, affricates always behave like one unit. For example, in a speech error such as key chain /ki tʃen/ becoming /tʃi ken/, the affricate /tʃ/ is interchanged with a single segment /k/; clusters, on the other hand, are separated in a comparable situation, as illustrated in scotch tape /skʌtʃ tep/ becoming /kʌtʃ step/ and not /tʌtʃ skep/ (see section 3.3 for more on this). Since affricates /tʃ/ and /dʒ/ contain sibilant fricatives in them (/ʃ/, /ʒ/, respectively), they are also sibilants. Stops, fricatives, and affricates, which are produced by a considerable amount of obstruction of the laryngeal airstream in the vocal tract, are collectively known as 'obstruents'.
- **Approximant:** Approximants are consonants with a greater opening in the vocal tract than fricatives, and thus do not create any friction. Identifying a sound as an approximant or a fricative includes acoustic/auditory and aerodynamic considerations as well as articulatory factors. Catford (1977) states that the typical cross-sectional areas of the maximum constriction in a fricative range about 3 to 20 mm^2, while it is greater than 20 mm^2 in an approximant. The sounds /l, ɹ, j, w/ (initial consonants of lay, ray, yes, and week) are the approximants of English. Both fricatives and approximants, because they let the airflow continue in the production, are called 'continuants'. Two of the English approximants, /l, ɹ/, are 'liquids', vowel-like consonants in which voicing energy passes through a vocal tract with a constriction greater than that of vowels. The liquid /l/, which is called the 'lateral' liquid, is produced with the tongue tip creating a closure with the alveolar ridge while maintaining an opening at the sides of the tongue where the air escapes. The non-lateral approximant, /ɹ/, which is described earlier in relation to retroflex place of articulation and is also known as the 'rhotic', will not be repeated here.

Table 1.2 Consonants of English

	Bilabial	Labio-dental	Inter-dental	Alveolar	Retroflex	Palato-alveolar	Palatal	Velar	Glottal
Stop	p b			t d				k g	
Fricative		f v	θ ð	s z		ʃ ʒ			h
Affricate						tʃ dʒ			
Nasal	m			n				ŋ	
Liquid				l	ɹ				
Glide	w						j	w	

The remaining two approximants, /j/ and /w/, are known as 'glides' (also 'semivowels' in some manuals). These are vowel-like sounds that function like consonants. In other words, /j/ is like the vowel /i/, and /w/ is like the vowel /u/ in production, while functioning like consonants, as they do not occupy the syllable nuclei and they always need a vowel to lean on.

• **Nasal:** If we compare the initial sounds of <u>beat</u> and <u>meat</u>, /b/ and /m/, we see that both sounds share the place of articulation (bilabial), and voicing (voiced). The difference between them lies in the velopharyngeal opening and the channels of the outgoing airflow. In the production of /m/, the velum is lowered and the velopharyngeal passage is open. Thus, upon release of the closure, the air goes out through the nasal cavity as well as through the oral cavity. In the production of /b/, on the other hand, the velum is raised and the passage is closed. Consequently, the only outlet for the airflow is the oral cavity. Sounds that are made with the former configuration, e.g. /m, n, ŋ/, are called nasals; the others are oral sounds.

Approximants (liquids and glides) and nasals, because they include a relatively unobstructed flow of air between the articulator and the place of articulation, collectively form the group of consonants that is known as 'sonorants'.

Table 1.2 shows the places and manners of articulation for English consonants. Whenever a cell has two consonants, the voiceless is placed to the left and the voiced is to the right.

1.3.5 Voice onset time

As stated earlier, a stop articulation consists of a closure formed by the two articulators followed by an abrupt release of this closure. In this section, we will look at the production of stop sounds and the timing of vocal cord

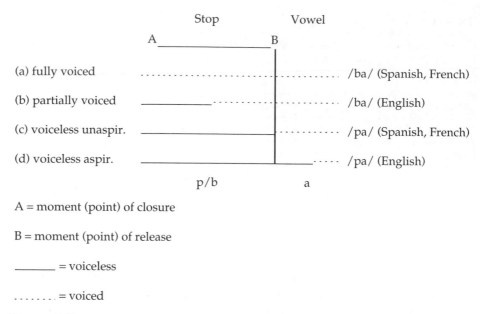

A = moment (point) of closure

B = moment (point) of release

_____ = voiceless

. . . . = voiced

Figure 1.5 VOT continuum

vibration which is relevant for voiced, voiceless, aspirated, and unaspirated distinctions. The differences for these various kinds of stops can be explained with the time difference between the release of the stop closure and the beginning of vocal cord vibration. This timing relationship is known as the 'voice onset time' (hereafter VOT). Figure 1.5 represents the different stop productions in the VOT continuum.

If the voicing starts before the release (i.e. during the closure period), as in the case of lines (a) and (b), then the situation is described as the 'voice lead' and given a negative VOT value (in milliseconds). Line (a) represents a fully voiced stop; we have the vocal cord vibration throughout the closure which continues after the release. The /b, d, g/ sounds of Romance languages are said to be typical examples of fully voiced stops.

Not all voiced stops are produced in this fashion. In some languages, English and other Germanic languages included, /b, d, g/ are subject to a certain amount of loss of voicing ('partially devoiced') during their production. Line (b) in figure 1.5 represents this configuration; the voicing starts some time into the closure stage and continues into the following vowel (the mirror image of this is seen in final voiced stops; these will be given in detail in chapter 3).

If, on the other hand, the voicing starts after the release of the stop closure, then it is said to have a 'voice lag' and is described with a positive VOT value (in milliseconds; ms). Cross-linguistically, the amount of the lag may be significant; while a lag greater than 30 ms results in stops that are called 'aspirated' (or 'long lag'), a shorter voice lag or voicing simultaneous with release results in stops that are known as 'unaspirated'. Lines (c) and (d) show these two possibilities. In neither case do we have vocal cord vibration during the stop closure (thus 'voiceless'). The difference between the two cases lies in the point at which the voicing starts with respect to the moment of release. In line (c), the vocal cord vibration is simultaneous with the stop release; the VOT is zero and we have a 'voiceless unaspirated stop'. The voiceless stops of Romance languages are given as examples for this.

In line (d) the lag is longer than the 30 ms threshold, and the resulting sound is a 'voiceless aspirated stop'. The diacritic used for aspiration is a small raised [ʰ] to the top right of the stop (e.g. [pʰ]). English initial [pʰ, tʰ, kʰ] sounds are produced in this way and we hear the resulting short burst before the buzz of voicing in the vowel. The degree of aspiration may be different in different languages. For example, while English voiceless stops are slightly aspirated, their counterparts in languages such as Mandarin, Thai, and Scots Gaelic are strongly aspirated.

In some languages (e.g. Hindi of India, Sindhi of Pakistan and India), the possibilities go beyond the three types of stops (voiced, voiceless unaspirated, voiceless aspirated) we discussed, by the addition of the so-called 'voiced aspirated stops'. These stops have, after the release of the stop closure, a period of breathy voice (murmur) before the regular voicing starts for the following segment. Thus we get the following four-way voicing distinction in Hindi.

[tal] 'beat'; [tʰal] 'plate'; [dal] 'lentil'; [dʰal] 'knife'

1.3.6 Vowels and diphthongs

When we examined consonants, we talked about the varying degrees of obstruction of the airflow in their production. As a general statement, we can say that the vocal tract is more open in vowels than in consonants. This, however, can be a tentative formulation, because as we saw in the discussion of glide/vowel separation, the consideration may be phonological and not phonetic.

For the characterization of vowels, we do not use the dimensions of place and manner of articulation, as there is no contact between the articulators. Instead, vowels are characterized by the position of the tongue and the lips. Since vowels are usually voiced, the voiced/voiceless distinction used for consonants is not relevant either.

If you examine the vowels of beat, bit, bait, bet, and bat in the order given, you will notice that your mouth opens gradually and the body of your tongue lowers gradually. A similar situation is observed if we go through the vowels of boot, book, boat, and bought; that is, gradual opening of the mouth and gradual lowering of the tongue. The difference between the two sets lies in the part of the tongue involved. While in the former set the front part of the tongue is involved (tongue pushed forward), the latter set focuses on the back of the tongue (tongue pulled back). The traditional type of chart used to plot vowel positions places the front vowels on the left, back vowels on the

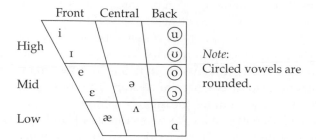

Figure 1.6 English vowels

right and the central vowels in the middle. There are height dimensions: 'high' (or 'close'), 'mid', and 'low' (or 'open'), while the 'mid' is frequently divided into 'high-mid' and 'low-mid'. Figure 1.6 shows the English vowels.

Another dimension of vowel description refers to the lip position. Four /ɔ, o, ʊ, u/ of the five back vowels, which are given in circles in the chart, are produced with rounded lips and thus are called 'round' (or 'rounded'); all other vowels are unrounded.

Finally, in addition to the height, backness and rounding characteristics, one other grouping, tense/lax, is given. This is a rather controversial issue and will be dealt with in detail in chapter 4. Here, suffice it to say that this book will follow the distributional criteria and group /ɪ, ɛ, æ, ʊ, ʌ/ as 'lax', while considering the rest 'tense'.

The vowels we have described so far are considered to have a single, unchanging quality and are called 'monophthongs'. (This is not uncontroversial for /i/, /u/, and especially for /e/ and /o/; see chapter 4 for details.) The vocalic elements of the words such as <u>bite</u>, <u>brown</u>, and <u>boy</u>, on the other hand, involve a complex articulation whereby we move from one vowel to another. More specifically, we have /aɪ/, /aʊ/, and /ɔɪ/, respectively. Such sounds are known as 'diphthongs'. The complete account of vowels and diphthongs, including their dialect variations will be discussed in chapter 4.

1.4 Additional Sounds

Our primary concern in this chapter has been the consonants and vowels of English. However, students of Speech Pathology and TESOL (teaching of English to speakers of other languages) as well as of applied linguistics frequently deal with speakers of other languages, either in the context of foreign language learning or in the context of bilingualism (or multilingualism). Such situations, needless to say, demand familiarity with several sounds that are not present in English. Thus, the following is intended to provide the necessary coverage.

1.4.1 States of glottis

Besides the two configurations (voiced and voiceless) we mentioned for the sounds of English, some languages use sounds that involve two additional states of glottis. These are **creaky voice** (also known as 'laryngealization' or 'vocal fry'), and **murmur** (also called 'breathy voice').

In creaky voice the arytenoid cartilages at the back of the glottis are together, and the cords vibrate at the other end. The result is a low-pitched sound. Many Chadic languages (e.g. Hausa, Bura, Margi of West Africa) use such sounds to make changes in meaning in opposition to a regularly voiced sound. Creaks can be transcribed by adding a subscript tilde to individual sounds (e.g. [a̰]).

Murmurs (or breathy voiced sounds) are produced in such a way that the vocal cords are apart at the back, while they vibrate at the front portions. The opening of the cords is narrower than in voiceless sounds, and the cords vibrate with high volume–velocity airflow through this gap that subsides soon because the high rate of flow cannot be maintained for long. Murmur sounds can be transcribed by placing two dots [..] under individual sounds (e.g. [d̤]). Niger-Congo languages in Africa (e.g. Zulu, Shona), and several languages spoken in India (Hindi, Sindhi, Marathi, Bengali, Gujarati) have murmured stops. Also, in Mazatec (an Oto-Mangean language spoken in Mexico) laryngealized vowels, breathy voiced vowels, and regular vowels can be found in contrast (substitutions for each other making meaning differences).

1.4.2 Places and manners of articulation

Stops

The bilabial, alveolar, and velar stops of English are very common in the languages of the world. Two additional places of articulation are noteworthy in stops. Voiceless and voiced *palatal* stops, which are transcribed as [c, ɟ] respectively, are found in Hungarian, Czech, Turkish, Basque, and Irish. *Retroflex* stops [ṭ, ḍ] (or [t, d]) are common in Hindi. As for *uvular* (the back of the tongue articulating against the uvula) stops, we can cite the voiceless [q] (found in Eskimo, Quechua), and the voiced [G] (found in Persian). Mention should also be made of *dental* stops [t̪, d̪], which are found in Romance languages (Spanish, Portuguese, Italian, etc.).

Fricatives

The fricative inventory of English is quite rich (nine fricatives), but there are many more possibilities that are entertained by several languages of the world. The voiceless *bilabial* fricative, [ɸ], is common in Greek and Hausa, while the voiced counterpart, [β], is found in Spanish. Ewe of West Africa has both of these bilabial fricatives. *Retroflex* fricatives (voiceless, which can be transcribed as [ṣ] (or [ʂ]), and voiced, which can be transcribed as [ẓ] (or [ʐ]) are found in Mandarin Chinese and in several Dravidian languages of India, such as Tamil and Malayalam. *Palatal* fricatives are also found in several languages. While the voiceless [ç] is found in Irish, Bengali, German, Norwegian, and Greek, the voiced counterpart, [ʝ], is found in Swedish, Greenlandic, and Margi. *Velar* fricatives can be found in Indo-European languages. We can cite Welsh, Irish, Bulgarian, Czech, German, Sindhi, and Slovene for the voiceless [x], and Greek, Spanish, Arabic, Persian, German, and Irish for the voiced [ɣ]. The voiceless *uvular* fricative, [χ], is common in Dutch and Semitic languages (e.g. Arabic, Hebrew), and several Amerindian languages (e.g. Tlingit), while the voiced counterpart, [ʁ], is frequent in Portuguese and French. Finally, *pharyngeal* fricatives, both voiceless, [ħ], and voiced, [ʕ] are commonly found in Semitic languages (e.g. Arabic, Hebrew).

Affricates

The two palato-alveolar affricates of English are, by far, the most common ones in the languages of the world. Besides these, *alveolars* are also relatively frequent. The voiceless member, [tˢ], of this group, which is the more common one, is found in Chinese, Croatian, Japanese, Slovene, and Czech, while the voiced [dᶻ] may be found in Bulgarian. Also worth mentioning is the voiceless *bilabial* fricative, [pᶠ], which is found in German.

Nasals

Just like the affricates, the nasals of English are among the most common in languages of the world. However, mention should be made of the next most common nasal, [ɲ], which is *palatal*. This sound is part of several languages such as French, Spanish, Portuguese, Vietnamese, Hungarian, Catalan, Irish, and Sundanese. Other nasals that are worth mentioning are the *uvular* [N], which is found in Japanese and in several Amerindian languages, and retroflex nasal [ɳ] (or [ɳ]) found in Malayalam.

Liquids

Under this group, we look at sounds that are known as 'l-sounds' and 'r-sounds', which present a wide variety. The voiced alveolar approximant [l], found in English, is one of the most common laterals in languages. Palatal [ʎ], which is found in languages such as Italian and Portuguese, is another common lateral approximant. Laterals are most likely to be approximants and voiced; however, neither of these qualities is necessarily the case. Fricative laterals are more commonly voiceless (e.g. voiceless, alveolar fricative [ɬ], as in Welsh).

The r-sounds, while they all are normally voiced, present a wider range in types than laterals. It is common to see a distinction between 'continuant' vs. 'interrupted' r-sounds. The r-sounds of English (retroflex approximant in American English, [ɻ], alveolar approximant in British English, [ɹ]) are examples of continuants.

More commonly, r-sounds belong to one of the 'interrupted' types (taps, flaps, trills). Both taps and flaps involve a momentary contact between the articulators. The Spanish [ɾ], in <u>caro</u> [kaɾo] "expensive" (or the American English intervocalic /t/, as in <u>writer</u>), is made with a flicking movement of the tip of the tongue against the upper articulator. Taps are sometimes equated with flaps, which is not accurate. First of all, taps are mostly dental/alveolar while flaps are retroflex. Also, these two sounds are different in direction of the movement; in taps we have a movement up to down, and in flaps back to front.

Trills are produced by the repeated tapping of one flexible articulator against the other. The dental/alveolar trill, [r], (e.g. Spanish <u>perro</u> [pero] "dog") is one of the most common in languages. Also noteworthy is the uvular trill, [R], which is found in German and in some varieties of French (e.g. [Ruʒ] "red"). In some other varieties of French (e.g. Parisian), this sound is a uvular fricative or approximant (e.g. [ʁuʒ] "red"). Sometimes a trill may be accompanied with friction. The Czech r-sound [r̝] is a good example of a voiced alveolar fricative trill (e.g. <u>Dvorak</u> [dvor̝ak]).

Glides

The sounds /j/ and /w/ that are found in English are by far the most common glides in languages. A noteworthy addition to this category is the labiopalatal approximant, [ɥ], found in French (e.g. [mɥɛt] "mute").

While the additional symbols are useful in dealing with sounds that are not found in English, they may not be sufficient to deal with data from a disordered population. Here, we may require extra refinement in the form of new symbols and/or diacritics to accurately reflect the atypical productions, which are rarely found in natural languages, or not found at all. Among such articulations we may find the following: *dentolabials*, which are the reverse of labiodentals, are articulated between the upper lip and the lower front teeth. These may include stops [p̪, b̪], nasal [m̪], and fricatives [f̪, v̪]. *Labio-alveolars*, which are common with speakers with excessive overbite for target labials and labiodentals, are articulated between the lower lip and the alveolar ridge (e.g. [p̞, b̞, m̞, f̞, v̞]. In clinical data, fricatives may be found with simultaneously median air flow over the center of the tongue and laterally (e.g. [l͡s, l͡z]), as well as fricatives with friction located within the nasal cavity (i.e. fricatives with nasal escape), [m̃, ñ, ŋ̃]. Also commonly cited are labiodental stops [p̪, b̪], and the velopharyngeal fricative (more commonly known as the velopharyngeal snort), [fŋ]. The sounds cited above do not constitute an exhaustive list of possible atypical articulations found in disordered speech. For a more detailed account and complete diacritics, including transcription conventions for phonatory activities and connected speech modes, the reader is referred to Ball and Lowry (2001).

1.4.3 Consonants made with non-pulmonic airstream mechanisms

The sounds we have described so far are all produced using air from the lungs, and thus are called 'pulmonic' sounds. While the sounds in many languages are exclusively made with this pulmonic egressive (outgoing airflow) airstream, several other languages may, in addition, utilize one or two other

Table 1.3 Consonants (English and other languages)

	Bilabial	Labio-dental	Dental / Interdental	Alveolar	Retroflex	Palato-alveolar	Palatal	Velar	Uvular	Pharyngeal	Glottal
Stop	p **b**		t̪ d̪	**t d**	ʈ(ṭ) ɖ(ḍ)		c ɟ	**k g**	q ɢ		ʔ
Fricative	ɸ β	**f v**	**θ ð**	**s z**	ʂ(ṣ) ʐ(ẓ)	**ʃ ʒ**	ç ʝ	x ɣ	χ ʁ	ħ ʕ	**h**
Affricate	pᶠ			tˢ dᶻ		**tʃ dʒ**					
Nasal	**m**			**n**	ɳ(ṇ)		ɲ	**ŋ**	N		
Liquid				**l r** ɾ ɹ	ɻ(ɽ)		ʎ		R		
Glide	**w**						**j**	w			

Sounds given in **bold type** occur in English.

airstream mechanisms, especially for the stop sounds. These mechanisms are 'glottalic' airstream (which employs the air above closed glottis, that is, pharynx air, and produces 'ejectives' and 'implosives', which are sometimes called 'glottalized' or 'laryngealized' consonants), and 'velaric' airstream (which employs the air in the mouth, and produces 'clicks').

Ejectives

In order to produce ejectives the closed larynx is raised. This is accompanied with a closure in the mouth (bilabial, alveolar, velar), and a raised velum. Raising the larynx squeezes the air trapped between the glottis and the consonant closure in the vocal tract and raises the air pressure in this chamber. Upon release of the consonant closure, the air rushes out. Stops produced this way are called 'ejectives'. Because there is no vocal cord vibration, ejectives are typically voiceless. They are symbolized by the appropriate consonant symbol with the addition of an apostrophe ([p', t', k']), and are common in many Amerindian languages (Nez Perce, Klamath, Nootka, Dakota), Circassian languages (Kabardian, Georgian), and African languages (Zulu, Hausa).

Implosives

The mechanism to produce implosives is the opposite to that of ejectives. Here, instead of squeezing the air and increasing the pressure, the downward-moving larynx sucks the air inward and reduces the air pressure. In general, the glottis cannot remain tightly closed during this downward movement of the larynx, and there is vocal cord vibration. When the closure in the vocal tract is released, the air rushes in, and thus 'implosives' are stops made by glottalic ingressive airstream. Implosives can be found in many African languages (e.g. Zulu, Hausa) and are symbolized by the addition of an upper rightward hook to the appropriate stop symbol ([ɓ, ɗ, ʄ, ɠ, ʛ]).

Clicks

The enclosed cavity for the production of a 'click' is created in the mouth, forming the back closure by raising the back of the tongue against the soft palate (velum), and the front closure somewhere more front in the mouth (e.g. alveolar ridge). The lowering of the body of the tongue rarefies the air, and when the front closure is removed, the air is sucked into the mouth. The result is a

Table 1.4 Stops made with pulmonic and non-pulmonic airstream mechanisms

	Bilabial	Dental	Alveolar	Palato-alveolar	Velar
Ejectives	p'		t'		k'
Implosives	ɓ		ɗ		ɠ
Clicks	ʘ	ǀ	ǁ	!	

clicking sound; 'tsk-tsk' is one that we hear for disapproval in English. Since the airflow is inward, clicks are known as sounds made with velaric ingressive airstream mechanism. Clicks, as speech sounds, are confined to languages of southern Africa. To symbolize clicks, we find the following ([ʘ] bilabial, [ǀ] dental, [!] post-alveolar, and [ǁ] alveolar lateral).

1.4.4   Vowels

American English has a rather rich vowel inventory that covers many of the positions on the vowel grid; however, there are many other possibilities that are entertained by other languages. UPSID (UCLA Phonological Segment Inventory Database) (Maddieson 1984), which looks at more than 300 languages that are representative of different language families, shows a grid with 37 different vowel symbols. We will not go into that detail here. Instead, we will first point out some non-English vowels that are common in several familiar languages, and then we will have a brief description of 'cardinal vowels', which are commonly used for reference points in talking about the vowels of other languages.

Although it is commonplace to find front vowels as unrounded in languages, there are some front rounded vowels that are found in several familiar languages. These are high front rounded, /y/ (/ü/), (the rounded counterpart of /i/), high-mid (close-mid) front rounded, /ø/ (/ö/), (rounded counterpart of /e/), and the low-mid (open-mid) front rounded, /œ/, (rounded counterpart of /ɛ/). All three are part of French and several Germanic languages (German, Swedish, Danish, Norwegian). Dutch and Hungarian have /y/ and /ø/, while Cantonese and Turkish have /y/ and /œ/. Another noteworthy vowel that is not part of English is the high back unrounded /ɯ/ (unrounded counterpart of /u/) which is found in Korean, Turkish, and many Amerindian languages.

1.5   Cardinal Vowels

Although we use similar traditional labels for vowel descriptions of different languages (e.g. high, front, rounded, etc.), we should not assume that vowels that are described the same way are identical in two languages. For example, both French and Galician have high front unrounded vowels, /i/, but their qualities are not the same. Similarly, identically transcribed vowels from different languages may not be the same. For example, if we look at /œ/ of Cantonese, French, and Dutch, we realize that they are all different; Cantonese has the highest tongue position, French is in the middle, and Dutch has the lowest. To avoid such problems in the description of vowels of different languages, phoneticians usually refer to the set of arbitrarily chosen vowels that is known as 'cardinal vowels' and describe the particular vowel of a language with reference to this system. The primary and secondary cardinal vowels are given in figure 1.7.

(1) i	y (9)		(17) ɨ ʉ (18)		(16) ɯ	u (8)
(2) e	ø (10)				(15) ɤ	o (7)
(3) ɛ	œ (11)				(14) ʌ	ɔ (6)
(4) a	ɶ (12)				(13) ɒ	ɑ (5)

Note: Primary cardinal vowels are outside the grid, and the secondary cardinal vowels are inside it.

Figure 1.7 Cardinal vowels

The front vowels (1–4) and (9–12), and the back vowels (5–8) and (13–16) are equidistant from one another. As such, they do not necessarily represent the vowels of any language; rather, they are arbitrary reference points that the vowels of any language can be described against. The top left corner of the vowel space defines the highest and most front possible vowel, (1). The bottom right corner (5) is the other extreme, which is the lowest and most back vowel. The other two corners represent the extremes in low front (4) and high back (8). The secondary cardinal vowels (the ones inside the grid) repeat the primary set with the opposite lip rounding. As such, (9) is high front rounded, (12) low front rounded, (13) low back rounded, and (16) high back unrounded.

Before we conclude this section, we will show how, using this system, we can describe vowels from different languages. Although, as stated above /œ/ is in the inventory of Cantonese, Dutch, and French, the realizations are not identical; this can be shown in figure 1.8.

Thus, we can say that /œ/ of Cantonese is a little lower than (10) and a little centralized. As for the French and Dutch counterparts, we can state the following: while French /œ/ is a little higher than (11), the Dutch sound is a little lower than (11) and more centralized.

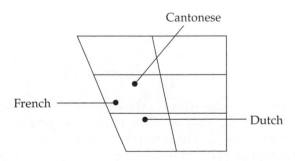

Figure 1.8 Realizations of /œ/ in Cantonese, Dutch, and French

1.6 Syllables and Suprasegmentals

What we have considered so far in this chapter have been the phonetic characteristics of individual speech sounds or segments. However, segments do not
exist in isolation and are part of larger units, such as syllables, which in turn
make up larger units of utterances.

Syllable

The syllable is a phonological unit consisting of segments around the pivotal
vowel or vowel-like (diphthong) sound, which is known as the *nucleus*. The
nucleus is the element that every syllable contains, and the other elements
are defined in relation to it; the consonant(s) we have before the nucleus are
called the *onset*, and the consonant(s) after it the *coda*. Thus, in the following
three words we have syllables with different elements. In 'a' [e], we have only
the nucleus with no onset and no coda; in 'at' [æt], the syllable consists of the
nucleus and the coda and there is no onset; finally, in 'cat' [kæt], we have
all three elements present. We will not go into greater details of various other
possibilities, as the detailed structure of English syllables will be discussed in
chapter 6.

Nucleus and coda together (elements after the onset) are known as the *rhyme*
(or *'rime'*), thus giving us the following hierarchical structure.

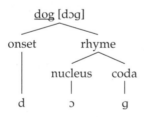

Depending on the structure of the rhyme, syllables are classified as *closed* (with
coda(s)), and *open* (lacking coda(s)). Thus, in the word beacon [bi.kən] we have
the open first syllable followed by the closed second syllable.

Suprasegmentals

In the context of utterances, certain features such as stress, length, and pitch
are contributing factors to the messages. Such features, which are used simultaneously with units larger than segments, are called 'suprasegmentals'.

Pitch: The pitch of the voice refers to the frequency of the vocal cord vibration. It is influenced by the tension of the vocal cords and the amount of air
that passes through them. In an utterance, different portions are produced
in different pitches. The patterns of rises and falls (pitch variation) across a
stretch of speech such as a sentence is called its *intonation*. The meaning of

a sentence may depend on its intonation pattern. For example, if we utter the sequence "her uncle is coming next week" with a falling pitch, this will be interpreted as a statement. If, on the other hand, the same is uttered by a rise in pitch at the end, it will be understood as a question.

In many languages, the pitch variation can signal differences in word meaning. Such languages, exemplified by several Sino-Tibetan languages (e.g. Mandarin, Cantonese), Niger-Congo languages (e.g. Zulu, Yoruba, Igbo), and many Amerindian languages (e.g. Apache, Navajo, Kiowa), are called *tone languages*. To demonstrate how tone can affect the lexical change, we can refer to the much-celebrated example of [ma] of Mandarin Chinese:

[ma] if uttered by a	*high level tone,*	/˥/,	"mother"
	high rising tone,	/˧˥/,	"hemp"
	low falling rising tone,	/˨˩˦/,	"horse"
	high falling tone,	/˥˩/,	"scold"

Such lexical changes cannot be accomplished in non-tonal languages such as English, Spanish, French, etc. In addition to the lexical differences, which are standard in all tone languages, some languages may utilize tonal shifts for morphological or syntactic purposes (e.g. Bini of Nigeria for tense shift, Shona of Zimbabwe to separate the main clause and the relative clause, Igbo of Nigeria to indicate possession).

Stress: Stress can be defined as syllable prominence. The prominence of a stressed syllable over an unstressed one may be due to a number of factors. These may include (a) loudness (stressed syllables are louder than unstressed syllables), (b) duration (stressed syllables are longer than unstressed syllables), and (c) pitch (stressed syllables are produced with higher pitch than unstressed syllables). Languages and dialects (varieties) vary in which of these features are decisive in separating stressed syllables from the unstressed ones. In English, higher pitch has been shown to be the most influential perceptual cue in this respect (Fry 1955, 1979).

Variation in syllable duration and loudness produce differences in rhythm. English rhythm (like most other Germanic languages) is said to be *stress-timed*. What this means is that stressed syllables tend to occur at roughly equal intervals in time (isochronous). The opposite pattern, which is known as *syllable-timing*, is the rhythmic beat by the recurrences of syllables, not stresses. Spanish, Greek, and Turkish are good examples of such a rhythm. One of the significant differences between the two types of languages lies in the differences of length between stressed and unstressed syllables, and vowel reduction or lack of it. We can exemplify this by looking at English and Spanish. If we consider the English word <u>probability</u> and its cognate Spanish <u>probabilidad</u>, the difference becomes rather obvious. Although the words share the same meaning and the same number of syllables, the similarities do not go beyond that. In Spanish (a syllable-timed language), the stress is on the last syllable, [proβaβiliðað]. Although the remaining syllables are unstressed, they all have full vowels, and the duration of all five syllables is approximately the same. In English (a stress-timed language), on the other hand, the word [prabəbɪləɾi] reveals a rather different picture. The third syllable receives the main stress (the most prominent) and the first syllable has a secondary stress (second most prominent syllable). The first, third, and the last syllables have full vowels, while the second and the fourth syllables have reduced vowels. Thus, besides the two stressed syllables, the last syllable, because it has a full vowel, has greater duration than the second and fourth syllables. Because of such differences in rhythm, English is said to have a 'galloping' rhythm as opposed to the 'staccato' rhythm of Spanish.

Several scholars (Dauer 1983; Giegerich 1992) object to the binary split between 'stress-timing' and 'syllable-timing', and suggest a continuum where a given language may be placed. For example, while French is frequently cited among 'syllable-timed' languages, it is also shown to have strong stresses breaking the rhythm of the sentence, a characteristic which is normally reserved for stress-timed languages.

A rather uncontroversial split among languages with respect to stress relates to 'fixed' (predictable) stress versus 'variable' stress languages. In English, similar to other Germanic languages, the position of stress is variable. For example, import as a noun will have the stress on the first syllable, [ímpɔrt], whereas it will be on the second syllable if it is a verb, [impɔ́rt].

In several languages, however, stress is fixed in a given word position. In such cases, the first syllable (e.g. Czech, Finnish), the last syllable (e.g. French), or the next-to-last syllable (e.g. Polish, Welsh, Swahili) is favored.

Length: Length differences in vowels or consonants may be used to make lexical distinctions in languages. Swedish, Estonian, Finnish, Arabic, Japanese, and Danish can be cited for vowel length contrasts (e.g. Danish [vilə] "wild" vs. [viːlə] "rest"). English does not have such meaning differences entirely based on vowel length. Examples such as beat vs. bit, and pool vs. pull are separated not simply on the basis of length, but also on vowel height and tense/lax distinctions.

In consonantal length, we again make reference to languages other than English. For example, in Italian and in Turkish different consonant length is responsible for lexical distinctions (e.g. Italian nonno [nɔnno] "grandfather" vs. nono [nɔno] "ninth"; Turkish eli [ɛli] "his/her hand" vs. elli [ɛlli] "fifty"). In English, we can have a longer consonant at word or morpheme boundaries: [k] in black cat, [f] in half full, and [n] in ten names are produced with one long obstruction.

Summary

In this chapter, we examined the basic elements of phonetics, which are prerequisites to understanding the patterning of sounds. We looked at the fundamentals of articulatory phonetics including voicing, places and manners of articulation, voice onset time, and dimensions that are relevant for vocalic articulations such as tongue height and backness, as well as lip positions. We also reviewed some common non-English sounds that might be of relevance. Finally, we had a brief account of syllable and suprasegmental features such as stress, tone, intonation, and length.

Exercises

1. Examine the following transcriptions. If you agree, do nothing; if the
    transcription is erroneous, correct it.

    injured [ɪnjerd]   gelatin [gɛlətɪn]
    measure [mɛshuɹ]   inches [intʃəs]
    caution [kɔʃən]   topical [topɪkəl]
    telephone [teləphon]   syllable [sələbəl]

2. How many segments are there in each of the following words?

    homophone   equestrian
    broach   writer
    thatched   middle
    knack   photographer
    lesson   imagination

3. State if the place of articulation is same (S) or different (D) in the
    initial consonants of each pair. In either case, state the place of
    articulation.

    Example: now – pneumonia   Same; alveolar
              sun – sugar   Different; alveolar vs.
                                 palato-alveolar

    (a)   goose – gerrymander
    (b)   simple – shackle
    (c)   curious – cereal
    (d)   phonetic – fictional
    (e)   manners – wicker
    (f)   normal – location
    (g)   wander – yesterday
    (h)   those – Thursday
    (i)   scissors – zipper
    (j)   temperate – chestnut
    (k)   chromosome – chief
    (l)   baker – delegate
    (m)   happened – usual
    (n)   neuron – market
    (o)   painting – broccoli

4. State if the manner of articulation is same (S) or different (D) in the *final consonants* of each pair. In either case, state the manner of articulation.

    Example: bomb – ten   Same; nasal
                 rough – zip   Different; fricative vs. stop

(a)   album – broken
(b)   ideal – keepsake
(c)   prologue – confine
(d)   aqueous – sociable
(e)   variable – watch
(f)   waste – adage
(g)   barometer – finish
(h)   inch – gauge
(i)   fiord – equip
(j)   barb – relief
(k)   alive – fiftieth
(l)   laughing – hydraulic
(m)   opulence – paramedic
(n)   outrage – swivel
(o)   dominion – eminent

5. State if the *vowels in the underlined portions* are same or different in the following words. In either case, state the phonetic description of the vowels, together with the phonetic symbols.

    Example: k<u>ee</u>l – cit<u>y</u>   Same: /i/ high, front, tense
                 m<u>e</u>ss – m<u>a</u>ss   Different: /ɛ/ mid, front – /æ/ low, front

(a)   prim<u>a</u>ry – n<u>u</u>trition
(b)   h<u>ea</u>l – electr<u>i</u>city
(c)   b<u>eau</u> – <u>a</u>perture
(d)   an<u>y</u>where – ph<u>a</u>ntasm
(e)   exp<u>o</u>sure – c<u>oa</u>ster
(f)   expl<u>i</u>cable – expl<u>i</u>cate
(g)   w<u>a</u>ve – irrig<u>a</u>te
(h)   m<u>ea</u>sure – f<u>i</u>nger
(i)   b<u>u</u>tter – t<u>ou</u>gh
(j)   ch<u>o</u>lesterol – b<u>o</u>ttom
(k)   n<u>y</u>mph – j<u>u</u>mp
(l)   ab<u>a</u>te – c<u>au</u>ght
(m)   hydr<u>o</u>gen – hydr<u>o</u>lysis
(n)   p<u>a</u>wn – h<u>a</u>rsh

6. Circle the words that:

   (a) start with a fricative
       foreign, theater, tidings, hospital, cassette, shroud
   (b) end in a sibilant
       wishes, twelfth, clutch, indicates, admonish, furtive
   (c) have an approximant
       winter, university, captive, ripe, little, mute
   (d) contain a back vowel
       putter, boost, roast, fraud, matter, hospital
   (e) start with a voiced obstruent
       government, pottery, taxonomy, jury, phonograph, sister
   (f) contain a lax vowel
       auction, redeem, ledger, cram, boat, loom
   (g) end in an alveolar
       went, atom, rigor, column, multiple, garnish

7. Give the phonetic symbols for the following English sounds.

   (a) voiceless stops   _____
   (b) voiced fricatives   _____
   (c) approximants   _____
   (d) alveolar obstruents _____
   (e) nasals _____
   (f) voiced obstruents   _____

   Now give the phonetic symbols for the following sounds that are
   not found in English.

   (g) alveolar affricates   _____
   (h) voiceless velar and uvular fricatives   _____
   (i) bilabial and palatal fricatives   _____
   (j) non-lateral liquids   _____
   (k) palatal and uvular stops   _____

8. The sounds in the underlined portions of the following pairs of words
   share some phonetic properties and are different in some other
   properties. Give the phonetic symbol for each sound and state the
   shared feature(s) and difference(s).

   Example: [p] 'park' – 'phone' [f]   Shared: voiceless, obstruent
                                          Difference(s):
                                          [p] bilabial, stop
                                          [f] labiodental, fricative

    (a)   telephone – television
    (b)   atop – wiser
    (c)   bitter – easy
    (d)   mister – enemy
    (e)   shipment – justice
    (f)   wait – root
    (g)   lime – window
    (h)   alone – elevate
    (i)   feather – fought
    (j)   limp – soccer

9.   The following groups consist of sounds that share a phonetic feature plus one sound that does not belong to this group. Circle the sound that does not belong to the group, and identify the feature shared by the remaining sounds of the group.

     Example: /l, ɹ, d, s, t, k, z/   /k/ is a velar, the rest are
                                              alveolars

    (a)   /f, ʃ, tʃ, z, θ, ʒ, ð/ _____
    (b)   /t, z, n, m, d, l, s/ _____
    (c)   /ɪ, ɛ, ʊ, u, æ, ʌ/ _____
    (d)   /n, g, v, s, z, ɹ, m/ _____
    (e)   /m, w, ŋ, p, b/ _____
    (f)   /i, ɪ, æ, ɑ, e, ɛ/ _____

10. Fill in the boxes with the appropriate label for the *final sounds* of each word.

	sipped	latex	triumph	bridge	rough	fought	dogs	palm
Upper articulator								
Lower articulator								
Voicing								
Manner of articulation								

11.   Do the same for the *initial sounds* of the same words.

	sipped	latex	triumph	bridge	rough	fought	dogs	palm
Upper articulator								
Lower articulator								
Voicing								
Manner of articulation								

12.   Fill in the boxes for the first vowels of the following.

	park	ocean	make	ember	hamper	fought	hypocrite	chew
Tongue height								
Frontness/ backness								
Lip position								
Tenseness/ laxness								

13.   Circle the correct alternative(s).

   (a)   Tensing the vocal cords makes them vibrate faster / slower, so that the pitch increases / decreases.
   (b)   In the production of stops / fricatives / glides / affricates, the air is blocked from going out through the nose and the mouth.
   (c)   In the production of stops / liquids / fricatives / nasals, the constriction of the vocal tract is such that a noisy airstream is formed.
   (d)   In the production of palato-alveolar sounds, the tip / front / blade / back of the tongue goes to the forward part of the hard palate / soft palate / uvula.
   (e)   In the production of labiodental / bilabial / labio-velar / velar sounds, the two lips approach one another, and the back of the tongue is raised towards the soft palate.

14. Transcribe the following (about 'the spread of English') *from* P. Trudgill and J. Hannah, *International English* (London: Edward Arnold, 2002).

The English language developed out of Germanic dialects that were
....

brought to Britain, during the course of the 5th and 6th centuries,
....

by Jutes (from modern Jutland, Denmark), Angles (from modern
....

Schleswig, Denmark/Germany), and Frisians (from modern
....

Friesland, Netherlands/Germany). By medieval times, this
....

Germanic language had replaced the original Celtic language of Britain
....

in nearly all of England as well as in southern and eastern Scotland.
....

Until the 1600s, however, English remained a language spoken by a
....

relatively small number of people and was confined geographically
....

to the island of Great Britain. Indeed, even much of Britain
....

remained non-English-speaking. The original Celtic language of
....

Britain survived in the form of Welsh in nearly all of Wales and as
....

Cornish in much of Cornwall. The Highlands and islands of western
....

and northern Scotland spoke Gaelic, another Celtic language which
....

had been brought across from Ireland in pre-medieval times. And
....

the populations of the Northern Isles – Orkney and Shetland – still
....

spoke the Scandinavian language, Norn, which they had inherited
....

from their Viking ancestors.
....

Phonology

2.1 Introduction

If we look at sound inventories of languages, we notice that several sounds are shared by a multiplicity of languages. Indeed, it is also possible that two or more languages have exactly the same sounds. However, having the same sounds does not mean that their phonologies (their patterning) are the same. Let us exemplify this with some concrete examples. If we present the words name, snail, panther, and invite to a native speaker of English and ask if there is any consonant sound that is shared by these words, we would invariably get a positive answer, and the consonant sound identified would be the one orthographically represented by n. In fact, the sounds that are identified as the same are not phonetically identical. In name [nem] we have a voiced alveolar nasal, which becomes partially devoiced in snail [sn̥el]. In panther, the nasal sound is dental [pæn̪θɚ], and finally, in invite, it is labiodental, [ɪɱvaɪt]. What is interesting and important here is the fact that, although there are phonetic differences among these sounds, native speakers of English do not pay attention to them, as the differences are functionally not relevant in their language.

If, on the other hand, we present the first and the third words in the above list (name and panther) to a speaker of Malayalam (a Dravidian language, spoken in the southwest of India), the situation would be entirely different. Since, in this language, employment of [n̪] instead of [n] in a given word can change the meaning of the word, the phonetic difference between the dental and alveolar nasals cannot be overlooked, and the speakers of Malayalam would perceive the phonetic difference under consideration immediately.

Let us now consider another example in which the sensitivity to a given phonetic difference between two sounds will come from the speakers of English, while it is overlooked in another language. If we give the following words, drama "drama", dolor "pain", comida "food", and lado "side", to native speakers of Spanish and ask them if there is any consonant sound shared by all these words, the unmistakable answer would be the sound that is orthographically represented by d. The fact is that while the sound that is represented by the orthographic d in the first two words is a stop, [d], the one

represented by the same grapheme in the third and the fourth words is a fricative, [ð]. Similar to what happened in the above case with different nasals in
English, Spanish speakers overlook the phonetically different sounds, because
their language does not employ the phonetic difference between these two sounds
in a structurally significant fashion. If, on the other hand, we give two words
containing the same two sounds to a speaker of English, the difference
between [d̪] and [ð] will be immediately noticed. The reason for this is that the
difference between these two sounds is very critical in English and can separate one word from another, as exemplified by the pair of words <u>day</u> [de] and
<u>they</u> [ðe].

When such mismatches are pointed out to the speakers of languages where
phonetic differences are overlooked, one very often does see an attempt to jus-
tify this by suggesting that whatever difference is overlooked presents a very
small difference phonetically, whereas the immediately noticed one is very obvious. That is, in the case of English, they would defend the situation saying that
the differences among the nasals [n, n̪, ɳ, m̩] is small and may not be percep-
tible, while the difference between [d] and [ð] is larger and is easily noticed.

That such explanations cannot be taken seriously becomes obvious when we
switch the cases around and ask the same questions to Malayalam speakers
for the difference between [n̪] and [n], and to Spanish speakers for [d̪] and [ð].
The answers we would get would be diametrically opposed to what we
receive from speakers of English. We are likely to hear how obvious the difference between the dental and alveolar nasals is by Malayalam speakers, and
how insignificant the difference is between [d̪] and [ð] by speakers of Spanish.
All these show that whether the users of a given language would be attuned
to a given phonetic difference simply depends on whether that difference is
contrastive (capable of changing the meaning of words) in that language.

Whether a given phonetic difference is meaningful (i.e. easily perceived, catches
the attention of the native speakers, etc.) has to do with the functional (contrastive) status in a language, and this has to do with the distribution of sounds
in a given sound system.

2.2 Complementary versus Overlapping Distribution

2.2.1 Overlapping distribution and contrast

In languages, sounds are in either of the two types of distribution. When two
sounds are capable of occurring in the same environment, we say that these
sounds are in overlapping distribution. For example, the sounds [l] and [ɹ] are
in overlapping distribution in English, because they can be found in the same
environment, as exemplified by the following pairs of words.

(a)   <u>lake</u> [lek] – <u>rake</u> [ɹek]
(b)   <u>mole</u> [mol] – <u>more</u> [moɹ]
(c)   <u>elect</u> [ɪlɛkt] – <u>erect</u> [ɪɹɛkt]

The examples above show that the sounds [l] and [ɹ] are capable of occurring in the same environment (in word-initial position, followed by the same sound in (a); in word-final position, preceded by the same sounds in (b); and medially, preceded and followed by the same sounds in (c)). It should be mentioned that the environments relevant for the distribution can be defined in terms of word or syllable position, neighboring sounds (preceding and/or following), or suprasegmentals.

When we have an overlapping distribution as shown above, we say that the sounds in question are in a non-predictable distribution. An overlapping distribution is not required to manifest itself in multiple positions; one environment will be enough to conclude the overlap. For example, the sounds [n] and [ŋ] in English may be found in an overlapping distribution only in a syllable-final position (kin [kɪn] – king [kɪŋ]). This is because [ŋ] can only be found in this environment in English.

When two sounds are found in an overlapping distribution, and the substitution of one sound for the other changes the meaning of the word ([lek] vs. [ɹek], [kɪn] vs. [kɪŋ]), we say that they are in *contrast*, and they are the manifestations of different phonemes.

The pairs of words used above to show the overlapping environments and contrast are known as *minimal pairs*. Simply defined, minimal pairs are pairs of words that have exactly the same sounds in the same order except for a single difference in sounds, and have different meanings. These are well exemplified in the pairs (a)–(c) above. Notice that the only way we can create a minimal pair with reference to the two sounds involved is to put them in exactly the same environment in terms of word position and the surrounding context. To clarify further, the pair: jail – Yale shows the contrast between /dʒ/ and /j/ in initial position, budge – buzz focuses on the contrast between /dʒ/ and /z/ in final position, while witch – wish contrasts /tʃ/ and /ʃ/ in final position. It should be noted that minimal pairs include forms that have different spellings, as evidenced in jail – Yale. In the following, we provide more examples with different spellings.

	Contrast
bite – light	/b/ and /l/ initially
bowl – soul	/b/ and /s/ initially
debt – dead	/t/ and /d/ finally
father – fodder	/ð/ and /d/ medially
broth – brought	/θ/ and /t/ finally
body – buddy	/a/ and /ʌ/ medially
scene – bean	/s/ and /b/ initially

While finding minimal pairs is very comforting and makes our job easy in concluding that the suspicious pair/group of sounds are in contrast and should belong to separate phonemes, this may not always be possible. The language simply may accidentally lack the needed vocabulary items. This is probably more common in languages with long words and large inventories. However, no language is immune to this. When we do not have the minimal pairs to prove that two or more sounds are in contrast, we look for the 'near-minimal pair'. This is a pair of words that would be a minimal pair except for some irrelevant difference. What this rather vague definition says is that the potentially influential elements in the linguistic environment are kept constant, while others that are unlikely to influence a change may be different. Essentially, we look at the immediately preceding and immediately following environments, because these are the primary sources of contextual conditioning of changes. For example, if we cannot find an exact minimal pair to show the contrast between [ʃ] and [ʒ] in English, we can use the words vision [vɪʒən] and mission [mɪʃən], or illusion [əluʒən] and solution [səluʃən]. Although these pairs do not constitute minimal pairs (because the difference is not solely on the suspicious pair of sounds, [ʃ] and [ʒ], but also related to others), the relevant 'preceding' and 'following' environments of the suspicious pairs of sounds are kept identical. Similarly, the pairs such as lethargy [lɛθɚdʒi] and leather [lɛðɚ] for [θ] and [ð], and lesion [liʒən] and heathen [hiðən] for [ʒ] and [ð] would serve as near minimal pairs. Thus, we can answer the question 'Do the two sounds occur in the same/similar environment?' affirmatively, and conclude that the pairs of sounds considered above are in contrast and belong to two separate phonemes.

2.2.2 Complementary distribution

The other distributional possibility, *complementary distribution*, presents the diametrically opposing picture. Here we never find the two or more sounds in the same environment. Simply stated, we can say that two sounds are in complementary distribution if /X/ never appears in any of the phonetic environments in which /Y/ occurs. Having said that, we can now go back to some of the examples we gave at the beginning of the chapter and re-examine them. The first one concerns the dental and alveolar nasal sounds [n̪] and [n]. In English the distribution of these two sounds is such that they never appear in the same environment (that is, they are *mutually exclusive*). We find the dental only before /θ/ or /ð/, as in tenth [tɛn̪θ], in the game [ɪn̪ ðə . . .], where the other one never appears. When we find the sound /X/ only in a certain environment, and the sound /Y/ in a completely different environment, then it would be impossible for the difference between these two sounds to be contrastive because a contrast requires an overlapping distribution. In such cases of complementary distribution, we say that these sounds are allophones of one and the same phoneme. We should be reminded, in passing, that the very same two sounds are capable of occurring in the same environment, as we saw in the case of Malayalam, and function contrastively (thus, belong to two separate phonemes) in that language.

Another example of complementary distribution of an allophonic relationship can be given for [d] and [ð] of Spanish. These two sounds can never occur in the same environment in Spanish; [ð] occurs between two vowels or after a nasal, [d] occurs in the remaining environments. This is clearly an example of a complementary distribution where the occurrences of the two members are mutually exclusive. Consequently, we say that in Spanish [d] and [ð] are the allophones (positional variants) of the same phoneme.

The best analogy (and, surely, a student favorite) for complementary distribution I have heard to date has been provided by the relationship between 'Superman' and 'Clark Kent' (I don't know who the credit is due to). Although these two characters belong to the same person, their presence is entirely mutually exclusive (they can never appear in the same environment). While we invariably see 'Superman' during the moment of danger, 'Clark Kent' is the fellow we encounter in the newspaper office. Thus, these two characters provide an excellent case of a complementary distribution.

While it is true to say that the allophones of the same phoneme are in complementary distribution, this assertion can only be unidirectional. That is, we cannot reverse the statement and say 'if two sounds are in complementary distribution, then they are the allophones of the same phoneme'. The reason for this may be due to some defective distribution of certain sounds. The distributions of English [h] and [ŋ] are a case in point. While [ŋ] occurs only as a coda (syllable-final), and never as an onset (syllable-initial), [h] is found only as an onset and never as a coda. The distribution displayed here is a perfect match for the 'Superman' and 'Clark Kent' situation. Because the contexts are mutually exclusive, the distribution will undoubtedly be labeled as 'complementary'. Despite this fact, no one has ever suggested (or will ever suggest) that these two sounds should be treated as the allophones of the same phoneme. This is because they do not satisfy the other important requirement of an allophonic relationship, 'phonetic similarity'. Allophones of the same phoneme always share phonetic features, and thus are phonetically similar. If we look at the two sounds in question, we hardly see any phonetic similarity; [h] is a voiceless glottal fricative, and [ŋ] is a voiced velar nasal. In other words, these sounds do not share anything with respect to place or manner of articulation; nor do they share the voicing. Thus, we can state the following generalization: two or more sounds are allophones (positional variants) of the same phoneme, if (a) they are in complementary distribution, and (b) they are phonetically similar.

While examining the environment that might be of relevance, there is one very important aspect to keep in mind, and this is the particular phonetic feature(s) that separate(s) the sounds in the suspicious pair/group. The reason for this is that different changes can and will be stimulated by different environments. For example, if we find one member, e.g. [b], of the suspicious pair in an exclusively intervocalic environment, and never find the other member, e.g. [p], in the same environment, we seem to have a very good case to conclude that these two sounds should be the allophones of the same phoneme. Besides satisfying the requirement of complementary distribution and phonetic closeness between the two sounds, the appearance of the voiced member in an intervocalic environment (surrounding two voiced sounds) is an excellent way to stimulate voicing. In other words, the context makes perfect phonetic sense for the change.

There is no magic formula to arrive at an airtight conclusion for phonetic similarity. However, the following can provide some useful guidelines as to what constitutes a suspicious pair (or group) of sounds which might prove to be the allophones of the same phoneme.

Obstruents
- Voiced–voiceless pairs with the same place and manner of articulation (e.g. [p–b], [s–z], [tʃ–dʒ]).
- Pairs of sounds with same voicing and manner of articulation, and rather close places of articulation (e.g. [s–ʃ], [f–θ]).
- Pairs of sounds with same voicing and place of articulation but different manner of articulation (e.g. [t–tʃ], [k–x], [p–ɸ]).

Sonorant consonants
- All nasals (especially the ones that are close in place of articulation).
- All liquids (within laterals, within non-laterals, and across these two subgroups).
- Glides [j] and [w] and high vowels [i] and [u] respectively. Glides may also have a relationship with the fricatives of the same or similar places of articulation.

The common theme in all the examples above is that there are more phonetic features that unite them than features that divide them. For example [s] is a voiceless, alveolar fricative, and [ʃ] is a voiceless, palato-alveolar fricative. In other words, both sounds are voiceless and fricatives. The only feature in which they differ is the place of articulation.

Having reviewed the relevant concepts regarding the contrastive and complementary distribution, we can now go back and re-examine the phonetic differences that were easily perceived or overlooked by speakers of certain languages. For example, the difference between the dental and alveolar nasals, [n] and [n̪], is overlooked by the speakers of English, but noticed immediately by speakers of Malayalam. In the case of [d] and [ð], the situation was different for speakers of English: while the difference is easily perceived by speakers of English, the same phonetic distinction is overlooked by speakers of Spanish. The reasons for different reactions for the same phonetic differences lie in the way these differences are employed in different languages. While [n–n̪] are in complementary distribution in English and the difference is allophonic, the same sounds are in a contrastive distribution and belong to separate phonemes in Malayalam. In English [d–ð] is contrastive, but it is allophonic in Spanish. There seems to be little doubt that contrastiveness plays a major role in the perception of language users. When two sounds are allophones of the same phoneme, a speaker of the language will feel that they are the same sound.

To sum up what has been reviewed so far, we can state that two or more phonetically similar sounds may have different phonemic (functional) status in different languages. Their status is determined solely by their distribution in a given sound system. If they are in overlapping distribution (that is, can occur in the same environment, which can be verified via existence of a minimal or near-minimal pair), and the substitution of one for the other results in a change of meaning, then these two or more sounds are in contrast and are phonetic manifestations of different phonemes (for example, <u>day</u> [de] and <u>they</u> [ðe] reveal that [d] and [ð] belong to separate phonemes, /d/ and /ð/ respectively). When two sounds are in contrast (i.e. when the difference is *phonemic*), the speakers of that language develop a high-grade sensitivity towards that difference, and notice any failure to observe it.

If, on the other hand, the distribution of two or more phonetically similar sounds is complementary (that is, they are found in mutually exclusive environments), they are said to be the allophones of the one and the same phoneme. The difference between the two or more sounds, then, is *allophonic* and not phonemic (e.g. [n], [ṇ], [n̪], [m̩] in <u>name</u>, <u>snail</u>, <u>panther</u>, and <u>invite</u>, respectively). In such cases, speakers' sensitivity to these phonetic differences is extremely low-grade, if it exists at all. The reason for this is that these differences are never utilized to make any meaning differences among words (cf. the difference between [n] and [ṇ] in Malayalam cited earlier).

Before we make an illustration of the points discussed with a mini-demo, it is useful to summarize the strategy we use to decide on the phonemic status of similar sounds (see figure 2.1).

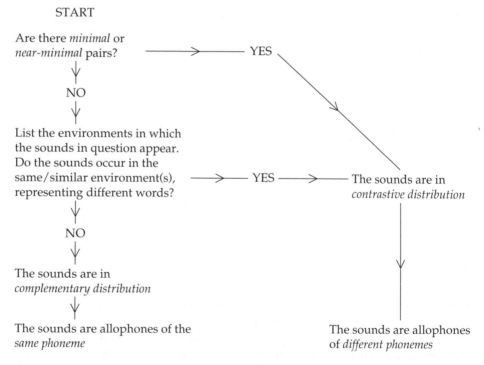

Figure 2.1 Flowchart for discovering the distribution of two or more phonetically similar sounds

2.3 Phonemic Analysis: A Mini-demo

In the following, we will review the points made thus far and briefly show the mechanics of the phonemic analysis. When we do a phonemic analysis to establish the phonological status of a pair or a group of sounds (phonetically similar sounds that can potentially be allophones of the same phoneme), it is necessary to examine their distribution. They are either in contrast and belong to separate phonemes, or represent allophones (positional variants) of a phoneme that are in complementary distribution. The first task is to spot the 'suspicious' pair or group of sounds. To exemplify this, we look at the sounds [s], [z], and [ʃ] in English and Korean. The three sounds [s, z, ʃ], which can be heard during the conversations of both English and Korean speakers, reveal the needed phonetic similarities. Namely, (a) they all share the manner of articulation features (sibilant fricatives); (b) [s] and [z] share the place of articulation (alveolar), differ only in voicing; (c) [s] and [ʃ] share the voicing (voiceless), differ only in place of articulation. The decision for their distributional character starts with the search for minimal pairs. When we look at English, we find these three sounds in an overlapping distribution, because we have the following minimal pairs: sip [sɪp] – ship [ʃɪp] – zip [zɪp]. In other words, the sounds in question do occur in the same word position (initial) before the same vowel, [ɪ], and the words mean different things. From this, we can conclude that the three sounds are in contrast and belong to three separate phonemes.

Now, let us examine the situation in Korean. The following data, although limited in size, are representative of the pattern in the language.

(1)	[us]	"upper"	(8)	[maʃi]	"delicious"
(2)	[sek]	"color"	(9)	[ʃigan]	"time"
(3)	[kasəl]	"hypothesis"	(10)	*[ʃilsu]	"mistake"
(4)	[saram]	"person"	(11)	*[ʃipsam]	"thirteen"
(5)	[sosəl]	"novel"	(12)	[ʃike]	"clock"
(6)	[sul]	"wine"	(13)	[paŋzək]	"cushion"
(7)	[ʃi]	"poem"	(14)	[inza]	"greetings"

   * words that have both [s] and [ʃ]

We start the search for the distribution of these sounds in Korean in exactly the same way we started for English, namely looking for minimal pairs. The examination of the data reveals, unlike English, that we do not have minimal pairs to establish contrasts. Our next step is to look for near minimal pairs whereby the immediately preceding and the immediately following environments are the same. We do not seem to have that either. Under such conditions, we list the environments in which the sounds in question appear, and ask the question whether the sounds occur in the same or similar environment. We do this by putting the preceding environment to the left of the blank, and the following environment to the right of it. The blank itself shows the place that the sound occupies. For example, # __ a indicates that [s] occurs in

word-initial position (# stands for the word boundary) before the vowel [a],
as exemplified in word number (4). When we have more than two sounds in
question in the group, it is customary to look at them pairwise. Thus, we start
with [s – ʃ]. The numbers next to each environment cited indicate the items
from the data above.

[s]	[ʃ]
u __ # (1)	# __ i (7, 9, 10, 11, 12)
# __ k (2)	a __ i (8)
a __ ə (3)	
# __ a (4)	
# __ o (5)	
l __ u (10)	
p __ a (11)	

When we examine the distribution of the two sounds in question, we see that
they can have the identical context for the preceding environment, namely the
beginning of a word. As for what comes after, we note the following: although
both sounds can be followed by a vowel, the vowels are not identical. While
[ʃ] always appears before [i], [s] is found before other vowels and never before
[i]. Before we decide if the difference in the following vowel can be significant
(that is, contextually create a change), we should remember what was said
earlier with regard to the difference between the two sounds. In the case of [s]
and [ʃ], the difference lies in the place of articulation only (alveolar and palato-
alveolar, respectively). The vowel [i] is known to cause alveolar sounds to change
in place of articulation and become palato-alveolar. Thus, what happens in
the Korean data is a good example of phonetically motivated contextual
change. The fact that we find [ʃ] only before [i], and never find [s] in the
same environment, satisfies the requirement of mutual exclusivity of a pair of
phonetically similar sounds that are in complementary distribution, and thus
the allophones of the same phoneme.

The next task is to examine the situation between [s] and [z], as these two
sounds share all features (alveolar, fricative) except for the voicing (voiceless
and voiced, respectively). Since we already have the environments for [s]
listed, we need to look at the occurrences of [z] alone.

ŋ __ ə (13)
n __ a (14)

The listing shows that the following environment is irrelevant, because it can
be shared by the two sounds in question ([s] can be followed by a [ə] as in (3)
and (5); it can also be followed by [a], as in (4). The examination of the preceding environment, however, reveals that [z] is always preceded by a nasal,
and [s] can never be. Thus, the complementary distribution exhibited by these
two phonetically similar sounds leads us to the conclusion that they are the
allophones of the same phoneme. Because we also said the same thing for the

relationship between [s] and [ʃ], the conclusion is that the three sounds are allophones of the same phoneme. At this juncture, we have another task that relates to the choice of the basic allophone that will represent the phoneme. To determine this, we look at the distribution of the three again and realize that [s] is the one that appears in the most different environments (the least restricted in occurrence). Because [ʃ] occurs only before [i], and [z] occurs only after nasals, [s] is clearly the choice and thus represents the phoneme.

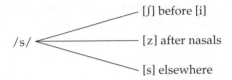

As shown above, the phoneme is represented with diagonal bars / /, and the allophones are represented with brackets, [ ]. Also, in giving the environments for the allophones, we write the more restricted one(s) first, so that we can say "elsewhere" for the basic (the least restricted) allophone of the phoneme.

If we compare the same three sounds in Korean and in English, we see a very different picture. While the sounds in question are in complementary distribution and are allophones of one and the same phoneme in Korean, they are in contrast and belong to three separate phonemes in English. We can illustrate these differences schematically in the following way.

English   **Korean**

Contrast: ship–zip–sip

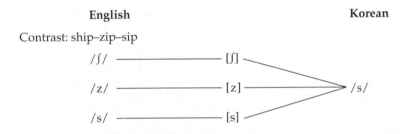

Phonetic similarity: [s] and [z] share the place and the manner of articulation, different in voicing; [s] and [ʃ] share the voicing and the manner of articulation, different in place of articulation.
Allophonic processes: change to [ʃ] before /i/. Change to [z] after nasal.

In the displays above, and below, we place the phonetically similar sounds that are shared by the two languages in the middle, between the brackets, [ ]. The language that makes the phonemic contrast has its two (or more) separate phonemes placed in between diagonal bars. With the phoneme symbols, we give a minimal pair to show the contrast. On the other side, the single phoneme of the language is placed. Underneath the display, we have more explicit statements regarding the phonetic similarity of the sounds (suspicious pair), and the type of process for the contextual variants (allophones) that are in complementary distribution. The processes that are responsible for the contextual variants are almost always assimilation processes. Simply defined, assimilation refers to the influence that one sound may have on another when they are contiguous in time. To exemplify this, let us look at the Korean triplet [s, z, ʃ] we discussed earlier. We saw that /s/ was realized phonetically as [ʃ] before /i/. The change shown here is that a voiceless alveolar fricative becomes a voiceless palato-alveolar fricative. If we think about the area that is relevant for the articulation of [i], we realize that it corresponds to the same area where palato-alveolars are made. In other words, the influence of [i] as a conditioning environment for [ʃ] is, phonetically, very plausible, and indeed not infrequent in languages. Since in this case, the conditioning sound, [i], is after the conditioned sound, the process is said to be an example of a *regressive assimilation* (the following sound influences the preceding sound; called *anticipatory coarticulation* in some books). If the influence comes from the preceding sound on to the following sound, it is termed a *progressive assimilation*. The other allophone of the Korean /s/ was [z], and the context it appeared in was always after a nasal. In other words, the voicing of the nasal seems to be the culprit for this change from a voiceless alveolar fricative to a voiced alveolar fricative. Since the conditioning sound, nasal, is before the conditioned sound, alveolar fricative, this is a case of progressive assimilation (called *perseverative coarticulation* in some books).

Contextual assimilatory changes are not restricted to consonants. For example, Totonac (an Amerindian language spoken in Mexico) has both voiced and voiceless vowels that are in complementary distribution. We find voiceless vowels in final position and the others elsewhere. The final devoicing of vowels can be considered as an assimilatory event, as it displays a situation whereby the vowel in final position is influenced by what comes after (i.e. 'silence', which does not have vocal cord vibration).

Another case of a complementary distribution relating to vocalic segments can be given from English. In certain dialects, the diphthong /aɪ/ has two phonetic manifestations, [aɪ] and [ʌɪ], as seen in the following.

nine	[naɪn]	rice	[ɹʌɪs]	rise	[ɹaɪz]	tight	[tʌɪt]
tire	[taɪɹ]	life	[lʌɪf]	side	[saɪd]	pipe	[pʌɪp]
buy	[baɪ]	Mike	[mʌɪk]				

What we see here is that [ʌɪ] is found before /s, t, f, p, k/, and [aɪ] is found elsewhere. Thus, the characterization of this systematic change is 'the diphthong is [ʌɪ] if it is followed by a voiceless sound; otherwise, it is [aɪ]'.

The conditioning environment is not always restricted to either the preceding or the following environment; sometimes the effects come from both environments. For example, in Cree (an Amerindian language spoken in Canada) [p] and [b] are in complementary distribution. We find [b] intervocalically (between two vowels) and [p] otherwise. This clearly tells us that the assimilatory conditioning environment is from both the preceding and the following environments; the voiced allophone [b] is found in between two vowels, which are voiced.

Now, let us examine the two cases – Malayalam–English for dental and alveolar nasals, and Spanish–English for dental/alveolar stops and fricatives – that we referred to earlier.

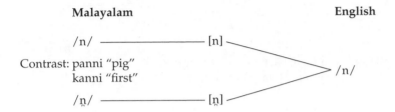

Malayalam   **English**

/n/ ——————— [n]

Contrast: panni "pig"   /n/
          kanni "first"

/n̪/ ——————— [n̪]

Phonetic similarity: shared voicing and manner of articulation; different in place
   of articulation.
Allophonic process: nasal becomes dental before /θ, ð/ (interdentals). Regressive
   assimilation.

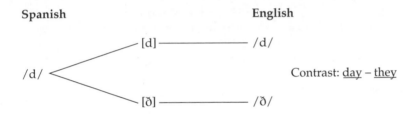

Spanish   **English**

                          [d] ——————— /d/

/d/   Contrast: <u>day</u> – <u>they</u>

                          [ð] ——————— /ð/

Phonetic similarity: shared place of articulation and voicing; different in manner
   of articulation.
Allophonic process: a stop becomes a fricative (more open articulation) between two vowels. Both the preceding and following environments are
   relevant.

The cases above, which show that the same phonetic reality is interpreted differently phonologically in different languages, are not limited to these pairs of sounds and contexts and can easily be multiplied cross-linguistically. The following are some examples between different pairs of languages.

(a) **Cree**   **English**

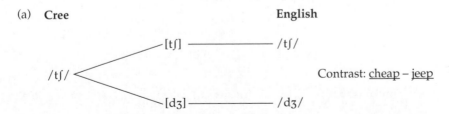

                          [tʃ] ——————— /tʃ/

/tʃ/   Contrast: <u>cheap</u> – <u>jeep</u>

                          [dʒ] ——————— /dʒ/

Phonetic similarity: shared place and manner of articulation; different in voicing.
Allophonic process: voicing between two vowels. Both the preceding and the
   following environments are relevant.

(b) **Lebanese Arabic**   **English**

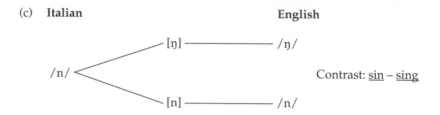

Phonetic similarity: both high, back, round; differ in tense/lax.
Allophonic process: lowering (laxing) in final position.

(c) **Italian**   **English**

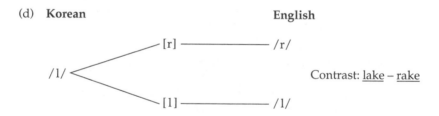

Phonetic similarity: shared manner of articulation and voicing; different in place
   of articulation.
Allophonic process: nasal becomes velar before velars. Regressive assimilation.

(d) **Korean**   **English**

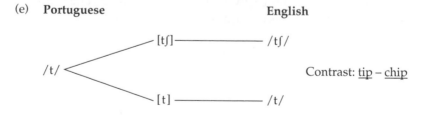

Phonetic similarity: share all features, except for lateral.
Allophonic process: liquid becomes non-lateral intervocalically. Both the preceding and following environments are relevant.

(e) **Portuguese**   **English**

Phonetic similarity: both voiceless obstruents; [tʃ] palato-alveolar affricate, [t] alveolar stop.
Allophonic process: an alveolar stop becomes a palato-alveolar affricate before
   /i/. (Since there are no palato-alveolar stops in Portuguese, the affricate is the
   closest sound. Palato-alveolar place is in the vicinity of the vowel area for /i/).
   Regressive assimilation.

(f)   **Biblical Hebrew**   **English**

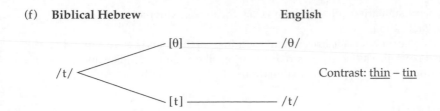

Phonetic similarity: dental/alveolar. Voiceless, obstruents; different in manner of
   articulation.
Allophonic process: a stop becomes a fricative (more open articulation) intervocalically. Both the preceding and the following environments are relevant.

(g)   **Sindhi**   **English**

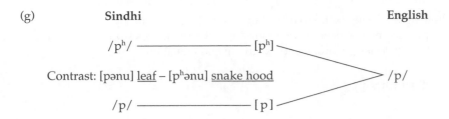

Phonetic similarity: all features same, except aspiration.
Allophonic process: aspirate a voiceless stop at the beginning of a stressed
   syllable.

   The following examples have some other relationships that do not have an
exact point of reference in English, but reveal certain phonetically significant
allophonic processes.

(h)   **Russian**

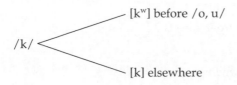

Phonetic similarity: both are voiceless velar stops; different in labialization.
Allophonic process: labialize (add lip rounding to) the velar stop before /o, u/
   (rounded vowels). Regressive assimilation.

(i)   **Russian**

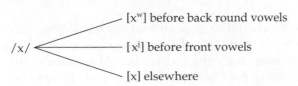

Phonetic similarity: all voiceless velar fricatives; different in labialization or
    palatalization.
Allophonic process: labialize (add lip rounding to) the sound before a round vowel,
    and palatalize it (more forward articulation, like adding an [i]-like quality) before
    a front vowel. Regressive assimilation.

(j)   **Czech**

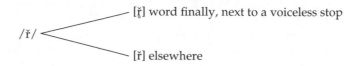

[ř̥] word finally, next to a voiceless stop

/ř/

[ř] elsewhere

Phonetic similarity: both alveolar r-sounds; different in voicing.
Allophonic process: devoice an r-sound next to a voiceless stop, or word-finally
    (also a voiceless environment). Regressive assimilation.

(k)   **Spanish**

[β] intervocalically

/b/

[b] elsewhere

Phonetic similarity: shared voicing and place of articulation; different in manner
    of articulation (stop/fricative).
Allophonic process: a stop becomes a fricative (more open articulation) between
    two vowels. Both the preceding and the following environments are relevant.

(l)   **German**

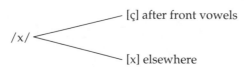

[ç] after front vowels

/x/

[x] elsewhere

Phonetic similarity: both are voiceless fricatives; different in place of articulation
    (velar/palatal).
Allophonic process: move a fricative to a more front articulation after a front
    vowel.

To sum up what has been said so far, we can say:

(a)   The goal of any phonemic (phonological) analysis is to determine the rela-
     tionship between two or more sounds in a language.
(b)   Two languages may share the same sounds, but arrange them differently.
     That is, phonetic identity does not result in phonemic identity.

(c)   Allophones of the same phoneme in a language must be phonetically similar and be in complementary distribution.
(d)   Realizations of different phonemes are in overlapping distribution, and are in contrast. That is, they must be capable of changing the meaning of a word if substituted by each other.

2.4 Free Variation

While the above generalizations are typically solid, there are two instances in English where the last two, (c) and (d), are violated. In the first, we see cases in which the allophones of a phoneme occur in the same environment. This is a violation of (c), because it does not follow the principle that the allophones should be in complementary distribution. For example, the final stops of American English are normally unreleased and unaspirated (see chapter 3 for details) as in bake [bek˺], dip [dɪp˺], etc. However, a speaker may pronounce these items with released final stops. Although these alternate productions are possible, they do not create any change in meaning. That is, in different speakers' pronunciations, we can find the released and unreleased allophones in an overlapping distribution. But, since the meaning of the word does not change, this is termed a free variation.

The second type of free variation is related not to the allophones of the same phoneme, but to the realizations of different phonemes. For example, the sounds [i] and [ɛ] belong to separate phonemes, /i/ and /ɛ/ respectively, because English possesses minimal pairs such as bead [bid] – bed [bɛd], Pete [pit] – pet [pɛt]. Since the change in meaning in these pairs of words is due to the substitution of these vowels for each other, there can be no question about their contrastiveness. However, for certain vocabulary items such as economics, which may be pronounced as [ɛkənamɪks] or [ikənamɪks], the two vowels in question occur in an overlapping distribution but without creating a change in meaning. A similar case can be cited between [aɪ] and [i], which are also normally in contrast. Thus, in cite [saɪt] versus seat [sit] the meaning change is due to these two vowels in contrast. However, alternate pronunciations for items such as either ([iðɚ] or [aɪðɚ]), neither ([niðɚ] or [naɪðɚ]) clearly show them in free variation (overlap but no meaning change). To summarize, we can say that free variation, however infrequent, can be found between the realizations of separate phonemes (phonemic free variation, as in [i] and [aɪ] of either), as well as between the allophones of the same phoneme (allophonic free variation, as in [k] and [k˺] of back).

2.5 Morphophonology

Up to this point we have looked at allophonic variations (contextual variation of the sounds belonging to the same phoneme), which take place within a single morpheme. We should also point out that several of the processes that are shown to be crucial in accounting for the allophonic variations in languages can also be found active across morpheme boundaries. A brief discussion of these is useful, because they are frequent sources of confusion for students. When morphemes are combined to form bimorphemic (two morphemes) or polymorphemic words, many of the assimilatory phenomena discussed can be present there too. Such things can also manifest themselves when two words are spoken consecutively. What we see in these instances, then, is the contextually determined alternations (different phonetic forms) of a morpheme.

To illustrate what has been said thus far, let us look at the nasal assimilation rule in Italian we cited earlier (in section 2.3). For explicitness, we give the relevant details below.

[dʒɛnte]	"people"	[aŋke]	"also"
[tinta]	"dye"	[staŋko]	"tired"
[tenda]	"tent"	[bjaŋka]	"white"
[nero]	"black"	[fuŋgo]	"mushroom"
[dansa]	"dance"		

As we see in the left column, [n] appears before [t, d, s, e] and, in the right column, [ŋ] appears before [k, g]. The sounds [n] and [ŋ] are in complementary distribution, since they share no phonetic environments. The velar, [ŋ], allophone appears only before velar stops, and the alveolar [n], appears elsewhere. The phonetically motivated (nasal assimilating to the place of articulation of the following segment) contextual variation occurs within a morpheme, and thus qualifies for allophonic variation.

The same/similar phonetically motivated nasal assimilation is also found across morpheme boundaries in several other languages. Observe the following:

impersonal [ɪmpɚsənəl]	independent [ɪndəpɛndənt]	incomplete [ɪŋkəmplit]
improbable [ɪmpɹabəbl]	intolerant [ɪntaləɹənt]	inconclusive [ɪŋkənklusɪv]
impossible [ɪmpasəbl]	inadvisable [ɪnædvaɪzəbl]	incapable [ɪŋkepəbl]

All the adjectives listed are preceded by the same negative prefix that manifests itself as either im or in orthographically. As for the phonetic manifestation, we have three forms: [ɪm] for the left column, [ɪn] for the middle column, and [ɪŋ] for the right column. That is, the pronunciation of the negative prefix is different only with respect to the nasal consonant which is bilabial, [m], before adjectives that start with a bilabial sound (left column), velar, [ŋ], before adjectives that start with a velar sound (right column). In other instances, the nasal is [n] in the prefix (middle column). This predictable alternation of the nasal is the result of the place of articulation assimilation that is reminiscent of the Italian example discussed above. Although the phonetic motivation (place of articulation assimilation for articulatory ease) of this alternation is the same in these two situations, they are different structurally. While the Italian contextual variation was allophonic in nature (occurring within one morpheme), the case of the English negative prefixes does not deal with allophones of the same phoneme, but rather shows contextually predictable alternations among separate phonemes. That English [m], [n], and [ŋ] are not allophones of the same phoneme but belong to separate phonemes /m/, /n/, and /ŋ/ can clearly be shown by the following triplet sum [sʌm], sun [sʌn], sung [sʌŋ]. Thus, what is revealed in the case of English negative prefixes is that there is an alternation of different phonemes for the same morpheme (indicators of the same meaning unit). Such cases are traditionally called morphophonemic alternations, and the different phonetic manifestations of the same morpheme (morpheme alternants) are called the allomorphs.

The previous case demonstrated the allomorphic alternations across morpheme boundaries in the same word. These cases, however, are not restricted to morpheme boundary situations in one word and can occur across the boundaries of two separate words. For example, if we examine the phonetic manifestations of the morpheme meaning 'one' in Spanish, we find the following.

un peso [um p . . .]   "one peso"
un taco [un t . . .]   "one taco"
un gato [uŋ g . . .]   "one cat"

While the morpheme meaning 'one' in Spanish is consistently spelt as un, its pronunciation varies among [um], [un], and [uŋ]. Here, again, we have a familiar picture regarding the nasals assimilating to the place of articulation of the following obstruent. This time, however, the allomorphs (phonetically conditioned variants of the same morpheme) of the meaning unit 'one' reveal the alternation across two words.

Another possibility is to find some feature-changing assimilatory processes that are restricted only across morpheme boundaries (i.e. acting only as morphophonemic processes), and with no parallels in allophonic processes of monomorphemic words. To illustrate this, examine the following past tense endings in English.

attempted [ətɛmptəd]   walked [wɔkt]   robbed [ɹabd]
blended [blɛndəd]   pushed [puʃt]   seemed [simd]
tested [tɛstəd]   sipped [sɪpt]   swayed [swed]

The above examples show that the regular past tense ending in English has three predictable phonetic manifestations. We have [-əd] if the last sound of the verb is an alveolar stop, /t, d/ (schwa insertion before another alveolar stop). However, if the verb-final sound is not an alveolar stop, then the shape of the past tense ending is an alveolar stop, [-t] or [-d], which is determined by the voicing of the verb-final sound. We have the voiceless [t] if the verb-final sound is voiceless (middle column); the form is the voiced [d] if the verb-final sound is voiced (right column). This is a clear case of voicing assimilation. However, this does not mean that this sequencing restriction occurs throughout. While the past tense of the verb ban [bæn] is necessarily [bænd] and cannot be [bænt], this does not mean that we cannot have a final consonant cluster with different voicing in its members ([-nt] sequence) in English. Words such as <u>bent</u>, <u>tent</u>, etc. reveal that there is no such restriction within a single morpheme, and that the assimilatory situation is at work only across morpheme boundaries. (See chapter 3 for similar situations regarding the allomorphs of the plural morpheme.)

In concluding this section, we should also mention that while morpho-phonemic alternations reveal several feature-changing assimilatory (phoneti-cally motivated) processes, they are not limited to those only. Several other processes, such as epenthesis (insertion), and deletion of segments, as well as metathesis (transposition) of segments can be cited among those.

2.6 Practical Uses of Phonological Analysis

Linguists are interested in finding out the patterned nature of speech for answers pertaining to psycholinguistics (the study of the interrelationship of language and cognitive structures, the acquisition of language), historical linguistics (the study of how languages change through time and the relationships among languages), and sociolinguistics (the study of the interrelationships of language and social structure of linguistic variation).

Besides its relevance in these areas, phonological analysis has great relevance in certain real world applications that go beyond the confines of linguistics. To start with, there is an intimate relationship between an alphabetic writ-ing system and the phonemic structure of a language. As such, the study of phonemics is highly useful for literacy experts, and to people devising orthographies for unwritten languages. This comes from the principle that assigns an orthographical letter for each 'phoneme' (not for each sound) in the lan-guage. Going back to the dental and alveolar nasals, [n̪] and [n], we discussed in relation to English and Malayalam, we can state that difference in the following manner. While the alphabetic representation of these two nasals will be sufficiently shown by one letter, <u>n</u>, in English (because the allophonic differences between [n̪] and [n] will be automatically supplied by the native speakers of English), in the orthographic system of Malayalam we will have to have two distinct orthographic letters because the two sounds are in con-trast in this language. When we consider the two sounds [d] and [ð], with reference to Spanish and English, we come to the following conclusion. Spanish is well served by a single grapheme, <u>d</u>, for the sounds [d] and [ð], as in <u>dedo</u> [deðo]. Since the two sounds are allophones of the same phoneme, speakers of Spanish automatically supply the predictable fricative allophone intervocalically. Thus, an additional grapheme for this predictable allophone will be an unnecessary duplication. When, on the other hand, we look at English, we realize that the language would require two distinct orthographical repre-sentations for these two sounds that are in contrast and belong to separate phonemes, as shown in the pair <u>they</u> [ðe] and <u>day</u> [de].

In chapter 1, the reader was urged to ignore spelling and focus only on the sounds in studying phonetics and phonology. The reason for this is the many discrepancies that exist between phoneme and grapheme correspondences in English. The orthographic th, which stands for two separate phonemes, /θ/ and /ð/ (e.g. ether [iθɚ] – either [iðɚ]) makes the point clearly. Had English spelling reflected an ideal alphabetic writing system (i.e. one grapheme to one phoneme), these two phonemes would be represented by two separate graphemes. We will have much more to say about English phonology and orthography in chapter 9.

We can summarize what has been said in the following manner: alphabetic writing systems are ideally phonemic in that they target one phoneme to one grapheme. However, due to several reasons during the history of a language many discrepancies may develop and the current state of the orthography of a language may be far from being ideal. Comparing the ir/regularity of the writing systems between languages, one does hear remarks such as 'the writing system of language X is phonetic'. Such remarks should not be taken seriously, because no alphabetic system ever targets or aspires to be phonetic. What we want from an efficient writing system is to represent only the relevant (functional/phonemic) distinctions made in the language, and this precludes the introduction of separate graphemes for every predictable allophonic variation; that would result in incredible complexity.

Besides the indispensable applications to devising alphabetical writing systems, the study of phonemics is a vital tool for foreign language teachers and speech and language therapists, who constitute the major targeted audience of this book. The common trait of the professionals in these two groups is that the populations they work with exhibit patterns (in sound systems, for our purpose) that are different from the ambient language, and thus should be remediated. Although the productions we observe in foreign language learners and individuals with phonological disorders are, to varying degrees, in disagreement with the norms of the ambient language, they nevertheless are not haphazard, but systematic. The importance of the application of phonological principles to the remediation setting stems from this patterned nature of the erroneous productions. The erroneous productions, in other words, are not random but are systematically organized. In the remediation setting, information on the patterned nature of the productions to be corrected is crucial for arriving at an accurate diagnosis, and this in turn serves as the basis for effective remediation.

In many cases of erroneous productions, both in foreign language learners and in individuals with phonological disorders, we find several errors related not to the complete lack of a particular sound in the client's system, but to the problems of distribution. To illustrate this, let us examine the following productions from a Japanese speaker who is learning English as a foreign language:

city [sɪtʃi], team [tʃim], totem [totɛm], tune [tˢun], tea [tʃi]

As we see, the renditions for the /t/ targets of English are varied: correct in totem, [tʃ] in city, team, and tea, and [tˢ] in tune. While the situation may initially look rather chaotic, a more careful look at the productions can show that the erroneous renditions in the form of [tʃ] and [tˢ] are not random, but systematic. Namely, the /t/ target of English is realized as [tʃ] if it is followed by /i/, and is realized as [tˢ] if it is followed by /u/. When the target /t/ is followed by any other sound, the learner's renditions are correct. The explanation for these phenomena is directly related to the learner's native language patterns, which can be illustrated as

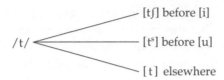

What the learner is doing is transferring the native rule to the English learning context. Such events, which are known as the native language interference, are in the central core of the field known as contrastive phonology, and will be dealt with in greater detail in chapter 8.

The importance of an accurate phonological profile of the learner for effective remediation has also been recognized in the clinical setting. A disordered system may also be a system with its own patterning and distribution that is not identical to the ambient system. The therapist, like the language teacher, needs to know the details of the system before any attempt at treatment is made. Consider the following data from a three-year-old who has the phonetic capacity to produce the target voiced stops /b, d, g/ but has distributional problems (Camarata and Gandour 1984).

bee [bi]	tea [di]	kite [gæ]
bath [bæ]	key [di]	tie [gæ]
bus [bʌ]	kick [di]	clown [gæn]
boot [bu]	two [du]	train [gæn]
book [bu]	cook [du]	cup [gʌ]
boat [bo]		duck [gʌ]
ball [ba]		goat [go]
pan [bæn]		car [ga]

We can see that the child has the contrast between the bilabial and alveolar voiced stops, as revealed by <u>bee</u> [bi] versus <u>tea</u> [di]. On the other hand, we do not have a contrast between the alveolar and the velar. What we gather from the productions is that the client shows a case of complementary distribution between these two; [d] appears before high vowels (second column), and [g] appears before non-high (low or mid) vowels (third column). Once again, we have a situation whereby the initially chaotic-looking productions that present mismatches with the ambient language have systematic patterns that could be exploited in the therapy.

Cases such as the ones described above can be easily multiplied in L₂ (second language) classroom and clinical contexts, and make it clear that the familiarity with the phonemic analysis is indispensable for L$_2$ teachers and therapists.

SUMMARY

In this chapter, we examined the functional values of sounds in different systems. Two or more sounds may be shared by two or more languages/systems, but the apparent phonetic identity of these sounds does not mean phonological identity, as they would be employed differently in different systems. We looked at the analytical technique (phonemic analysis) to discover the functional values of sounds. It is commonly observed that while two sounds are allophones of the same phoneme (complementary distribution) in one system, the very same two sounds can belong to separate phonemes (contrastive distribution) in another system. Phonemic analysis, which deals with the distributional function of sounds, is not only a tool for linguists, but a very important and helpful means for professionals (language teachers and therapists) who deal with the mismatch of systems in remediation.

1. Circle the correct alternative(s).

   (a) If two languages have the same sounds, then they (sometimes / always / often / never) have different phonologies.
   (b) If the phonetic difference between two sounds serves as the basis for distinguishing words, then the difference is (distinctive / phonemic / non-predictable / allophonic / predictable).
   (c) Occurrences of the allophones of a single phoneme are (always / sometimes / often / never) predictable.
   (d) Allophones of a single phoneme are (sometimes / often / always / never) phonetically similar.
   (e) If two phonetically similar sounds are in complementary distribution, then they are (sometimes / often / always / never) the allophones of the same phoneme.
   (f) If two sounds are in free variation, then they are (sometimes / always / never) the allophones of the same phoneme.
   (g) Speakers of a language tend to be (more / less / equally) consciously aware of phonemes than allophones.
   (h) Two sounds that appear in a minimal pair (sometimes / always / never) belong to distinct phonemes.
   (i) If two sounds are not phonemically distinct, their distribution overlaps / does not overlap.

2. Create two minimal pairs with each given word in different word positions.

	Initial	Medial	Final
Example: /t/	tea: 'pea', 'sea'	charter: 'charmer', 'charger'	seat: 'seed', 'seal'
/p/	pack:	mapping:	ape:
/m/	mate:	slimming:	room:
/s/	seek:	leasing:	class:
/ʃ/	sheet:	mashed:	bash:
/l/	lash:	rolling:	coal:
/f/	feel:	refined:	staff:
/n/	knee:	sneak:	bone:
/d/	dash:	budding:	bed:
/g/	gain:	plugging:	wig:
/ɹ/	rain:	roaring:	four:
/z/	zip:	buzzing:	seize:

3. Create three words with contrasts by supplying different vowels (diphthongs) in the following consonantal frames.

   Example: [b t]: 'beat', 'bait', 'bet'

   (a) [s l]:
   (b) [pl]:
   (c) [sp k]:
   (d) [m θ]:
   (e) [l n]:
   (f) [k n]:
   (g) [d m]:
   (h) [t k]:
   (i) [gɹ nd]:

4. Identify the sounds in contrast in the following minimal pairs.

   Example: eke – ache   /i/ – /e/

   (a) ceased – cyst / / – / /   (b) sinned – send / / – / /
   (c) gym – jam / / – / /   (d) phase – fuzz / / – / /
   (e) laugh – life / / – / /   (f) rot – wrote / / – / /
   (g) how – hi / / – / /   (h) limp – lymph / / – / /
   (i) white – right / / – / /   (j) miff – myth / / – / /
   (k) rough – rush / / – / /   (l) phi – high / / – / /
   (m) thigh – shy / / – / /   (n) wit – witch / / – / /

5. Identify the sounds that are alternating in the following morpho-
   phonemically related pairs.

   (a) profane / profanity
   (b) serene / serenity
   (c) pedagogue / pedagogy
   (d) receive / receptive
   (e) mine / mineral
   (f) verbose / verbosity
   (g) consume / consumption
   (h) public / publicity
   (i) sign / signature

6. Examine the distribution of [s] and [ʃ] in the speech of T (4;3), a child
   with phonological disorders, and determine if their distribution is

(a)   complementary
(b)   contrastive

State your evidence.

sail [ʃel]	pushy [puʃi]	seek [ʃik]
save [ʃev]	Sam [ʃæm]	gas [gæs]
grass [gɹæs]	fasten [fæsən]	crash [kɹæs]
ship [ʃɪp]	Irish [aɪɹɪs]	fashion [fæʃən]

7. Examine the following data from B (4;1), a child with phonological disorders. The /ɹ/ targets show three different realizations: [ɹ], [w], or 'zero' (i.e. deleted). What kind of distribution do these realizations reveal? State your rationale.

rich [ɹɪtʃ]	raise [ɹez]	red [ɹɛd]
more [mo]	door [do]	deer [di]
wrong [ɹɔŋ]	correct [kɔwɛk]	mirror [mɪwə]
rain [ɹen]	room [ɹum]	parrot [pæwət]
roller [ɹɔlə]	parade [pəwed]	Henry [hɛnɹi]

8. (a) Examine the following data from Maasai, a Nilotic language spoken in Kenya and Tanzania, and determine the phonemic status of [t], [d] and [ð] (that is, whether they belong to one, two, or three phonemes). State your evidence.

[ɓaða]	dangerous	[endorop]	bribe him
[tasat]	disabled	[tisila]	sift it
[taruɓini]	binoculars	[oltuli]	buttock
[iltoi]	barrel	[ɗalut]	mischievous
[endaraða]	fight each other	[indai]	'you' plural
[endulelei]	apple	[eŋgiruðoðo]	fright
[emɓiðir]	female wart hog	[enɗaraða]	thunder

(b) Note that the same three sounds are also found in English. Are their distributions in the two languages the same or different? Explain.

(c) In learning each other's language (English speaker learning Maasai – Maasai speaker learning English), who do you think will have greater difficulty with respect to the three sounds in question? Why?

9. (a) Examine the following data from Hindi and determine the phonemic status of [t], [tʰ], and [d] (i.e. if they belong to one, two, or three phonemes). State your evidence.

[tantrik]	tantra	[tʰan]	a bolt of cloth
[dan]	donate	[batʰ]	words
[tal]	beat	[tʰal]	plate
[patʰak]	one who studies	[bad]	later
[dal]	lentil	[pʰatak]	a gate

(b) Note that the same three sounds are also found in English. Are their distributions the same or different in the two languages? Explain.

(c) In learning each other's language (English speaker learning Hindi – Hindi speaker learning English), who do you think will have greater difficulty with respect to the three sounds in question? Why?

10. Examine the following data from German and determine the phonemic status of [ç] and [x] (that is, whether they are the allophones of the same phoneme or belong to separate phonemes). State your evidence.

[abmaxə]	to remove	[ɛçtə]	to ban
[axt]	eight	[ɛːnliç]	like, resembling
[blɛːçən]	small blister	[drɔliç]	amusing
[ɛlç]	elk	[fraxt]	carriage
[fruxt]	fruit	[glaɪç]	equal
[knoplaʊx]	garlic	[mɛçtiç]	powerful
[hoːx]	high	[laxən]	to laugh
[lox]	hole	[fɛçtən]	to fence

11. Examine the following data from Persian (Farsi) and determine the phonemic status of [r], [ɽ], and [ɾ] (that is, whether they belong to one, two, or three phonemes). State your evidence.

[aɾam]	calm	[arezu]	wish	[kæɾim]	giving
[ræhim]	giver	[ʃiɽ]	lion	[pæniɽ]	cheese
[ziɾe]	cumin	[zærd]	yellow	[farsi]	Persian
[musafiɽ]	traveler	[kæbiɽ]	grand	[bæɾe]	sheep
[nærm]	soft	[ræht]	laundry	[ræʃid]	strong
[modeɽ]	mother	[sefeɽ]	trip	[pæɾiveʃ]	angel looking

12. Transcribe the following (about 'spread of English', cont.) *from*
     P. Trudgill and J. Hannah, *International English* (London: Edward
     Arnold, 2002).

     It was not until the 17th century that the English language began
     ....

     the geographical and demographic expansion which has led to the
     ....

     situation in which it finds itself today, with more non-native speakers
     ....

     than any other language in the world, and more native speakers than
     ....

     any other language except Chinese. This expansion began in the late
     ....

     1600s, with the arrival of English-speakers in the Americas – North
     ....

     America (the modern United States and Canada), Bermuda, the
     ....

     Bahamas, and the Caribbean – and the importation of English from
     ....

     Scotland, into the northern areas of Ireland. Subsequently, during the
     ....

     1700s, English also began to penetrate into southern Ireland, and it
     ....

     was during this time, too, that Cornish finally disappeared from
     ....

     Cornwall, and Norn from Orkney and Shetland. During the 1800s,
     ....

     English began making serious inroads into Wales, so that today only
     ....

     twenty percent of the population of that country are native Welsh
     ....

     speakers; and in the Highlands and islands of Scotland, English also
     ....

     began to replace Gaelic, which today has around 70,000 native
     ....

     speakers.
     ....

three

English Consonants

3.1 Stops

We will start our account of the English consonants and their allophones with the most versatile group, stops. As we saw in chapter 1, articulation of stops can be analyzed in three stages (closing stage, closed stage, and release stage).

English has six stop phonemes, /p, b, t, d, k, g/. Their differences can be examined in different dimensions. Firstly, with respect to **place of articulation**, there is a three-way distinction: bilabials /p, b/, alveolars /t, d/, and velars /k, g/. Bilabials /p/ and /b/ are made by forming the closure with upper and lower lips and, after building up the pressure necessary, releasing the closure abruptly, as in pay [pe] and bay [be]. Alveolar stops /t/ and /d/ utilize the tip of the tongue to form the closure with the alveolar ridge, as in tip [tɪp] and dip [dɪp]. Finally, for velars /k/ and /g/, we raise the back of the tongue to make a contact with the soft palate (velum), as in cap [kæp] and gap [gæp].

While the account of the places of articulation for stops is very straightforward, the characteristics related to their **voicing** are not so. It is customary to see labels such as 'voiceless' and 'voiced' for /p, t, k/ and /b, d, g/, respectively, in several manuals. Although this definitely reflects the truth for /p, t, k/ which are always voiceless, and may indeed be true for /b, d, g/ of several languages (Spanish, French, etc.), it will hold in English only for the intervocalic position in such words as aboard [əboɹd], adore [ədoɹ], eager [igɚ]. In initial and final positions (following or preceding silence) /b, d, g/ are partially, if at all, voiced.

(a) bay   (b) cab   (c) bib
     day   sad   did
     gay   sag   gig

In (a) words we may have partially voiced (and indeed little voiced) /b, d, g/ in initial positions. In (b), the words contain partially voiced final stops. In (c), each word has a /b, d, g/ in both initial and final positions which are not fully voiced. Because English /b, d, g/ are fully voiced only in intervocalic position, several phoneticians prefer the classification in terms of fortis and lenis to differentiate /p, t, k/ from /b, d, g/. Accordingly, fortis stops, /p, t, k/ are pronounced with more muscular energy (force), higher intra-oral pressure, and a stronger breath effort than their lenis counterparts /b, d, g/. Following the popular usage, we will employ the labels 'voiced' and 'voiceless', but the reader should remember the more accurate lenis vs. fortis distinction in initial and final positions.

Before we leave the discussion of initial and final devoicing, some clarifications are needed. Firstly, it should be stated that devoicing in these positions is not total, and does not make these stops indistinct from their voiceless counterparts. Thus, partially devoiced [b̥, d̥, g̥] are not [p, t, k], respectively. Secondly, there is almost always a difference in the degree of voicing; final devoicing is greater than initial devoicing. Thus, in the (c) words above, [b̥ɪb̥], [d̥ɪd̥], [g̥ɪg̥], the final stops normally have greater devoicing than their initial counterparts. Finally, it should also be pointed out that final devoicing is present if there is no voiced sound coming immediately after; if there is a voiced sound immediately after, the devoicing does not take place. For example, while the final sound of <u>dog</u> is partially devoiced, the same is not observed in <u>dog meal</u>, because in the latter /g/ is immediately followed by a voiced sound, /m/ (cf. <u>dog-food</u>).

When a stop is preceded by a /s/, the distinction between /p, t, k/ and /b, d, g/ is not in voicing, but lies in fortis/lenis. For example, the velar stops /k/ and /g/ are not in any way different in voicing in the following pairs of words, <u>discussed</u> – <u>disgust</u>, <u>misspell</u> – <u>miss Bell</u>, <u>disperse</u> – <u>disburse</u>; the difference lies in fortis and lenis productions respectively.

The type of stop (/p, t, k/ or /b, d, g/) influences the length of the preceding vowel in that vowels are longer before voiced (lenis) stops than when before voiceless (fortis) stops. This difference seems to be much more noticeable when the syllable contains a long vowel or a diphthong. Pairs such as <u>lobe</u> – <u>slope</u>, <u>nab</u> – <u>nap</u> (/b/ – /p/), <u>wide</u> – <u>white</u>, <u>ride</u> – <u>right</u> (/d/ – /t/) <u>league</u> – <u>seek</u>, <u>dog</u> – <u>dock</u> (/g/ – /k/) illustrate the difference in the length whereby the first member of each pair has the longer vowel because it is followed by a voiced stop. The influence on the length of the preceding segments is not restricted to vowels and diphthongs, and can also be observed with the nasals and the lateral. If we compare the following pairs, <u>killed</u> – <u>kilt</u>, <u>send</u> – <u>sent</u>, <u>amber</u> – <u>ampere</u>, we see that the sonorants in the first member of each pair are longer.

Another dimension that differentiates /p, t, k/ from /b, d, g/ in English is the feature of **aspiration**. The voiceless set of stops is pronounced with aspiration at the beginning of stressed syllables (<u>pay</u> [pʰeɪ], <u>take</u> [tʰeɪk], <u>cab</u> [kʰæb]). That this characteristic is not restricted to word-initial position can be verified in words such as <u>apart</u> [əpʰaɪt], <u>attack</u> [ətʰæk], <u>occur</u> [əkʰɝ], where the aspirated stops are not word-initial, but in initial positions of stressed syllables. In American English (AE), this is the most common pattern. In addition, voiceless stops may be produced with weak aspiration in the following positions:

(a) in an unstressed syllable: polite [pəláɪt], vacuum [vǽkjum]
(b) before a syllabic consonant: pickle [pɪkl̩]
(c) if released in final position: sit [sɪt], sick [sɪk]

In their release stage, syllable-final (especially word-final) single coda stops are often produced with no audible release. The following examples illustrate the point with the appropriate diacritic for unreleased stops: mop [mɔp˥], sit [sɪt˥], sack [sæk˥], mob [mab˥], sad [sæd˥], bag [bæg˥]. When not following a vowel, most speakers release the final /t/ (e.g. fast).

When we have a word with two non-homorganic (i.e. not from the same place of articulation) stops in a row, there is no audible release for the first stop; the closure of the second stop in sequence is made before the release of the first stop.

sipped [sɪp˥t] /p + t/	good girl [gʊd˥gɜ˞l] /d + g/
light coffee [laɪt˥kɑfi] /t + k/	cheap date [tʃip˥det] /p + d/
sobbed [sab˥d] /b + d/	soft breeze [sɔft˥bɹiz] /t + b/

When we have two homorganic (i.e. sharing the same place of articulation) stops in a sequence, there is no separate release for the first stop; rather one prolonged closure for the two stops in question. This is valid for the cases where there is voicing agreement (gemination), as in big girl, black cat, sad dog, stop please, as well as sequences with different voicing, as in top block, white dog, black girl.

The stop closure is maintained and nasally released in cases in which the stop is followed by a homorganic nasal. In this process, which is known as 'nasal plosion', the air is released through the nasal cavity. This happens in the following environments:

(a) the nasal is syllabic: button [bʌtn̩] /t + n/, sudden [sʌdn̩] /d + n/, taken [tekŋ̩];
(b) the nasal is in the initial position of the following syllable of the word: submarine [sʌbməɹin], /b + m/, madness [mædnəs] /d + n/;
(c) the nasal is in the initial position of the next word: hard nails [hɑɹdnelz] /d + n/, sad news [sædnuz] /d + n/.

A comparable release, this time laterally, is provided when the stop is followed by a homorganic lateral. This process, which is known as 'lateral plosion', can be observed in the following words, cattle [kætl̩] /t + l/, middle [mɪdl̩] /d + l/, as well as in the sequences of words, bud light [bʌdlaɪt] /d + l/, at last [ətlæst] /t + l/. That this event requires the homorganicity is further shown by an example such as tickle [tɪkl̩], or nipple [nɪpl̩], which have no lateral release.

Putting all this information together, we can say that the following parameters need to be looked at in differentiating the stops /p, t, k/ from /b, d, g/. In initial position, fortis vs. lenis, and/or aspirated vs. unaspirated should be considered. Medial position is the only one in which voicing is a distinguishing factor; in addition, length of the preceding sound (longer vowels and sonorant before /b, d, g/), and aspiration if the stop is at the initial position of a stressed syllable would be considered. In final position, the length of the preceding sound would be the most crucial aspect.

Apart from these general patterns exhibited, certain stops have characteristics of their own. Alveolar stops are realized as dental when they occur immediately before interdentals, as illustrated in the following: bad [bæd] – bad things [bæd̪ θɪŋz]; great [gɹet] – great things [gɹet̪θɪŋz].

For many speakers of American English, words such as letter, atom, header, and ladder are pronounced as [lɛDɚ], [æDəm], [hɛDɚ], [læDɚ], respectively. This process, which is known as *flapping* (*tapping* in some books, which is a more correct characterization), converts an alveolar stop to a voiced flap/tap. The most conducive environment for this process is intervocalic, when the second syllable is not stressed. Thus, while attic [ǽDɪk] has a flap, attack [ətʰǽk] does not because, in the latter, the alveolar stop is the onset of a stressed syllable. This pattern is also revealed in morphologically related but prosodically different word pairs. Thus, while the /t/ targets in the left column below (in unstressed syllables) undergo this process, they do not do so in the morphologically related words in the right column (in stressed syllables).

Italy [ɪDəli]	Italian [ɪtæljən]
autumn [ɔDəm]	autumnal [ətʌmnəl]
rhetoric [ɹɛDəɹɪk]	rhetorical [ɹətɔɹəkəl]
notable [noDəbl]	notation [noteʃən]

The principle is also valid across word boundaries, because we get at all [əDɔl] (flapped because /t/ is the coda of the unstressed syllable), but a tall [ə tɔl] (not flapped because /t/ is the onset of the stressed syllable). Similarly, the /t/ target in eat up is flapped, but in e-top [i tap] it is not. Although in a great majority of cases of flapping (all the above included) the first vowel is stressed, this is not a necessary condition. For example, in words such as nationality [næʃənǽləDi], sorority [səɹɔɹəDi], calamity [kəlǽməDi] flapping occurs between two unstressed vowels. Thus, the only condition related to stress is that the target alveolar stop cannot be in a stressed syllable (this condition also includes the secondary stress; thus, we don't have flapping in words such as sanitary, sabotage, latex, etc., in which /t/ targets are in syllables with secondary stress, which will be discussed in chapter 7). Besides the clear intervocalic environments that were given above, there are two other environments that seem to provide the context for this process. These are (a) the r-coloring of the first vowel, as exemplified in porter [pɔɹDɚ], border [bɔɹDɚ], and (b) following syllabic liquid, as in little [lɪDḷ], cattle [kæDḷ], bitter [bɪDɚ], and butter [bʌDɚ].

Before finishing the discussion of flapping, mention should be made regarding the cases of homophony created by the neutralization of the distinction between the alveolar stops, as illustrated by the pairs writer – rider [ɹaɪDɚ], grater – grader [gɹeDɚ], latter – ladder [læDɚ], bitter – bidder [bɪDɚ]. While many speakers of American English pronounce such pairs homophonously, there are others who make a distinction between these words. However, whenever the distinction is made, it is not related to the pronunciation of the alveolar stop, but to the preceding vowel/diphthong. Following the generalization we looked at earlier, where it was stated that vowels/diphthongs were longer before voiced than before voiceless stops, we could predict that the diphthong /aɪ/ would be longer in rider and grader than in writer and grater respectively. Similarly, the vowels /æ/ and /ɪ/ would be longer in ladder and bidder than in latter and bitter. The phenomenon described above is not limited to the retroflex liquid, and is also observed with the lateral liquid. Pairs such as petal – pedal [pɛDl̩], futile – feudal [fjuDl̩], metal – medal [mɛDl̩] illustrate this point well.

Alveolar stops of English are produced with considerable affrication as onsets when they are followed by /ɹ/ (e.g. train, drain). The diacritic used for this is a _ under the stop [t̠]. The tongue tip touches behind the alveolar ridge, exactly to the point where affricates /tʃ, dʒ/ are produced (note children's frequent spelling mistakes for the target train as chrain or chain).

Also noteworthy is the fact that /t, d/ may turn into palato-alveolar affricates when they are followed by the palatal glide in the following word. Thus, we get did you . . . ([dɪd ju . . .] or [dɪdʒ ju . . .]).

Another characteristic of American English in informal conversational speech is the creation of homophonous productions for pairs such as planner – planter [plænɚ], canner – canter [kænɚ], winner – winter [wɪnɚ], tenter – tenor [tɛnɚ]. The loss of /t/ in the second member of these pairs is also seen in many other words, as in rental, dental, renter, dented. In all these examples we see that the /t/ that is lost is following a /n/. However, that such an environment is not a guarantee for this process is revealed by examples such as contain, interred, entwined in which /t/ following an /n/ cannot be deleted. The difference between these words and the earlier ones is that /t/ is deleted only in an unstressed syllable.

Finally, mention should be made of the glottal stop or the preglottalized /t/ and the contexts in which it manifests itself. A glottal stop is the sound that occurs when the vocal cords are held tightly together. In most speakers of American and British English (AE, BE), glottal stops or the preglottalized /t/ are commonly found as allophones of /t/ in words such as Batman, [bæʔmæn], Hitler [hɪʔlɚ], atlas [æʔləs], Atlanta [əʔlæntə], he hit me [hihɪʔmi], eat well [iʔwɛl]. While the glottal stop can replace the /t/ in these words, it is not allowed in atrocious [ætɹoʃəs] (not *[æʔɹoʃəs]), attraction [ətɹækʃən] (not *[əʔɹækʃən]). The reason for this is that the glottal stop replacement requires the target /t/ in a syllable-final position ([bæʔ.mæn], [əʔ.læn.tə]). The words that do not allow the replacement have their /t/ in the onset position ([ə.tɹo.ʃəs], [ə.tɹæk.ʃən]), as /tɹ/ is a permissible onset in English. We should point out, however, that /tɹ/ being permissible is not carried over across words as the compound court-room illustrates. The expected production of this sequence is with a glottal replacement, [kɔɹʔ rum], because the syllabification is not [kɔɹ.tɹum]. The glottal stop replacement of /t/ is also observable before syllabic nasals, which also provides the occurrence in coda position, as in beaten [biʔn̩], kitten [kɪʔn̩]. The process under discussion is most easily perceived after short vowels (e.g. put, hit), and least obvious after consonants (e.g. belt, sent). As pointed out above, in absolute final position, some speakers do not replace the /t/ with a glottal stop entirely, but insert a glottal stop before /t/, as in hit [hɪʔt]. It is also worth pointing out that this process, which is sometimes called 'preglottalization' (or 'glottal reinforcement') may be applicable to other voiceless stops for many speakers, as shown in tap [tæʔp], sack [sæʔk].

Velar stops of English, /k, g/, have appreciably different contact points in the beginning of the following two-word sequence, car key [kaɹ ki]. The initial stop of the first word is made at a significantly more back point in the velum area than that of the initial sound of the second word, which is almost making the stop closure at the hard palate. The reason for such a difference is the back/front nature of the following vowel. Thus, velars are more front when before a front vowel than when before a back vowel.

The other assimilatory process velar stops undergo relates to the different lip positions in geese and goose. While in the latter example the lips are rounded during the stop articulation, they are not so in the former. Again, the culprit is the rounded/unrounded nature of the following vowel. The stop is produced with lip rounding if it is followed by a rounded vowel. Putting together the two assimilatory processes we have just discussed, we can see why the velar stops in the following sequence, keep cool, are produced differently. Predictably, the /k/ of the first word, followed by /i/, is unrounded and more front, while that of the second word, followed by /u/, is back and rounded.

Dialectal variation

The most significant dialectal changes regarding stop consonants of English center around the alveolars. As mentioned earlier, the process of flapping is restricted to American English (also in Irish English (IrE), Australian English (AuE), and New Zealand English (NZE)). Thus, in other varieties of English /t/ and /d/ are unchanged. Related to this process, we can point out the differences in aspiration. Since the following syllabic lateral provides a conducive environment for flapping in American English (bottle [baDl̩], little [lɪDl̩]), there is no aspiration in this word. However, in varieties without flapping, /t/ may be released with some aspiration. Also noteworthy is the frequent unaspirated realization of the voiceless stops in Scottish English (ScE). In African American Vernacular English (AAVE), final voiced stops may be devoiced (e.g. bad [bæd] → [bæt], pig [pɪg] → [pɪk]), or may be deleted (e.g. hat [hæt] → [hæ], bad [bæd] → [bæ]). In addition, /d/ may be deleted before the /z/ of the following plural/possessive morpheme (e.g. kids [kɪdz] → [kɪz]).

3.2   Fricatives

English has nine fricative phonemes occupying five places of articulation. Eight of these fricatives are pair-wise matching in voiceless/voiced for labio-dental

/f, v/, inter-dental /θ, ð/, alveolar /s, z/, and palato-alveolar /ʃ, ʒ/ places of articulation. The remaining /h/ is a voiceless glottal fricative.

Although the labels 'voiceless/voiced' are commonly used to separate certain fricatives, as with stops, the situation of voicing needs to be looked at carefully. The picture presented by the voiced fricatives echoes what we saw in stops; they are fully voiced only in intervocalic position, and partially voiced in initial and final positions.

(a) sip [sɪp]   (b) assume [əsum]   (c) bus [bʌs]
     zip [zɪp]   resume [ɹəzum]   buzz [bʌz]

Thus, among the three words with a voiced alveolar fricative, only the word-medial /z/ in resume is fully voiced. Because of this, as with the stops, several phoneticians prefer the terms 'fortis vs. lenis' for the voiceless vs. voiced distinction. The fortis fricatives are produced with louder friction noise than lenis counterparts.

There are other parallels between fricatives and stops. The length of the preceding vowel, or sonorant consonant is dependent on the following fricative. Thus, the first member of each of the following pairs has a longer vowel/sonorant than the second member, as it is followed by a lenis (voiced) fricative:

save [sev] – safe [sef], fens [fɛnz] – fence [fɛns], shelve [ʃɛlv] – shelf [ʃɛlf]

Similarly to stops, when a word ends in a fricative and the next word starts with the same fricative, we get one longer narrowing of the vocal tract, as the one long /s/, in tennis socks [tɛnɪs:ɑks], and a long /f/ in half full [hæf:ʊl].

A subgroup of fricatives (alveolars, /s, z/, and palato-alveolars /ʃ, ʒ/) which are known as 'sibilants' are very important for certain regularities in English phonology. These fricatives are produced with a narrow longitudinal groove on the upper surface of the tongue; acoustically, they are identified by noise of relatively high intensity (hissing, hushing noise). In the formation of the regular noun plurals, third person possessive marking, and the marking of the third person verb ending in simple present, sibilants play an important role. In all these events, English has three possible markings [s], [z], and [əz], as shown in the following:

Plural	Possession	Simple present
cats [kæts]	Jack's [dʒæks]	s/he jumps [. . . dʒʌmps]
dogs [dɔgz]	John's [dʒɑnz]	s/he runs [. . . ɹʌnz]
buses [bʌsəz]	George's [dʒɔɹdʒəz]	s/he catches [. . . kætʃəz]

All the above can be accounted for by stating one rule: if the last sound of the singular noun (in the left column) / possessor (in the middle column) / verb (in the right column) is a sibilant (affricates /tʃ/ and /dʒ/ are sibilants because they have in them the sibilant fricatives /ʃ/ and /ʒ/ respectively) then the ending is [əz]; if the last sound is not a sibilant, then it is either a [s] or a

[z], and this is determined by its voicing. This pattern repeats itself in the contractions with 'is' and 'has' in connected speech.

Pam's very angry [pæmz vɛ.ɹi æŋg.ɹi]   Pam's been very angry [pæmz bɪn vɛ.ɹi æŋg.ɹi]
What's your name? [wʌts jɔ.ɹ nem]   It's been a long time [ɪts bɪn ə lɔŋ taɪm]
Ross is here [ɹɔs ɪz hiɹ]   Mitch has been there [mɪtʃəz bɪn ðɛɹ]

We can show all these with the following tree diagram.

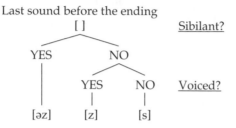

Apart from these characteristics that are general to the fricatives, there are certain other points worth making for certain fricatives. To start with, palato-alveolar fricatives /ʃ, ʒ/ differ from the others by having an appreciable lip rounding (labialization). Another pair, alveolars /s, z/, echoing the alveolar stops, may undergo palatalization and turn into [ʃ, ʒ] respectively, when they occur before the palatal glide /j/. Commonly heard forms such as [aɪmɪʃju] (I miss you), [ðɪʃjiɹ] (this year), [aɪpliʒju] (I please you), [huʒjuɹ bɑs] (who's your boss?) demonstrate this clearly. Thus, we can put together the behavior of /t, d, s, z/ and state that the alveolar obstruents of English become palato-alveolar when followed by a word that starts with the palatal glide /j/. (Since there are no palato-alveolar stops in English, the replacements are affricates for /t, d/.)

Interdental fricatives /θ, ð/ undergo the elision process (i.e. they are left out) when they occur before the alveolar fricatives /s, z/, as exemplified by clothes [kloz], months [mʌns].

Certain fricatives are subject to some distributional restrictions. Firstly, the voiced palato-alveolar /ʒ/, although it is well established in medial position (e.g. vision [vɪʒən], measure [mɛʒɚ]), is not found in word-initial position. Very few seemingly contradictory cases are found in loan words in the speech of only a limited number of speakers (e.g. genre [ʒɑn.ɹə]. The standing of /ʒ/ in final position is relatively better established, although one can still observe several fluctuating forms, such as massage [məsɑʒ/məsɑdʒ], beige [beʒ/bedʒ], garage [gəɹɑʒ/gəɹɑdʒ] ([gæ.ɹɪdʒ] in BE).

The other fricative that has a defective distribution is the glottal /h/, which can only appear in syllable-initial (never syllable-final) position. This sound is different from the other voiceless fricatives, as the source of the noise is not the air being forced through a narrow gap. The origin of /h/ is deep within the vocal tract, and the turbulence is caused by the movement of air across the surfaces of the vocal tract. Also worth mentioning is its voicing status; while it is voiceless word-initially, as in <u>home</u> [hom], <u>his</u> [hɪz], etc., it is pronounced with breathy voice intervocalically, as in <u>ahead</u>, <u>behind</u>, and <u>behave</u>.

The distribution of the voiced interdental fricative /ð/ may also deserve some comment in that, in initial position, it is restricted to grammatical morphemes. It is important to note that although we have fewer than twenty words that begin with this sound (the case forms of the personal pronouns <u>they</u> and <u>thou</u>, the definite article, the demonstrative pronouns such as <u>this</u>, <u>that</u>, and so on, and a handful of adverbs such as <u>then</u>, <u>thus</u>), these are words of high frequency in use.

Finally, we should mention the process whereby initial /ð/ in words such as 'the', 'this', 'that' becomes assimilated (with or without complete assimilation) to previous alveolar consonants (e.g. <u>what the heck</u> [wɑtdəhɛk]/ [wɑttəhɛk], <u>run the course</u> [ɹʌndəkɔɹs]/[ɹʌnnəkɔɹs]).

Dialectal variation

While we do not see much of a difference across varieties regarding the labio-dental and alveolar fricatives, interdentals and palato-alveolars present some notable variations. One does find dentalized realization of interdentals before vowels in New York City, as in <u>think</u> [t̪ɪŋk], <u>they</u> [d̪e]; the same has been reported in Southern Irish English. In African American Vernacular English (AAVE), they turn into alveolar stops in the same environment (<u>think</u> [tɪŋk], <u>they</u> [de]), but are realized as labio-dental fricatives in intervocalic and postvocalic environments in AAVE (<u>nothing</u> [nʌfɪŋ], <u>with</u> [wɪf], <u>mother</u> [mʌvɚ], <u>smooth</u> [smuv]). In AAVE, and also in some southern dialects of England one does see a labio-dental replacement for the voiceless /θ/ before /ɹ/, as in <u>three</u> [fɹi]. Also notable is the stopping of voiced fricatives /v/ and /z/ preceding nasals (e.g. <u>seven</u> [sɛvən] → [sɛbm], <u>isn't</u> [ɪznt] → [ɪdnt]).

In certain words, AE and BE show appreciable differences regarding the palato-alveolar fricatives. While targets such as <u>Asia</u>, <u>Persia</u>, <u>version</u> all have /ʒ/ in AE, they may have either /ʒ/ or /ʃ/ in BE. In <u>issue</u>, <u>sensual</u>, we invariably find /ʃ/ in AE; in BE these words may have either /ʃ/ or /sj/. Similarly, <u>seizure</u> and <u>azure</u> are pronounced with a /ʒ/ in AE, while they may have either /ʒ/ or /zj/ in BE.

Finally, although it was stated above that alveolars do not reveal any patterned dialectal variation, from personal observation this author created a list of respectable length containing words that could have either of the two alveolar fricatives /s, z/ (e.g. <u>resources</u>, <u>Exxon</u>, <u>citizen</u>, <u>absorb</u>, <u>representing</u>, <u>greasy</u>, <u>absurd</u>, <u>desolate</u>, <u>disburse</u>, <u>Texas</u>, <u>Renaissance</u>) among AE speakers.

3.3 Affricates

The two English affricates, /tʃ, dʒ/ follow the patterns of stops and fricatives with regard to fortis/lenis (voiceless/voiced). Thus, we can state that /dʒ/ is fully voiced only in intervocalic position (e.g. <u>agent</u> [edʒənt], <u>ledger</u> [lɛdʒɚ]);

in initial and final position it is only partially voiced (e.g. Jane [dʒen], fudge [fʌdʒ]).

Also, similar to stops and fricatives, sonorants (vowels, diphthongs, and sonorant consonants) are longer preceding the voiced (lenis) affricate than when preceding the voiceless (fortis) affricate. The vowels in ridge [ɹɪdʒ] and badge [bædʒ] are longer than the ones in rich [ɹɪtʃ] and batch [bætʃ]; we obtain a similar difference for the nasal consonant in binge [bɪndʒ] and pinch [pɪntʃ], and lunge [lʌndʒ] and lunch [lʌntʃ]. Since the above two generalizations are valid for stops, fricatives, and affricates, we can reformulate the rule and make it general for all obstruents. Thus, we can state that (a) lenis obstruents are voiced only when they occur intervocalically; they are partially voiced in initial and final position, unless immediately followed by a voiced sound; and (b) sonorants are longer preceding a voiced (lenis) obstruent than when preceding a voiceless (fortis) one.

There is, however, a notable difference between the affricates on the one hand and the stops and the fricatives on the other with respect to lengthening in geminates. Unlike stops and fricatives, in which one long articulation with no separate release is observed in cases of two adjacent identical segments (e.g. stop Peter [stɑp:itɚ], rough features [ɹʌf:itʃɚz]), affricates have separate releases. Thus, sequences such as much cheaper [mʌtʃ tʃipɚ], orange juice [ɔɹəndʒ dʒus] cannot be pronounced as *[mʌtʃ:ipɚ], and *[ɔɹəndʒ:us]. The same principle also holds when the two affricates are different in voicing (e.g. much jollier [mʌtʃ dʒɔliɚ], large chair [lɑɹdʒ tʃɛɹ]).

Although affricates are phonetically made up of two sounds /t + ʃ/ and /d + ʒ/, phonologically they behave like one segment and not like consonant clusters. There are several supporting arguments for this assertion. Firstly, English does not allow any onsets with a stop + fricative combination. Secondly, as indicated earlier in section 1.3.4, data from speech errors (spoonerisms) show that affricates, when transported from one position to another, fill the space that is vacated by a single segment, as illustrated by key chain [ki tʃen] becoming [tʃi ken], Ray Jackendoff [ɹe dʒækəndɔf] becoming [dʒe ɹækəndɔf], and last cigarette Tim had in June [. . . tɪm hæd ɪn dʒun] becoming [. . . dʒɪm hæd ɪn tun] (Fromkin 1973). Thus, if roughly cheaper [ɹʌfli tʃipɚ] were to suffer a spoonerism, the likely form would be [tʃʌfli ɹipɚ], and never *[tɹʌfli ʃipɚ]. Lastly, sounds representing an affricate are noticeably shorter than the sequence of the sounds that make up the affricate. Thus, /tʃ/ in watch ear is shorter than a sequence of [t] + [ʃ] in what sheer.

Dialectal variation

Affricates do not present any variation among AE dialects. However, there are some notable differences between AE and BE with respect to the pronunciation of certain words. In AE words such as statue, virtue are always pronounced with /tʃ/, they may have either /tʃ/ or /tj/ in BE. A similar thing is found in the voiced counterpart: individual, education are with /dʒ/ in AE, but may be either with /dʒ/ or /dj/ in BE. Also, in BE, we note a tendency to the use of /ʃ/ for /tʃ/ after an /n/, as in pinched, lunch, wrench.

3.4 Nasals

English has three nasals in the following places of articulation: bilabial /m/, alveolar /n/, and velar /ŋ/. The first two of these can occur in all word and syllable positions, but the last one has defective distribution in that it can only occur in syllable-final position.

Similar to the stops, a nasal will have one prolonged closure in cases where it is followed by an identical nasal, as in <u>ten names</u> [tɛn:emz], <u>some more</u> [sʌm:ɔɹ].

The alveolar nasal, /n/, is articulated in a more forward fashion (dental) when it is followed by an interdental (/θ, ð/): <u>tenth</u> [tɛn̪θ], <u>ban the film</u> [bæn̪ðəfɪlm], <u>when they</u> [wɛn̪ðe].

Bilabial and alveolar nasals become labio-dentals when they are followed by a labio-dental sound, as in <u>emphasis</u> [ɛɱfəsɪs], <u>comfort</u> [kʌɱfɚt], <u>invite</u> [ɪɱvaɪt], <u>infant</u> [ɪɱfənt]. This assimilation is not restricted to the adjacent sounds in the same word and still occurs when the labio-dental fricative is at the beginning of the next word, for example <u>come first</u> [kʌɱ fɚst], <u>on fire</u> [aɱfaɪɹ], <u>warm feet</u> [wɔɹɱ fit].

The susceptibility of nasals to assimilation is further demonstrated by total change in place of articulation in the following: <u>ten pairs</u> [tɛmpɛɹz], <u>one piece</u> [wʌmpis], <u>ten girls</u> [tɛŋgɚlz], <u>you can go</u> [jukəŋgo].

The above-mentioned cases of regressive assimilations which nasals go through do not exhaust all the assimilatory possibilities. The alveolar nasal /n/ is also retroflexed when it occurs after /ɹ/ (progressive assimilation), as in <u>burn</u>, <u>barn</u>. Finally, /m/ and /n/ are also subject to progressive assimilation in cases of partial devoicing after voiceless obstruent /s/, as in <u>snail</u> [sn̥el], <u>small</u> [sm̥ɔl].

As mentioned earlier, nasals, together with liquids, can be syllabic in English. In words such as <u>sudden</u>, <u>button</u>, <u>open</u>, <u>taken</u>, and <u>chasm</u>, the second syllables may be represented solely by nasal consonants ([sʌdn̩], [bʌtn̩], [opm̩], [tekŋ̩], [kæzm̩]). Although these forms are possible, and indeed are preferable over the ones with an [ə] in the second syllables in running speech, the same is not possible in words such as <u>felon</u>, <u>carom</u> which are pronounced only as [fɛlən] and [kæɹəm] (not [fɛln̩] and [kæɹm̩]) respectively. Neither is it possible to have a syllabic nasal in <u>film</u> or <u>charm</u>. Why? The key issue appears to be the manner of articulation of the segment preceding the nasal. For a nasal to be syllabic, it has to be immediately preceded by an obstruent. Since the segments preceding the nasal in <u>film</u> and <u>charm</u> are sonorants, the nasals cannot be syllabic. It should also be stated that when the consonant preceding the nasal is preceded by another consonant, the nasal tends not to be syllabic, as we normally insert an [ə] in that syllable, as exemplified by [kændəl] not [kændl̩], <u>piston</u> [pɪstən] not [pɪstn̩], <u>Lincoln</u> [lɪŋkən] not [lɪŋkn̩].

One issue that has been subject to some controversy is the homorganicity of the syllabic nasal and the preceding obstruent. The overwhelming majority of examples of syllabic nasals come from homorganic sequences such as <u>bidden</u>

[bɪdn̩], golden [goldn̩], Latin [lætn̩], kitten [kɪtn̩], etc. Indeed, the motivation for homorganicity is further revealed by examples such as ribbon [ɹɪbən] vs. [ɹɪbm̩], open [opən] vs. [opm̩], bacon [bekən] vs. [bekŋ̩], broken [bɹokən] vs. [bɹokŋ̩], in which the syllabic nasal assimilates to the place of articulation of the preceding obstruent in colloquial speech. While these examples support the homorganicity view, it should be pointed out that we can also encounter words such as madam [mædm̩], modem [modm̩] with [dm], and chasm [kæzm̩], prism [pɹɪzm̩] with [zm], which present notable exceptions, because their syllabic nasals are not homorganic with the preceding obstruent, and they are not subject to further assimilation to become *[mædn̩] *[modn̩], *[kæzn̩], *[pɹɪzn̩].

   Finally, mention needs to be made of some points unique to the velar nasal. As stated above, /ŋ/ can occur only in coda position in English. However, even in that position there are further restrictions: it can only be preceded by /ɪ, ɛ, æ, ʌ, ʊ/ (lax vowels). Another point worth mentioning is related to the orthographic correspondences for this phoneme. While /ŋ/ is typically represented by the ng sequence orthographically, this is a unidirectional relationship. While some words with orthographic ng in the middle have the pronunciation /ŋ/ only, others will have /ŋg/. Morphology seems to be a factor. For example, while ng in finger and anger stand for /ŋg/ ([fɪŋgɚ], [æŋgɚ]), it stands for /ŋ/ in singer and hanger ([sɪŋɚ], [hæŋɚ]). The difference between the two groups of words is that while the former are monomorphemic words, the latter have two morphemes. There are, however, other monomorphemic words such as sing and hang in which ng stands for /ŋ/ ([sɪŋ], [hæŋ]). Thus, the generalization will have to be made in the following manner: the orthographic ng stands for /ŋ/ at the end of a morpheme, or when inside a polymorphemic word. Such a generalization will have one notable exception related to comparative and superlative suffixes. While adjectives such as long, strong are pronounced with a /ŋ/ [lɔŋ], [stɹɔŋ], their comparatives and superlatives have /ŋg/ ([lɔŋgɚ], [stɹɔŋgɚ], and [lɔŋgəst], [stɹɔŋgəst]).

Dialectal variation

In AAVE, final nasals may be deleted and the preceding vowel is nasalized (e.g. den [dɛn] → [dɛ̃]). In the North of England, there is dialectal variation between /ŋ/ and /ŋg/; the old /ŋg/ survives, especially before vowels (e.g. singer). Similar cases can be found in the US southern mountains. The most obvious variation in the US is the substitution of /n/ for /ŋ/ in the unstressed -ing, as in going, something, and so on. This appears to occur, at least for several speakers, more commonly in the progressive (e.g. 'he is reading') than in gerunds (e.g. 'reading is fun').

3.5 Approximants

Liquids and glides form the category of approximants. These sounds are made in such a way that one articulator is close to another without narrowing the vocal tract to create any friction. Approximants are joined with stops in two-member English onset clusters, as in play [ple], green [gɹin], twin [twɪn], beauty [bjuti]. In addition to this general pattern, certain members of this class have specific combinatorial characteristics. The lateral liquid /l/ can be combined with /s/ (sleep [slip]) and /f/ (fly [flaɪ]), and the non-lateral liquid /ɹ/ can combine with /f/ (free [fɹi]), /θ/ (three [θɹi]), and /ʃ/ (shrimp [ʃɹɪmp]). The labio-velar glide /w/ can follow a /s/ (sweet [swit]), and /θ/ (thwart [θwɔɹt]) in clusters, while the possibilities are more numerous for the palatal glide /j/ (/m/ music [mjuzɪk], /f/ few [fju], /v/ view [vju], and /h/ hue [hju]). When the first member of the cluster is a voiceless obstruent, approximants are devoiced ([gɹin] but [pɹ̥e], [glu] but [sl̥ip], [dwɪndl̩] but [sw̥it]).

The palatal glide /j/ is articulated with an audible friction before /i/ or /ɪ/ (year [jiɹ], yip [jɪp]), while there is no friction with other vowels (yes [jɛs], yacht [jɑt], yawn [jɔn]). Another point to be made for /j/ is that it is restricted to appearing before /u/ in initial clusters (music [mjuzɪk], pure [pjuɹ]).

The labio-velar glide /w/ is unique among the consonants of English, as it involves two places of articulation. While we have the lip rounding (thus, labial) on the one hand, the back part of the tongue is also raised towards the velum in the production (thus, velar) of this sound.

The liquids, /l, ɹ/, differ from the glides in one important respect: they can be syllabic in English. The conducive environment for the syllabicity of the liquids is similar, but not identical, to that of the nasals we examined earlier. Nasals required an obstruent as the preceding segment to become syllabic, while liquids can accept any consonant for this condition. For example, in words such as channel [tʃænl̩], kennel [kɛnl̩], the final syllable has the syllabic liquid after a sonorant consonant. Also worth mentioning is the lack of the requirement of homorganicity between the syllabic liquid and the preceding consonant. Unlike nasals that overwhelmingly require homorganicity with the preceeding obstruent, syllabic liquids have the freedom of occurring after consonants with different places of articulation, as exemplified by apple [æpl̩], removal [ɹəmuvl̩], pickle [pɪkl̩], eagle [igl̩].

We should also add, similar to what was said in relation to nasals, that whenever the consonant that precedes the lateral is yet preceded by another consonant, we normally insert an [ə] between the liquid and the consonant preceding it, and thus, the liquid does not become syllabic. Examples such as pistol [pɪstəl] not [pɪstl̩], and tingle [tɪŋgəl] not [tɪŋgl̩] illustrate this clearly.

The retroflex approximant /ɹ/ is produced with the tip of the tongue curled back toward the hard palate in AE. However, this is not the only way to produce the /ɹ/ in AE. Some speakers have no retroflexion and use a 'bunched' articulation. The /ɹ/ is produced with friction (affricated) in onset clusters after the alveolar stops (try, dry). It is commonplace to use a 'retracted' diacritic for this phenomenon ([tɹ̠aɪ]).

The alveolar lateral liquid, /l/, which is produced with varying degrees of 'velarization' (raising the back of the tongue) is articulated in a more forward (dental) fashion when it is followed by an interdental fricative (e.g. wealth [wɛl̪θ], kill them [kɪl̪ðɛm]).

Dialectal variation

In BE, the /ɹ/ has no retroflexion; the tip of the tongue approaches the alveolar area in a way similar to that of alveolar stops, but does not make any contact with the roof of the mouth. This is commonly described as a post-alveolar approximant. Besides the difference in production, the distribution of this sound varies greatly. Whereas in AE and other so-called 'rhotic' (or 'r-ful') dialects, such as IrE, ScE, CnE, /r/ can occur without much restriction, in BE (except the southwest of England) and in other 'non-rhotic' (or r-less) dialects, such as New England and the Southern US, Australia, New Zealand, and Wales, it can occur only before vowels. Thus, we observe differences such as car ([kɑ] / [kɑɹ]), farm ([faːm] / [fɑɹm]). When a word ending in r is followed by a word beginning with a vowel, we see a 'linking r' in non-rhotic dialects (player of the game [pleəɹ əv . . .]). Another aspect of the r-less, non-rhotic dialects is the 'intrusive r' whereby an /ɹ/ is inserted between a word ending in /ə/ and the following word starting with a vowel, as in India and Pakistan [ɪndiəɹ ænd . . .], the idea is [. . . aɪdiə·ɹɪz]. In AAVE, /ɹ/ may be deleted intervocalically (e.g. during [dʊɹɪŋ] → [dʊɪŋ], Carol [kæɹəl] → [kæʊ], more [moɹ] → [mo]), as well as in clusters (e.g. professor [pɹəfɛsəʳ] → [pəfɛsəʳ]).

The other liquid, alveolar lateral approximant /l/ also presents appreciable differences among different varieties. While it is customary to see the groupings of 'dark l' and 'clear l' ('light' or 'bright' in some publications) in referring to both AE and BE, the reality is rather different. In BE, we find the 'clear l' which is articulated with the tongue tip in contact with the alveolar ridge (resembling an /i/ vowel, with no raising of the back of the tongue) in prevocalic (onset) position, as in like, law; in postvocalic (coda) position (e.g. fall, belt) the realization is the velarized 'dark l' which has a quality similar to /u/ with raising of the back of the tongue towards the velum. In AE, as well as ScE, and IrE, however, we may hardly find the 'clear l'; most commonly, the realizations differ in terms of the shades of the 'dark l'. Thus, we find a 'dark l' before front vowels (e.g. left), a more velarized darker variety before back vowels (e.g. loose, low), and the darkest one is found in postvocalic position (e.g. bolt, full). The syllabic [l̩] is invariably 'dark' in AE. In Welsh English (WeE), the /l/ is always 'clear'. In AAVE, postvocalic /l/ may vocalize to [u] or [ʊ], as in bell [bɛl] or [bɛʊ], and /l/ may be deleted before a labial consonant (e.g. help [hɛlp] or [hɛp], wolf [wʊlf] or [wʊf]).

Words such as music [mjuzɪk], museum [mjuziəm], pure [pjuɹ], cure [kjuɹ], cute [kjut] have to have the same sequence of two sounds in their onsets in both AE and BE. However, the two dialects vary when we examine words such as tune, nude, dune, news, lute. While in BE, and to a lesser degree in New England, we see a /j/ after the first consonant in these words ([tjun], [njud], [djun], [njuz], [ljut]), the expected AE pronunciations are without a /j/ ([tun], [nud], etc.). The same difference is also observed in words such as assume, resume ([əsjum], [ɹəzjum] in BE, and [əsum], [ɹəzum] in AE). These examples may suggest that /j/ may not follow an alveolar in the same morpheme in AE (across morphemes this is possible, as in would you, bet you). This generalization, however, has to be amended, because words such as <u>onion</u> [ɑnjən], <u>tenure</u> [tɛnjɚ], <u>annual</u> [ænjuəl], <u>value</u> [vælju], <u>failure</u> [feljɚ], <u>million</u> [mɪljən] have alveolars /n/ or /l/ followed by a /j/ in AE as well as in BE. Thus, the correct characterization of the AE restriction on alveolars should read as '/j/ cannot follow an alveolar obstruent; it can follow an alveolar "sonorant" when in an "unstressed" syllable'.

For several speakers of AE, as well as ScE, IrE, and NZE, /w/ has a voiceless version (phonetically shown as [hw] or [ʍ]) in words spelled with <u>wh</u>. Thus, these speakers make the following distinctions in pairs such as <u>Wales</u> – <u>whales</u> [welz] – [hwelz], <u>witch</u> – <u>which</u> [wɪtʃ] – [hwɪtʃ]. In AAVE, /j/ can be deleted in a [CjV] sequence (e.g. <u>computer</u> [kəmpjutɚ] [kəmputɚ]).

Summary

In this chapter, we looked at the consonant phonemes of American English and their contextual variants. The variants clearly attest the highly rule-governed nature of language and are critical for practitioners who need to identify the mismatches of their population with the norm. We also noted the differences among the varieties, which are also systematic. Information gathered from these is particularly helpful to remediators who may otherwise confuse some dialect features with disordered speech.

1. Complete the following statements and give examples (in phonetic transcription). Your examples should be different from the ones provided in the chapter.

    (a) Vowels/diphthongs are longer before _____ stops than before _____ stops.
         e.g. _____/_____   _____/_____

    (b) Voiceless (fortis) stops are aspirated when _____
         e.g. _____   _____   _____

    (c) Stops are unreleased when _____
         e.g. _____   _____   _____

    (d) Stops are nasally released when _____
         e.g. _____   _____   _____

    (e) Alveolar stops become dental when _____
         e.g. _____   _____   _____

    (f) Alveolar stops are flapped when _____
         e.g. _____   _____   _____

    (g) /t/ is deleted when _____
         e.g. _____   _____   _____

    (h) /t/ may be replaced by a glottal stop when _____
         e.g. _____   _____   _____

    (i) Velar stops are more front when _____
         e.g. _____/_____   _____/_____   _____/_____

    (j) Velar stops are rounded when _____
         e.g. _____/_____   _____/_____   _____/_____

    (k) Vowels, nasals, and /l/ are longer before _____ fricatives than before _____ fricatives.
         e.g. _____/_____   _____/_____   _____/_____

    (l) Interdental fricatives are elided when _____
         e.g. _____   _____   _____

(m) Stops, fricatives, and nasals are long when _____

e.g. _____   _____   _____

(n) Alveolar sonorants become dental when _____

e.g. _____   _____   _____

(o) Non-velar nasals become labio-dental when _____

e.g. _____   _____

(p) Nasals may be syllabic when _____

e.g. _____   _____   _____

(q) Approximants / /, / /, / /, / / are devoiced when _____

e.g. _____   _____   _____   _____

(r) Approximants / / and / / may be syllabic when _____

e.g. _____   _____   _____   _____

2. /t/ is probably the most versatile of all stops of English, as it can undergo several processes such as becoming dental, preglottalization, glottal stop replacement, deletion, flapping, aspiration, etc. Examine the following list of words and indicate the various possibilities for the /t/ targets together with the phonetic transcription.

Example: entity [ɛntɪti]
t-deletion: [ɛnɪti], flapping [ɛntɪDi], t-deletion and flapping [ɛnɪDi]

mentality   _____
scientist   _____
stunting   _____
betting   _____
attest   _____
trustable   _____
tractor   _____
don't think _____
mortality   _____
quarter   _____
battle   _____
at large   _____

3. Transcribe the following and discuss the release of the stops.

(a) skip town [_____] _____
(b) sheep dog [_____] _____
(c) great dane [_____] _____
(d) drip blood [_____] _____
(e) light bulb [_____] _____
(f) fake gun [_____] _____
(g) ship mate [_____] _____
(h) club member [_____] _____
(i) cat tail [_____] _____

4. Circle the items that qualify for lateral plosion. State the generalization.

puddle, bottle, goggle, apple, head lice, deep lake, red light, pickle

5. Transcribe the following. Pay special attention to the nasals.

keep him here _____
looking good _____
I can go _____
lamb meat _____
green thumb _____
citizen Kane _____
pen-pal _____
home free _____
run there _____
blame me _____
in Greece _____

6. If the following were to undergo spoonerisms, what would be the likely and unlikely results, and why?

red jeep _____
just right _____
cheap rate _____

7. Transcribe the following (about 'spread of English', cont.) *from* P. Trudgill and J. Hannah, *International English* (London: Edward Arnold, 2002).

It was also during the 1800s that the development of Southern Hemisphere varieties of English began. During the early 19th century, large-scale colonization of Australia began to take place and, at a slightly later date, New Zealand, South Africa, and the Falkland Islands also began to be colonized from the British Isles. The South Atlantic islands of St Helena and Tristan da Cunha also acquired English-speaking populations during the 1800s, as did Pitcairn Island and, subsequently, Norfolk Island in the South Pacific. Not surprisingly, these patterns of expansion, settlement and colonization have had an effect on the relationships, similarities and differences between the varieties of English which have grown up in different parts of the world. For example, there are very many similarities between Scottish and northern Irish English. North American English and the English of southern Ireland also have many points of similarity. And the English varieties of the Southern Hemisphere (Australia, New Zealand, South Africa, Falklands), which were transplanted relatively recently from the British Isles, are very similar to those of the south-east of England, from where most emigrants to Australasia and South Africa came. They are quite naturally much less different from the English of England than are the varieties spoken in the Americas, which were settled much earlier.

English Vowels

4.1 Introduction

Describing the vowels of English is a much more complex task than doing the same for the consonants. The main reason for this is the magnitude of variation and differences in the inventories of different varieties of English. The number of consonant phonemes is the same in all varieties of English (24), and the dialectal variations are relatively small. When we look at the vowels, however, we see that the number of phonemes varies, and the phonetic realizations of these phonemes may be different from one variety to another. Thus, in order not to overwhelm the primary readership of this book, students and practitioners of Applied Linguistics, TESOL (teaching of English to speakers of other languages), and Communication Disorders in the United States, our main focus will be American English. At the end of the chapter, we will also present a comparison of American English with some other major varieties spoken outside the US.

4.2 Vowel Set of American English

The vowel set of American English can be described with the following key words. To the left of the key word, we place the symbol that is used in this book; the symbols to the right of the word can be found in other publications. The following list contains what is commonly described as monophthongal vowels, mostly flanked between obstruents:

/i/	beat	(/iː/, /ij/, /iy/)
/ɪ/	bit	
/e/	bait	(/eɪ/, /ej/, /ey/)
/ɛ/	bet	
/æ/	bat	
/ʌ/	bus	(/ə/ in unstressed syllables)
/ɑ/	pot	(/ɑː/)

/ɔ/   cloth   (/ɔ:/)
/o/   boat   (/ou/, /ow/)
/ʊ/   book
/u/   boot   (/uw/, /u:/)

Although these vowels are commonly described as 'simple', we have to mention that /i/ and /u/ are slightly diphthongized (thus, the symbols /ij/, /iy/ and /uw/, respectively, in some books and manuals), and /e/ and /o/ are even more diphthongized (thus, the symbols /ej/, /ey/, and /ou/, /ow/, respectively, in some books and manuals).

Diphthongs

The following three are the main diphthongs of American English:

/aɪ/   bite   (/aj/, /ay/, /ai/)
/aʊ/   bout   (/aw/, /au/, /aʊ/)
/ɔɪ/   void   (/oy/, /oj/, /ɔj/, /ɔy/, /oɪ/, /oi/)

4.2.1   Phonetic properties of vowels

As we saw in chapter 1, in the description of vowels, tongue position plays a very important role. Accordingly, one of the important dimensions is related to the part of the tongue involved, and the other is related to the height of the tongue in the production of a specific vowel. According to the former criterion, English vowels can be classified as:

Front: /i/, /ɪ/, /e/, /ɛ/, /æ/
Central: /ʌ/
Back: /u/, /ʊ/, /o/, /ɔ/, /ɑ/

As for tongue height, we have the following groupings:

High: /i/, /ɪ/, /u/, /ʊ/
Mid: /e/, /ɛ/, /o/, /ɔ/
    In some publications, a separation between 'high–mid' and 'low–mid' is given
    to separate /e/ and /o/ from /ɛ/ and /ɔ/.
Low: /æ/, /ʌ/, /ɑ/

If we put these two dimensions together, we obtain the vowel chart shown in figure 4.1.

Besides the tongue height and the tongue part involved, the vowels of English are also grouped according to the lip position. The binary split is between the rounded vowels (/u, ʊ, o, ɔ/), and the unrounded vowels (the remainder). All rounded vowels of English are back; in fact we can make the following generalization: all non-low back vowels are rounded in English.

	FRONT	CENTRAL	BACK
HIGH	beat i		u boot
	bit ɪ		ʊ book
MID (high-mid)	bait e		o boat
(low-mid)	bet ɛ		ɔ cloth
LOW		bus ʌ	
	bat æ		ɑ pot

Figure 4.1 American English vowels

4.2.2 Tense–lax

It is also customary to see another binary grouping between the 'tense' and 'lax' vowels of English. This issue requires more detailed attention, as we may find different rationales and classifications in different publications. In some manuals, the tense–lax distinction is present to account for the two vowels that are otherwise described identically. For example, vowels /i/ and /ɪ/, according to the dimensions discussed above, will both be described as 'high, front, unrounded' vowels; the same problem is present with regard to /u/ and /ʊ/, because both are 'high, back, rounded'. Similarly, the front and back mid vowels /e, ɛ/ and /o, ɔ/, if not separated as high-mid and low-mid, will end up being described identically To solve these problems, tense and lax are introduced; the first member in each of these pairs of vowels is called 'tense', because (a) it has a higher tongue position, (b) it has greater duration than its 'lax' counterpart, and (c) it requires a greater muscular effort in production (hence, the term 'tense') than the lax vowel. This phonetic definition, however, is not universally adopted. Rather, one finds a phonologically defined 'tense–lax' separation more popular in the literature. This distributionally based classification is more useful, because it divides the vowels into two groups that are distinguished by the environments in which they occur. Also, as we will see later in chapter 7, this division will play an important role in the stress rules of English.

The following describes the tense–lax rationale in terms of the different kinds of syllables in which the vowels can occur. Since all English vowels can occur in closed syllables (as shown in the list at the beginning of this chapter), this cannot be used as a criterion. However, when we examine the vowels and diphthongs that can occur in stressed open syllables, we find /i, e, ɑ, ɔ, o, u, aɪ, aʊ, ɔɪ/ (tense vowels); however, /ɪ, ɛ, æ, ʊ, ʌ/ (lax vowels) are absent in such syllables. Another syllable type that is said to favor the occurrence of tense vowels and, thus, generally rejects lax vowels is closed by /ɹ/. This, however, is a somewhat complex issue, because the contrasts between the tense vowels and their closest lax counterparts are generally lost before /ɹ/ for many speakers of American English. We will have more to say about this later. As for the syllable types that favor the occurrence of the 'lax' vowels of English, we can cite the syllables closed by /ʃ/ or by /ŋ/. To summarize the mutually exclusive environments, we can say that tense vowels are found in stressed open syllables (and syllables with /ɹ/ coda), while 'lax' vowels are found in syllables with /ʃ/ or /ŋ/ coda.

This distributionally based phonological classification of tense–lax does come into conflict with the earlier mentioned phonetically based classification. First of all, both /o/ and /ɔ/ are 'tense' in the latter classification, while they were separated ('tense' for the former, 'lax' for the latter) in the phonetic classification. Secondly, there will be a problem with regard to 'duration', which the phonetically based criterion focuses on. While it is true that several of the lax vowels (/ɪ, ɛ, ʊ, ʌ/) are short, /æ/ is not. Indeed, this vowel has equal or even greater duration than typically long and tense vowels such as /ɑ, e, o/. We will not go into further details in this introductory text and, following the widespread usage, will utilize the 'tense' and 'lax' grouping as defined by the occurrences in different syllable types.

Now we can revise the vowel chart and incorporate all that has been said.

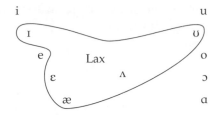

Before we examine in detail the different subgroups of vowels and their dialectal variation, we look at some other characteristics that are relevant to all vowels.

4.2.3 Nasalized vowels

The words <u>bead</u> and <u>bean</u> form a minimal pair, and any native speaker of English can tell that the final consonants in these words are responsible for the contrast. Besides this obvious fact, however, there lies another difference between these two words and that has to do with the vowel sounds. While both vowels belong to the phoneme /i/, the phonetic manifestation of the vowel of the second word, <u>bean</u>, is nasalized and, phonetically, an [ĩ]. This predictable allophonic rule of English is valid for all vowels; that is, English vowels (and diphthongs) are nasalized when they occur before a nasal consonant.

4.2.4 Length

Length of vowels (and diphthongs) varies predictably according to the context they appear in. More specifically:

(a) Vowels are longer before voiced consonants than before their voiceless counterparts. Thus, the phonetic realization of the vowel /æ/ in <u>bag</u> [bæg] is longer than its realization in <u>back</u> [bæk].

(b) Vowels are longer before sonorant consonants than before obstruents. Thus the phonetic realization of the vowel /o/ in <u>goal</u> [gol] is longer than its realization in <u>goad</u> [god].
(c) Vowels are longer in open syllables than in closed syllables. Thus, the phonetic realization of the vowel /e/ in <u>bay</u> [be] is longer than its realization in <u>bait</u> [bet].

We can combine the three rules above and say that we find a vowel longest in an open syllable (/i/ in <u>knee</u> [ni]); next longest before a syllable closed by a sonorant consonant (/i/ in <u>kneel</u> [nil]); next longest in a syllable closed by a voiced obstruent (/i/ in <u>need</u> [nid]); and shortest in a syllable closed by a voiceless consonant (/i/ in <u>neat</u> [nit]).

(d) Vowels are longer in stressed syllables than in unstressed syllables. Thus, the phonetic realization of the phoneme /i/ in the stressed (bold-faced) syllable of the word <u>appreciate</u> [ə.p**ɹi**.ʃi.et] is longer than its realization in the following unstressed syllable.

4.2.5 Vowels before /ɹ/

Earlier we mentioned that vowels are affected by the surrounding consonants, and this effect is much more noticeable with certain consonants, especially with liquids. In this section, we will examine the vowels before /ɹ/. In most forms of American English some form of r-sound after a vowel is permitted. When the following /ɹ/ is the same syllable (as in <u>ear</u>, <u>cure</u>, <u>work</u>, <u>party</u>), the vowel takes on some retroflex quality, which is commonly known as 'r-coloring'. When this happens, several otherwise well-established vowel contrasts of English are neutralized (i.e. lost) with many speakers of American English. For example, the contrast between the two high front vowels, /i/ and /ɪ/ seems to disappear in words such as <u>ear</u>, <u>fear</u>, <u>beard</u>, <u>pier</u>, etc. The r-colored production resembles neither /i/ nor /ɪ/; it is somewhere in between (traditionally transcribed as [iɹ]). A similar situation can be observed between the two high back vowels /u/ and /ʊ/ in words such as <u>tour</u>, <u>mature</u>, <u>endure</u>, and <u>poor</u>. The r-colored vowel is not identical to either /u/ or /ʊ/. This phenomenon of neutralizations of contrasts continues with full force in the front and back mid vowel series. For many speakers of American English, the r-colored vowel in <u>Mary</u>, <u>merry</u>, and <u>marry</u> is the same, thus revealing a neutralization of the contrasts between /e/, /ɛ/, and /æ/. As for the back vowels, words such as <u>pork</u>, <u>bore</u>, <u>horn</u>, and <u>fork</u> do not seem to reveal any distinction between /o/ and /ɔ/ as the /ɹ/ has the effect of raising the /ɔ/ toward /o/ (cf. <u>morning</u> vs. <u>mourning</u>). Similarly, with respect to the high back vowels, the contrast between /u/ and /ʊ/ may be neutralized in words such as <u>poor</u> and <u>cure</u>.

Besides neutralizing the above-mentioned distinctions, the r-coloring is present in the following two diphthongs: /aɪɹ/ (<u>fire</u>, <u>entire</u>, <u>inspire</u>), and /aʊɹ/ (<u>sour</u>, <u>devour</u>). Finally, the central vowel schwa has two r-colored manifestations; [ɝ]

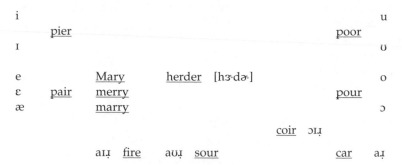

Figure 4.2 Vowels before the tautosyllabic /ɹ/

in stressed syllables, and [ɚ] in unstressed syllables (e.g. herder [hɝˑdɚ]). We summarize the r-colored vowels with the tautosyllabic /ɹ/ in figure 4.2.

Before we end this section, we should mention that an additional neutral-ization is present in some varieties of General American, and especially in east-ern New England, New York City, and Southern American, whereby /ɔɹ/ may shift to /aɹ/, when the vowel and the following /ɹ/ are not tautosyllabic. In words such as foreign, moral, forest, and horrible, the vowel shown with the orthographic o may be pronounced as /a/, thus giving us [faɹən], [maɹəl], [faɹəst], and [haɹəbl]. Note that this shift is not possible if the vowel is in the same syllable with the following /ɹ/, as exemplified in score, shore, organized, and storm. The following example, observed in its multiple occurrences with several speakers, makes the point succinctly. The word forehead may be heard as [fɔɹhɛd] or [faɹəd]; in the first rendition, [ɹ] is the coda of the first syllable (tautosyllabic with the preceding vowel), and thus is not lowered to [a] (not [faɹhɛd]). However, the second rendition, which has the lower vowel, [a], necessarily puts the [ɹ] in the onset position of the second syllable.

4.2.6 Vowels before /l/

The effect of /l/ on the preceding tautosyllabic vowel, although not as drastic as that of /r/, is still noticeable. As we saw in the preceding chapter, postvocalic /l/ is highly velarized (dark) in American English, and this has a retracting effect on the front vowels. As a result, we have a more centralized vowel in the second word of each pair below.

/i/   meat – meal
/ɪ/   Mick – milk
/e/   pay – pale
/ɛ/   bet – belt
/æ/   tack – talc

The effect of the postvocalic /l/ on the remaining vowels (central and back) and diphthongs is more of a raising and backing, but might be less noticeable.

/ɑ/   <u>dot</u> – <u>doll</u>
/ʌ/   <u>hut</u> – <u>hull</u>
/o/   <u>so</u> – <u>sole</u>
/ʊ/   <u>foot</u> – <u>full</u>
/u/   <u>food</u> – <u>fool</u>
/aɪ/   <u>might</u> – <u>mile</u>
/aʊ/   <u>bout</u> – <u>bowel</u>
/ɔɪ/   <u>coin</u> – <u>coil</u>

4.3 Front Vowels

High front: The two American English high front vowels, /i/ and /ɪ/, differ in height, length, and tense–lax dimension. The /i/ is longer and higher and slightly diphthongal (thus, the symbols such as /i:/, /ij/, /iy/ in some books). In the production, the highest point of the tongue is a little lower and centralized, and is raised and fronted in articulation. This is most noticeable in the final position, as in <u>see</u>, and least noticeable before voiceless stops, as in <u>feat</u>, where the duration is shortest. For some speakers, [i] may be in free variation with [ɪ] in final position (e.g. <u>city</u> [sɪti/sɪtɪ], <u>happy</u> [hæpi/hæpɪ]). The use of final unstressed [ɪ] is most common to the south of a line drawn west from Atlantic City to northern Missouri, thence southwest to New Mexico.

The vowel /ɪ/ has several different phonetic manifestations; it may undergo 'tensing' and be realized as [i] before palato-alveolar fricatives (e.g. <u>fish</u> [fiʃ]). In AAVE and in Southern American English, /ɪ/ tends to be lowered to [ɛ] before nasals (<u>thing</u> [θɛŋ]). Also observed in the same region is the tendency that converges the front vowels to [ɪ] (<u>gater</u>, <u>kettle</u>, <u>daddy</u>). Finally, we should note the free variation of [ɪ] with [ə] in unstressed syllables (<u>believe</u> [bəliv/bɪliv], <u>kitchen</u> [kɪtʃən/kɪtʃɪn]), and in suffixes <u>-ed</u>, <u>-es</u>, <u>-est</u>, as in <u>tempted</u> [tɛmpt(ə/ɪ)d], <u>bushes</u> [bʊʃ(ə/ɪ)z], <u>longest</u> [lɔŋg(ə/ɪ)st].

Mid front: The difference between the mid front vowels /e/ and /ɛ/ is similar to that between the high front vowels /i/ and /ɪ/; /e/ is longer, higher, and tense, and /ɛ/ is lower, shorter, and lax. The diphthongal nature of the tense one, however, is more pronounced; this is most obvious in open stressed syllables, such as <u>say</u>, or before voiced consonants (<u>game</u>, <u>grade</u>) than before voiceless consonants (e.g. <u>gate</u>) or in weak syllables (e.g. <u>create</u>). A more monophthongal (or very narrow) diphthong can be found in northernmost Midwest (Wisconsin, Minnesota).

The vowel /ɛ/, similar to the tensing of /ɪ/ to [i], may be realized as diphthongal [e] before /ʃ, ʒ/ (e.g. <u>special</u> [speʃəl], cf. <u>spatial</u>) in the South. This is also extended to contexts before voiced stops (e.g. <u>bed</u>, <u>dead</u>), and as a result the contrast between /e/ and /ɛ/ is lost, and <u>egg</u> rhymes with <u>vague</u>. Besides the free variation that exists before a tautosyllabic [ɹ], there is also a free variation between /e/ and /æ/ (e.g. <u>apricot</u>, <u>matrix</u>); this also exists in the negative prefix, as in <u>amoral</u>, <u>asymmetric</u>. Similar to the southern variety, /ɛ/ may be raised to /ɪ/ before a nasal in AAVE (e.g. <u>pen</u> [pɛn] → [pɪn]).

Low front: English has one low front vowel, /æ/, which has different real-izations in different regions. In Eastern American, especially in some New England varieties (Boston), the lower and more back vowel [a] is common (e.g. half [haf], rat [ɹat]). In the south, a diphthongal allophone is frequently heard (e.g. glass [glæɪs], bad [bæɪd]).

Before an [ɹ] plus another vowel, as in carry, Paris, Arabic, [æ] occurs along the Atlantic and Gulf Coast and in the South, but [ɛ] occurs more frequently in other areas. This vowel can be diphthongal, especially before /ʃ, ʒ, k/, in the South (e.g. splash [splæɪʃ], back [bæɪk]).

4.4   Central Vowels

The central, low-mid, lax vowel of English is /ʌ/ (e.g. bus [bʌs]). This vowel is found only in stressed syllables; in unstressed syllables, a higher vowel, [ə] "schwa" [ʃwɑ], is the realization (around [əɹaʊnd]).

Before a tautosyllabic [ɹ] in stressed syllables, as in nurse, her, etc., a slightly higher, r-colored vowel, [ɝ] is found. Its corresponding unstressed version is [ɚ]. These are the two r-colored vowels of the word herder [hɝdɚ]. When /ɹ/ is intervocalic, as in courage, this may be represented as [kɝɹədʒ] to show that the vowel is not in the same syllable with /ɹ/. In some such words (e.g. hurry, worry), [ʌɹ], instead of [ɝɹ], may be found along the Atlantic seaboard, throughout most of Pennsylvania ([hʌɹi], [wʌɹi]). There are several different treatments of these central vowels in different manuals with respect to the num-ber of phonemes. Without going into these controversies, we will adopt the following in our transcriptions.

[ʌ] in stressed syllables (e.g. bus [bʌs])
[ə] in unstressed syllables (e.g. sofa [sofə])
[ɝ] in stressed syllables before a tautosyllabic [ɹ] (e.g. bird [bɝd])
[ɚ] in unstressed syllables before a tautosyllabic [ɹ] (e.g. father [fɑðɚ])
[ɝɹ] in stressed syllables before a heterosyllabic [ɹ] (e.g. courage [kɝɹədʒ])
[əɹ] in unstressed syllables before a heterosyllabic [ɹ] (e.g. parade [pəɹed])

4.5   Back Vowels

Low back: The low back vowel in American English is /ɑ/, as in father. While many speakers of American English make a distinction between /ɔ/ and /ɑ/, as in the following pairs of words (collar – caller [kɑlɚ] – [kɔlɚ], cot – caught [kɑt] – [kɔt], Don – dawn [dɑn] – [dɔn]), many others do not make this dis-tinction and use /ɑ/ for both. In such cases, some books suggest that /ɑ/ has two allophones: [ɑ] and [ɒ]. The vowel [ɒ], which is heard mainly in the Eastern seaboard, has slight lip rounding and lies between [ɑ] and [ɔ]; it is not used by all Americans. For those people who use it, the distribution is as follows: [ɑ] occurs in both open syllables (e.g. spa) and syllables closed by a sonorant consonant (e.g. car, prom), and [ɒ] in syllables closed by an obstruent (e.g. hot, posh).

Mid back: The relationship between the mid back vowels of American English, /o/ and /ɔ/, is similar to that of their front counterparts /e/ and /ɛ/. The vowel /o/, like /e/, is somewhat diphthongized and has a movement higher towards the end in production (thus, the symbols /oʊ/, /ow/ in some books). It is monophthongal (or very narrowly diphthongal) in the northernmost Midwest (Wisconsin, Minnesota). As mentioned earlier, before a tautosyllabic /ɹ/, the distinction between the two vowels is lost for speakers in the New York City area and across the northern US west of New England. In the south and upper New England, however, the distinction is maintained. Thus, pairs such as hoarse – horse, morning – mourning may or may not be homophonous depending on the region.

High back: The high back vowels, /u/ and /ʊ/, behave very similarly to their front counterparts /i/ and /ɪ/. The vowel /u/ is slightly diphthongal (thus, the symbol /uw/ in some books). While /u/ is centralized in the southeastern US (e.g. school, good), /ʊ/ may undergo 'tensing' and be realized as [u] before a palato-alveolar fricative coda, as in bush [buʃ], which rhymes with douche. As mentioned earlier, the distinction between /u/ and /ʊ/ is lost before a tautosyllabic /ɹ/ (e.g. tour); a similar situation may be observed in some other words spelled with oo (e.g. hoof, roof, root) where either vowel is acceptable. Finally, in unstressed syllables preceding another vowel, /u/ may become lax [ʊ] (e.g. gradual [gɹædʒʊəl]).

4.6 Diphthongs

The three diphthongs of American English, /aɪ, aʊ, ɔɪ/ can appear in all word positions, all are stressed on the first vowel, and all end in a high vowel. While the end points are pretty well established across the varieties of American English, the first element of these diphthongs may show considerable variation.

- /aɪ/:   The most common beginning point for this diphthong is [a], but it may shift to a more back [ɑ]. In the southern US /aɪ/ becomes [ɑː] if not followed by a voiceless consonant (e.g. buy [bɑː], miles [mɑːlz]). In southern Philadelphia and parts of New York City, one hears [ʌɪ] instead. In midland and south, it is often reduced to a monophthong before /ɹ/ (e.g. fire [faɹ]).
- /ɔɪ/:   For this diphthong, the starting point is back lower-mid, and the tongue glides from /ɔ/ towards /ɪ/. The lips are slightly rounded for the first element and neutral for the second. In Pennsylvania, Maryland, and Delaware, /ɔɪ/ sometimes approximates to [oɪ]. In AAVE and in the south, we normally get a monophthongized [ɔː] (e.g. oil [ɔːl], foil [fɔːl]).

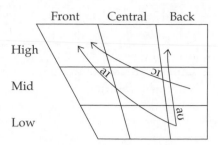

Figure 4.3 American English diphthongs

- /aʊ/: The starting point for this diphthong is normally not as front as that of /aɪ/, but not as back as /ɑ/ either, although the latter may be the case across the north from New England through the Great Lakes, and on into Minnesota. In the south, [aʊ] and [æʊ] are common, while in Nebraska and Iowa [æʊ] predominates. In Virginia and to some extent in northern New England, Wisconsin, and Minnesota, the allophone [ʌʊ] is found before voiceless consonants (e.g. <u>house</u> [hʌʊs], <u>out</u> [ʌʊt]).

Besides these diphthongs, in non-rhotic varieties (eastern New England, New York City, lower Southern), the targets with V + /r/ turn into centering diphthongs. Thus, we have the following correspondences:

	Rhotic	**Non-rhotic**
/i/		
	<u>pier</u>	[pɪə]
/ɪ/		
/ɛ/	<u>pear</u>	[pɛə]
/u/		
	<u>poor</u>	[pʊə]
/ʊ/		
/o/		
	<u>pour</u>	[pɔə]
/ɔ/		

In the case of [aɹ], we get a prolonged [a:] rather than [aə] (e.g. <u>car</u> [ka:]). The remaining three diphthongs show the following centralizations:

[aɪɹ]	<u>fire</u>	[faɪə]
[aʊɹ]	<u>sour</u>	[saʊə]
[ɔɪɹ]	<u>coir</u>	[kɔɪə]

In addition to the differences we observed within the United States, the non-US varieties show significant variations. Tables 4.1 to 4.4 show the differences between American English and some other Englishes.

Table 4.1 Comparison of the vowels and diphthongs of American English with those of the non-Caribbean varieties

	AmE	CnE	RP	ScE	IrE	WeE	AuE	NZE
beak	i	i	i	i	i	i	i	i
pit	ɪ	ɪ	ɪ	ɪ	ɪ	ɪ	ɪ	ɨ
hate	e	e	e	e	e	e	ʌɪ	ʌɪ
pet	ɛ	ɛ	ɛ	ɛ	ɛ	ɛ	e	e
sat	æ	æ	æ	a	æ	a	ɛ	ɛ
bath	æ	æ	ɑ	a	a	a	a:	a:
bus	ʌ	ə	ʌ	a	a	ə	a	a
pot	ɑ	ɑ	ɒ	ɔ	ɑ	ɔ	ɒ	ɒ
calm	ɑ	ɑ	ɑ	a	a:	a:	a:	a:
loft	ɔ	ɑ	ɒ	ɔ	ɒ	ɒ	ɒ	ɒ
bought	ɔ/ɑ	ɑ	ɔ:	ɔ	ɔ:	ɔ:	ɔ:	ɔ:
soak	o	o	əw	o	o	o	ʌʊ	ʌʊ
book	ʊ	ʊ	ʊ	ʉ	ʉ	ʊ	ʊ	ʊ
boot	u	u	u	ʉ	ʉ:	ʉ:	ʌʉ	ʌʉ
bike	aɪ	ʌɪ	aɪ	ʌɪ	aɪ	əɪ	aɪ	aɪ
about	aʊ	ʌʊ	aʊ	ʌʉ	aʊ	əʊ	æʊ	æʊ
coin	ɔɪ	ɔɪ	ɔɪ	ɔe	ɔɪ	ɔɪ	ɔɪ	ɔɪ

AmE = American English   IrE = Irish English
CnE = Canadian English   WeE = Welsh English
RP   = Received pronunciation   AuE = Australian English
         (British English)   NZE = New Zealand English
ScE = Scottish English

Table 4.2 Vowel and diphthong variations before /r/, and the [i – ɪ], [ə – ʌ] variations in final position between American English and non-Caribbean varieties

	AmE	CnE	RP	ScE	IrE	WeE	AuE	NZE
sneer	ɪɹ	iɹ	iə	ir	ir	iə	ɪə	ɪə
pear	ɛɹ	eɹ	ɛə	er	er	ɛə	eə	eə
heart	ɑɹ	ɑɹ	ɑ:	ar	ar	a:	a:	a:
nurse	ɝ	ɝ	ɜ:	ər	ɛr	ə:	ɜ:	ɜ:
runner	ɚ	ɚ	ə	ər	ər	ə	ə	ə
poor	ʊɹ	ʊɹ	ʊə	ʉr	ur	uə	ʊə	ʊə
sore	ɔɹ	ɔɹ	ɔə	or	or	ɔ:	ɔ:	ɔ:
fire	aɪɹ	ʌɪɹ	aɪə	ʌɪr	aɪr	əɪə	aɪə	aɪə
sour	aʊɹ	ʌʊɹ	aʊə	ʌʉr	aʊr	əʊə	æʊə	æʊə
coir	ɔɪɹ	ɔɪɹ	ɔɪə	ɔer	ɔɪr	ɔɪə	ɔɪə	ɔɪə
baby	i	i	ɪ	ɪ	i	ɪ	i	i
coma	ə	ə	ə	ʌ	ə	ə	ə	ə

Table 4.3 Comparison of the vowels and diphthongs of American English with those of the Caribbean varieties

	AmE	Jamaica	Guyana	Barbados	Trinidad	Bahamas
beak	i	i	i	i	i	i
pit	ɪ	ɪ	ɪ	ɪ	ɪ	ɪ
hate	e	e	e	e	e	e
pet	ɛ	ɛ	ɛ	ɛ	ɛ	ɛ
sat	æ	a	a	a	a	a
bath	æ	aː	aː	aː	a	aː
bus	ʌ	ʌ	ʌ	ʌ	ʌ	ʌ
pot	ɑ	a/ɑ	ɑ	aː	a	aː/ɑ
calm	ɑ	aː	aː	aː	ɑ/a	aː/ɑ
loft	ɔ	aː/ɔː	aː/ɔː	ɒː	ɒ/ɔ	ɑː
bought	ɔ/ɑ	ɔː	aː/ɑː	ɒ	ɔ	ɑː
soak	o	o	o	o	o	o
book	ʊ	ʊ	ʊ	ʊ	ʊ	ʊ
boot	u	u	u	u	u	u
bike	aɪ	aɪ	aɪ	ʌɪ	aɪ	ʌɪ
about	aʊ	ɔʊ	ɔʊ	ʌʊ	ɔʊ	aʊ
coin	ɔɪ	ɔɪ	aɪ/ɔɪ	ʌɪ/oɪ	ɔɪ	əɪ

Table 4.4 Vowel and diphthong variations before /r/, and the [i – ɪ], [ə – ʌ] variations in final position between American English and the Caribbean varieties

	AmE	Jamaica	Guyana	Barbados	Trinidad	Bahamas
sneer	ɪɹ	ɛːr	eː(r)	eːr	ɛə	ea
pear	ɛɹ	ɛːr	eː(r)	eːr	ɛə	ea
heart	ɑɹ	ɑː(r)	ɑː(r)	ɑːr	a/ɑ	ɑː
nurse	ɝ	ʌ/ʌr	ʌr	ɝ	ɒ/3	əi
runner	ɚ	a/ʌr/ə	a/ə	ɚ	a/ə	ə
poor	ʊɹ	oːr	oː(r)	oːr	ɒ/ɔ	oa
sore	ɔɹ	oːr	oː(r)	oːr	ɒ/ɔ	oa
fire	aɪɹ	aɪr	aɪ(r)	ʌɪr	aɪə	ʌɪə
sour	aʊɹ	ɔʊr	ɔʊ(r)	ʌʊr	ɔʊə	ʌʊə
coir	ɔɪɹ	ɔɪr	ɔɪ(r)	ʌɪr	ɔɪə	əɪə
baby	i	ɪ	i	i	i	ɪ
coma	ə	a	a/ə	ə	a/ə	ə

The tables are intended to provide some basics regarding the vowel (and diphthong) variations among several varieties of English. However, they are neither comprehensive descriptions of all varieties of English, nor do they pretend to give the details of variations within a single variety.

It should also be remembered that the symbols in tables 4.1 to 4.4 are abstract in that the use of the same symbol for a sound in two or more varieties does not mean the sound is identical in different varieties. For example, when we consider AE, RP, ScE, IrE, and WeE, we see that all have the same symbol /e/ for a word such as hate [het]. This may give the impression that the phonetic qualities are identical in all varieties. This is definitely not the case. While the vowel is definitely diphthongal in RP, its degree of diphthongization is very slight in AE, or basically monophthongal in ScE, IrE, and WeE. The vowel /o/ is another case where the same symbol is used for different qualities; in AE, this sound is often diphthongal, whereas in ScE, IrE, and WeE, it is monophthongal. Besides these monophthongal/diphthongal differences, there may be other variations. For example, although we use the same symbols /ɛ/, /æ/, and /ʌ/ for the words pet [pɛt], sat [sæt], and bus [bʌs], respectively, we realize that these sounds are different in AE and RP. While the first two have higher tongue position in RP than in AE, the situation is the reverse for /ʌ/, that is, it has higher tongue position in AE than RP.

4.7 Full Vowels–Reduced Vowels

Although stress is the topic we will discuss in the next chapter, there is one issue that we will take up here, and this relates to the reduced vowels. While all vowels of English (except [ə]) can occur in stressed syllables, many of these vowels reveal alternations with an [ə] in unstressed syllables in a morphologically related word.

	Stressed syllable with a full vowel	Reduced syllable with [ə]
/i/	homogeneous [homodʒiniəs]	homogenize [həmadʒənaɪz]
/ɪ/	implicit [ɪmplɪsət]	implication [ɪmpləkeʃən]
/e/	rotate [ɹotet]	rotary [ɹotəɹi]
/ɛ/	perpetuate [pɚpɛtʃuet]	perpetuity [pɚpətʃuəti]
/æ/	enigmatic [ənɪgmætɪk]	enigma [ənɪgmə]
/a/	stigmata [stɪgmatə]	stigma [stɪgmə]
/o/	photograph [fotaɡɹæf]	photography [fətaɡɹəfi]
/ʌ/	confront [kənfɹʌnt]	confrontation [kanfɹənteʃən]
/aɪ/	design [dəzaɪn]	designation [dɛzɪgneʃən]

We should immediately point out, however, that a vowel's appearance in an unstressed syllable does not necessarily result in a reduced vowel [ə]. It is perfectly possible for the English vowels to appear in full (unreduced) form in unstressed syllables, as shown in the following:

/i/   labial
/ɪ/   implicit
/e/   rotate
/ɛ/   centennial
/æ/   sarcasm
/ɑ/   October
/ɔ/   causality
/o/   location
/ʊ/   boyhood
/u/   acoustician
/aɪ/   titration
/aʊ/   outside
/ɔɪ/   exploitation

Thus, the unidirectional generalization to be made is the following: while a reduced vowel is necessarily in an unstressed syllable, a vowel in an unstressed syllable is not necessarily reduced.

Although we have consistently used the [ə] in reduced syllables, it is not uncommon to see an [ɪ] in several people's speech. In other words, for a word such as implication we can get [ɪmplɪkeʃən] as well as [ɪmpləkeʃən]. In general, [ɪ] is found before palato-alveolars (e.g. selfish [sɛlfɪʃ], sandwich [sændwɪtʃ], marriage [mæɹɪdʒ]) and velars (e.g. metric [mɛtɹɪk], running [ɹʌnɪŋ]). It should be noted, however, that the syllable structure is also a factor. The influence of palato-alveolar/velar consonants is more visible when there is tautosyllabicity. For example, we tend to find [ɪ] in topic [tɑpɪk], which is likely to change to an [ə] in a related word such as topical [tɑpəkəl], because the velar, [k], is the onset of the following syllable. Individuals should check their pronunciation of such syllables and transcribe the vowels accordingly. However, since reduced syllables are necessarily unstressed, and [ə] cannot appear in a stressed syllable (but [ɪ] can), for these practical reasons, we encourage our students to use the [ə] for such vowels.

Besides having this relationship with the unstressed [ɪ], we should also point out that [ə] has a special relationship with three other vowels, /i, o, u/. In unstressed syllables, the range of pronunciation values of these three vowels extends to the central [ə] area, as shown in the following.

	[i]	[ə]
record	[ɹikɔɹd]	[ɹəkɔɹd]
denounce	[dinaʊns]	[dənaʊns]
eleven	[ilɛvən]	[əlɛvən]

	[o]	[ə]
produce	[pɹodus]	[pɹədus]
romantic	[ɹomæntɪk]	[ɹəmæntɪk]
protest	[pɹotɛst]	[pɹətɛst]

	[u]	[ə]
regular	[ɹɛgjuləˑ]	[ɹɛgjələˑ]
graduate	[gɹædʒuet]	[gɹædʒəet]
circular	[sɝˑkjuləˑ]	[sɝˑkjələˑ]

4.8 Full Forms versus Reduced Forms of Function Words

The pronunciations of words do reveal differences, whether we consider them in isolation (i.e. citation form) or in connected speech. The latter is a very fertile context to accommodate many changes, especially for unstressed monosyllabic function words (free grammatical morphemes). The class of function words includes auxiliaries, prepositions, articles, conjunctions, and pronouns. In connected speech utterances, such words are typically not the focus of information (they are unstressed), and thus they readily lend themselves to reduction. The reduced forms are very common in connected speech, and their under-use (i.e. employing the strong (full) forms) does quickly strike the native speaker's ear as unnatural. Also, learners who have no familiarity with these forms are likely to have difficulty understanding native speakers who use them regularly in connected speech. Thus, learners should be frequently reminded of this aspect of English phonology. As will be obvious from the list below, some of these function words have more than one weak form. While some of these variations are predictable (e.g. [ðə] before consonants as in the book [ðə bʊk], and [ði] before others as in the apple [ði æpəl]), many others are far from being invariable. Also noteworthy are the cases where two identically spelt words behave differently. For example, while that as a relative pronoun, as in "You said that she ate", is reduced to [ðət], the identically spelt demonstrative that, as in that boy is not reduceable, and is always pronounced as [ðæt].

Before we list the items in question, we would like to remind the reader that the citation form in isolation is not the only context that the strong (full) forms of these words can be used in. They are also expected when these words become the focal point in the exchange. For example, when given special emphasis, as in

A: 'We can serve strawberries or grapes for dessert.'
B: 'I think we should serve strawberries **and** grapes.'

or to make a contrast, as in

A: 'I can't finish this job by Tuesday.'
B: 'Yes you **can**.'

While the reduced forms [ən] and [kən] are the expected forms in normal running speech, in the above examples they will be uttered in their full form [ænd] and [kæn] respectively when they become the focus of the exchange.

Strong and weak forms of some common function words in English

	Strong	**Weak**		
a	[e]	[ə]	'a book'	[ə bʊk]
that (rel.pr)	[ðæt]	[ðət]	'you said that . . .'	[ju sɛd ðət . . .]
but	[bʌt]	[bət]	'it's good but late'	[ɪts gʊd bət . . .]
and	[ænd]	[ənd, ən, ɛn]	'boys and girls'	[bɔɪz ən gɜˑlz]
than	[ðæn]	[ðən]	'better than ever'	[bɛDə ðən . . .]
his	[hɪz]	[ɪz]	'put his name down'	[pʊt ɪz . . .]
her	[hɜˑ]	[əˑ]	'put her name down'	[pʊt ə . . .]
your	[jʊɹ]	[jəˑ]	'put your name down'	[pʊt jə . . .]
he	[hi]	[hɪ, i, ɪ]	'will he read?'	[wɪl i ɹid]
him	[hɪm]	[ɪm]	'I told him to come'	[aɪ tɔld ɪm . . .]
you	[ju]	[jə]	'do you eat this?'	[djə ɪt . . .]
them	[ðɛm]	[ðəm]	'leave them alone'	[liv ðəm . . .]
us	[ʌs]	[əs]	'leave us alone'	[liv əs . . .]
just	[dʒʌst]	[dʒəst]	'he's just arrived'	[hiz dʒəst . . .]

In addition to these, the words in the following group occur in their strong forms when they are final in a sentence:

at	[æt]	[ət]	'at home'	[ət h . . .]
for	[fɔɹ]	[fəˑ]	'this is for me'	[. . . fə mi]
to	[tu]	[tə]	'he went to school'	[hi wɛnt tə . . .]
from	[fɹʌm]	[fɹəm]	'back from work'	[bæk fɹəm . . .]
of	[av]	[əv, ə]	'a cup of coffee'	[ə kʌp ə kafi]
some	[sʌm]	[səm]	'have some coffee'	[hæv səm . . .]
as	[æz]	[əz]	'as funny as . . .'	[əz fʌni əz]
do	[du]	[də, d]	'do you eat this?'	[djə ɪt . . .]
had	[hæd]	[əd]	'we had done that'	[wi əd . . .]
has (prf.)	[hæz]	[əz]	'John has gone'	[dʒan əz gan]
has (pos.)	[hæz]	[həz, əz]	'she has two of those'	[ʃiəz t . . .]
can	[kæn]	[kən, kŋ]	'I can do it'	[aɪ kŋ du . . .]
will	[wɪl]	[wəl, əl]	'I'll be there'	[aɪəl bi . . .]
would	[wʊd]	[wəd, əd]	'he would like to come'	[hɪəd . . .]
should	[ʃʊd]	[ʃəd]	'I should go'	[aɪ ʃəd . . .]
must	[mʌst]	[məst (before vowels), məs, ms]	'you must tell me'	[ju məs tɛl . . .]
have	[hæv]	[həv, əv]	'The kids have done it'	[ðə kɪdzəv dan . . .]
am	[æm]	[əm]	'I'm going'	[aɪ (ə)m . . .]
are	[aɹ]	[əˑ]	'students are going'	[studənts ə . . .]
was	[wʌz]	[wəz]	'He was there'	[hi wəz . . .]
were	[wɜˑ]	[wəˑ]	'We were just leaving'	[wi wə . . .]

Some of these function (minor) words also have contracted forms by losing their vowel and consequently merging with the preceding syllable.

'He will come' → /hɪl . . . /   'I have seen it' → /aɪv . . . /
'They are here' → /ðɛɹ . . . /   'Bill has done it' → /bɪlz . . . /

It is worth mentioning that prepositions and auxiliary verbs have certain requirements for their reduced forms. Thus, for example, the preposition 'by' behaves differently in the following two sentences.

(a)   He walked <u>by</u> the other day.
(b)   He walked <u>by</u> the other route.

The reduced form occurs only in (b) because the preposition is followed by a noun phrase (i.e. 'by' has an object noun phrase and thus is a 'transitive' preposition). The 'intransitive' (with no object) preposition 'by' in (a) is stressed and does not reduce.

    Auxiliary verbs are typically unstressed and are reduced or contracted, except

(a)   when they occur with the 'negative particle *not*'; in such cases, only one of them can reduce/contract, not both.
       'The game hasn't started' (*not* is contracted, *has* is not)
       'The game's not started' (*has* is contracted, *not* is not)
      The following two are not possible:
       * 'The /gemzənt/ started' (*has* is reduced and *not* is contracted)
       * 'The game /əzənt/ started' (both *has* and *not* are contracted)
(b)   when they occur in final position.
      'Is she coming?'   'She <u>is</u>'
      'Has she returned?'   'She <u>has</u>'
      'Do they like it?'   'They <u>do</u>'
      'Who will read?'   'John <u>will</u>'

    Finally, we should point out that reduced vowels are not restricted to function words only, and are found in lexical morphemes (nouns, verbs, adjectives, adverbs) too. These will be looked at in the next chapter.

Summary

In this chapter, we looked at the vowels and diphthongs of American English and their contextual variants. Since the dialectal variations in vowels are far greater than those of consonants, the discussion was focused on the US varieties. Non-US varieties are given in summary lists. Similar to what was noted in the previous chapter regarding the consonants, knowledge on the highly rule-governed nature of vowel variations is invaluable for the practitioners in the fields of communication disorders and foreign language teaching.

EXERCISES

1. In some words, the sequence represented by orthographical <u>or</u> has the phonetic realization [ɔɹ], which may be shifted to [aɹ]. In which of the following words would this be possible? Explain your reasoning.

   forge, ignore, divorce, bore, horoscope, Oregon, explore, tomorrow, lord

2. As we saw in section 4.8, [ə] has a special relationship with /i, o, u/ whereby the pronunciation of the word can be with an [ə] as well as with one of these vowels. Examine the following words and state which one(s) would qualify for this alternation:

   devoid, satisfactory, photography, progress (v), episcopal, calculate, statutory, reserve, meaning, gratefully, supremely, obscene, consumer, vocation

3. Circle the words that contain:

   [i]:   audible, hitter, lisp, pity, foreign, Nancy, horrible, slowly, leave, heed, crease, Greek

   [ɪ]:   seen, pitch, sneaker, feast, knit, cheap, sing, fist, greed, simmer, evening, each, eat

   [e]:   sense, aide, starved, sensational, amaze, enough, nation, revolver, nervous, forgiven

   [ɛ]:   locate, perceive, slapped, said, maid, adept, laughed, check, came, tread, grained

   [æ]:   panda, peptic, cabin, delta, cobra, bandit, camel, alone, inept, coma, acted, dragon

   [a]:   hopper, dole, hotter, father, tranquil, market, polar, bargain, magnify, organizer, vanity

   [o]:   could, groan, brook, flowed, boiling, cook, told, boat, crook, poised, posed, bowling

   [ʊ]:   should, most, coin, could, poled, good, stood, broke, soul, hoop, cooled, wood, booking

   [u]:   goodness, groom, foot, cooled, woman, root, broom, shook, school, coiled, couch, under

   [aɪ]: imply, ironic, point, arrive, halve, advice, save, thyself, fatherly, breath, decide, lake

   [ɔɪ]: spoiling, beside, guile, pointless, boil, Norwegian, soil, voyages, official, soy, continent [aʊ]:   bought, laundry, bound, owl, vowed, old, nose, cow, ploy, toad, Joan, foul, drowsy

4. Circle the words that have both [ʌ] and [ə]:

undone, luckily, abundance, Monday, rushing, redundant, trouble, Paris, plaza, suspend

5. Circle the words that have both [ʌ] and [ɚ]:

mustard, award, wonderful, support, guarded, thunder, serpent, walker, tremor, barley, harbor, rubber, custard, under, others

6. Which words have:

(a)   both [ɝ] and [ə]
(b)   both [ɝ] and [ɚ]
(c)   only [ɝ]
(d)   only [ɚ]
(e)   only [ə]

Example: bourbon a

cursor ____, person ____, career ____, abort ____, verses ____, whisper ____, suburb ____, carat ____, convert (v) ____, surprise ____, heard ____, Herbert ____, under ____, shivered ____, birthday ____, worker ____, serviced ____

7. Transcribe the following (about 'English as a world language') from David Crystal, *The Cambridge Encyclopedia of the English Language* (Cambridge: Cambridge University Press, 1995).

The movement of English around the world began with the pioneering
....
voyages to the Americas, Asia, and the Antipodes, continued with the
....
19th century colonial developments in Africa and the South Pacific,
....
and took a significant further step when it was adopted in the 20th
....

century as an official or semi-official language by many newly

independent states. English is now the dominant or official language

in over 60 countries, and is represented in every continent. It is this

spread of representation which makes the application of the term 'world

language' a reality. The present-day world status of English is primarily

the result of two factors: the expansion of British colonial power, which

peaked towards the end of the 19th century, and the emergence of

the United States as the leading economic power of the 20th century.

It is the latter factor which continues to explain the position of the

English language today. The USA contains nearly four times as many

English-mother-tongue speakers as the next most important nation

(UK), and these two countries comprise 70 percent of all English-

mother-tongue speakers in the world.

Acoustics of Vowels
and Consonants

5.1 Introduction

The aim of this chapter is to present information that will be helpful to teachers of English and/or speech therapists in their assessment and planning of remediation. As such, it does not deal with the details of speech acoustics. Rather, it is intended to supply some basic knowledge concerning the spectrographic analysis of speech. In order to make a reliable assessment, we need an accurate and adequate description of the client's speech. The affordable software currently available makes such procedures a real possibility both in therapy centers and in classrooms. Since speech that requires remediation reveals patterns that are different from the 'norm' (average speaker), the professional who works with remediation may compare the speech of the client with the 'norm' to determine the amount of deviation. Speech spectrograms or 'voice prints', as many people refer to them, are a very convenient means of displaying the acoustic characteristics of speech in a compact form. Learning to interpret them is also relatively easy with practice. The spectrographic data can also be utilized to monitor the changes in remediation and can guide the practitioner in adjusting the remediation plan.

Before we begin a spectrographic description of speech, we need to alert the reader regarding the following important points. Firstly, while spectrograms provide detailed information about several aspects of speech and can be very helpful in assessment and remediation, it should be noted that not all acoustically distinct phenomena are perceptually distinct. Thus the practitioner must be able to pinpoint the information in the spectrographic data that is pertinent for a particular case. It is also important to emphasize the fact that perceptual cues interact with each other, and often, coexistence of more than one cue is required to reliably identify an opposition with respect to a single feature. Secondly, it is important to emphasize that there are inherent problems associated with recognizing words from acoustic information in a spectrogram. In addition to the expected differences because of inter- and intra-talker variations, two other issues – 'linearity' and 'invariance' – are particularly relevant. Although in our phonetic transcriptions we represent the sounds in a linear fashion, this is simply an abstraction. Speech articulations typically overlap each other in time, and result in sound patterns that are in transition much of the time. The boundaries are blurred and the individual sounds can lose some of their distinctive characteristics. Thus, one should not expect that sounds be linearly mapped on to spectrographic displays. Also, as we will see in detail later in the chapter, characteristics of a given sound change in different phonetic environments (e.g. the nature of adjacent segments, the length of the word, position of the word in a phrase, stress, rate of speech, and so on), and consequently, one should not assume that sounds exhibit invariant characteristics in all contexts.

Production of every sound sets a body of air in vibration. Two factors influence the sounds produced. One of these is the size and the shape of the air. When a short and narrow body of air vibrates, it results in a higher pitch than a body of air which is longer and wider. The other factor is related to the intensity of the sound. The waveforms created by these differences may result in simple (periodic) or complex (aperiodic) patterns, the former showing regular vibrations, and the latter resulting in turbulent patterns. The sound source for vowels is always periodic. For consonants, it may be periodic (glides, nasals), or aperiodic (fricatives), determined by the narrowness of the consonantal constriction. Too much narrowing results in turbulent airflow.

The three acoustic properties of speech sounds are frequency, time, and amplitude.

- **Frequency:**   Frequency relates to the individual pulsations produced by the vocal cord vibrations for a unit of time. The rate of vibration depends on the length, thickness, and tension of the cords, and thus is different for child, adult male, and female speech. A speech sound contains two types of frequencies. The first, *fundamental frequency*, (f0), relates to vocal cord function and reflects the rate of vocal cord vibration during phonation (pitch). The other, *formant frequency*, relates to vocal tract configuration.
- **Time:**   Time as a property of speech sounds reflects the duration of a given sound. For example, the duration of an alveolar fricative such as /s/ is greater than the corresponding alveolar stop /t/.
- **Amplitude:**   The amplitude of a sound refers to the amount of subglottal (beneath the vocal cords) air pressure.

These three acoustic properties can be analyzed in a spectrographic display. A spectrogram analyzes a speech wave into its frequency components and shows variation in the frequency components of a sound as a function of time. This allows us to see more detail regarding the articulation of the sounds. On a spectrogram, time is represented by the horizontal axis and given in milliseconds (ms). The vertical axis represents the frequency, which is the acoustic characteristic expressed in cycles per second, or Hz. Each horizontal line on this axis indicates 1,000 Hz (or 1 kHz). The intensity (amplitude) is marked by the darkness of the bands; the greater the intensity of the sound energy present at a given time and frequency, the darker will be the mark at the corresponding point on the screen/printout.

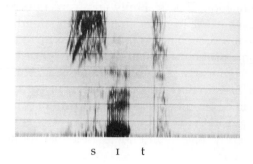

s   ɪ   t

Figure 5.1 Spectrogram of <u>sit</u>

If we look at the spectrogram of the monosyllabic word in figure 5.1, we can make the following observations. The vowel portion of the word, /ɪ/, contains a series of thin vertical lines (striations) whose darkness varies with loudness. These lines represent the vocal cord vibrations. The space between the lines is in inverse relationship with the fundamental frequency (pitch), given in Hz. For example, with a fundamental frequency of 220 Hz (typical for the female voice), the vertical lines indicating voicing will be 1/220 second, or 4.5 ms apart in time. The same vowel, with a fundamental frequency of 125 Hz (typical for the male voice), will have its vertical lines 8 ms apart in time. The vowel portion also shows very clear horizontal dark bands. These are the resonance frequencies, called formants. The portion before the vowel /ɪ/ represents the fricative /s/ with its high-amplitude frication noise in the higher frequencies. The portion after the vowel represents the stop /t/. This is shown with a gap, which is the closure portion for /t/, followed by a vertical spike indicating the release of the final /t/. Each of these points will be made more explicit when we examine the spectrograms of different classes of sounds.

Adjustment of the spectrograph can create two different kinds of spectrograms. *Broad-band spectrograms* have good time resolution, but blur frequency. *Narrow-band spectrograms*, although they are not as clear on the time dimension, have good resolution for frequency, and are generally the ones we see in books and manuals.

5.2 Vowels

As shown in the case of [sɪt], vowels have their frequency components grouped into broad horizontal bands, called formants. Different formants characterize different vowels and are the result of the different ways in which the air in the vocal tract vibrates. Every time the vocal cords open and close, there is a pulse of air exiting the lungs, and these pulses act like sharp taps on the air in the vocal tract. The resonance patterns created by the vibration of this body of air are determined by the size and the shape of the vocal tract. In a vowel sound, the air in the vocal tract vibrates at a number of different frequencies simultaneously. These are the resonance frequencies of the particular vocal tract shape. A formant frequency, then, is a bandwidth containing a concentration of energy. Irrespective of the rate of vibration, the air in the vocal tract will continue to resonate at these frequencies as long as the shape of the vocal tract remains the same. The precise acoustic makeup of each sound will differ for each individual speaker, but there are certain core features that make it possible for us to identify the general categories. This is exactly the reason why we can recognize the same vowel produced at different pitches by different individuals. Since vowels are associated with a steady-state articulatory configuration and a steady-state acoustic pattern, they are the simplest sounds to analyze acoustically. Customarily, formants are represented from the lower end of the spectrogram to the upper end. The clearly marked dark bandwidth at the lower end of the spectrogram is the first formant, denoted as F_1. The subsequent bands of similarly marked energy locations are the second (F_2) and third (F_3) formants. Vowel spectra have at least 4–5 obvious spectral peaks. In general, the frequencies of the first three formants are sufficient to identify the vowels, and the frequencies of F_4 and higher formants vary among speakers because they are primarily determined by the shape and size of the speaker's head, nasal cavity, sinus cavities, etc.

Differences between the vowels of English can be explained in terms of the different locations and widths of the formant frequencies. It is commonly stated that there is a clear relationship between the frequency of the first formant and the height of the vowel. This happens to be an inverse relationship; high vowels have low first formants, and low vowels have higher first formants. As for the front/back distinction, the frequency of second formants is often mentioned; we see that the frequency of the second formant is much higher in front vowels than in back vowels. However, the correlation between the second formant frequency and the backness of the vowel does not seem to be as solid as the correlation between the first formant frequency and the vowel height. This is primarily due to the fact that rounding in the case of back vowels can affect the frequency of the second formant too. Thus, backness of a vowel can better be related to the difference between F_2 frequency and F_1 frequency. The simple formula is as follows. A vowel is more front when the difference between F_2 frequency and F_1 frequency is greater than the same difference for another vowel. Whatever has been said above can be illustrated in the differences between beat and bet (see figure 5.2).

When we consider the 'height' dimension, the expected inverse relationship with the frequency of F_1 is very clear. The sound /i/, which is higher than /ɛ/, has its F_1 around 300 Hz, whereas the frequency of F_1 of /ɛ/ is around 550 Hz.

As for the difference between F_2 and F_1 determining the degree of backness, we can look at the two words again. The resulting numbers from F_2 minus F_1 frequencies for the vowels /i/ in beat (around 2,150 minus 300 = 1,850), and for /ɛ/ in 'bet' (around 1,700 minus 550 = 1,150) quite clearly confirm that /i/ is, by nature, more front than /ɛ/.

/i/ More front vowel; greater F_2–F_1 distance

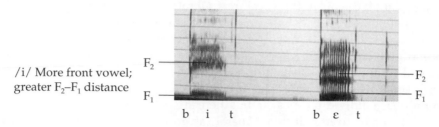

Figure 5.2 Spectrogram of <u>beat</u> and <u>bet</u>

To better understand how changes in the vocal tract shape results in different formant frequencies, think of the 'highest point of the tongue' dividing the vocal tract into two cavities (front/back). In a movement from the high front vowel /i/ to the low front vowel /æ/, the body of the tongue is retracted, making the front cavity larger (this results in a smaller back cavity). Since the resonating frequency is higher for the smaller vibrating cavity than the larger one, such a movement will have the effect of lowering the resonating frequency of the front cavity (the cavity which has become larger), and increasing the frequency of the back cavity (the cavity which has become smaller). If we think that the F_1 frequency is representative of the back cavity, and the F_2 frequency is representative of the front cavity, we can understand how the changes in the vocal tract shape can result in the changes in formant frequencies. Thus, there is a gradual increase in F_1 frequency as we move from /i/ to /ɪ/ to /ɛ/ to /æ/.

A similar argument can be said to explain the lowering of both F_1 and F_2 frequencies as we move from /a/ to /u/. As the tongue root is raised towards higher back vowels, the back cavity enlarges, resulting in the lowering of the frequency of F_1. Also, the highest point of the tongue is moving farther back from /a/ to /u/, and this creates a larger front cavity which results in lowering the frequency of F_2. While the above statements are quite solid for the gradual lowering of F_1 frequency for the back series, /a/ to /ɔ/ to /ʊ/ to /u/, it is not so for the lowering of the frequency of F_2. We consistently see higher F_2 frequencies for /ʊ/ than /ɔ/. This is primarily due to the more front production of /ʊ/ than /ɔ/. Table 5.1 shows the formant frequencies of the first three formants in ten American English vowels. It should be remembered that these values are given as guidelines, not as absolute values. However, they are useful because they indicate the typical vowel patterns in relation to each other. For the front vowels, we see a gradual rise in values for F_1 and gradual decrease for F_2. For the back vowels, we see a decrease in the values of F_1 and F_2 as we move from the lowest back vowel to the highest.

If the frequency of F_1 is plotted against the distance between F_1 and F_2, a chart is obtained which strongly resembles the traditional vowel height charts. This further attests that these diagrams have acoustic correlates (see figure 5.3).

The frequency of F_3 has no simple articulatory correlates, but is useful in the identification of labial consonants, and retroflexion. The F_3 frequency for the

Table 5.1 Frequencies of the first three formants in ten American English vowels (averages of three adult male speakers)

Vowel	F₁	F₂	F₃
i	270	2,200	2,900
ɪ	400	1,900	2,500
ɛ	550	1,700	2,450
æ	670	1,670	2,450
ɑ	700	1,100	2,500
ɔ	600	870	2,450
ʊ	450	1,000	2,300
u	320	850	2,250
ʌ	600	1,250	2,450
ɝ	500	1,400	1,650

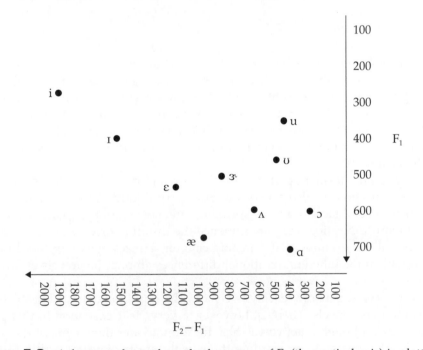

Figure 5.3 A formant chart where the frequency of F_1 (the vertical axis) is plotted against the distance between F_1 and F_2 (the horizontal axis)

English vowels can be predicted fairly accurately from the frequencies of their F_1 and F_2. The single exception to this is [ɝ], as in <u>bird</u>. Although its first two formants are very similar to that of /ʊ/, the frequency of its F_3 is very low; this will be clear in the discussion of /ɹ/ later in the chapter.

The frequencies given in figure 5.3 represent male speech. The men's vowels typically have lower formant frequencies than those of women, and those, in

Table 5.2 Comparisons between men, women, and children in 10 vowels

Vowel	Men			Women			Children		
	F_1	F_2	F_3	F_1	F_2	F_3	F_1	F_2	F_3
i	270	2,300	3,000	300	2,800	3,300	370	3,200	3,700
ɪ	400	2,000	2,550	430	2,500	3,100	530	2,750	3,600
ɛ	530	1,850	2,500	600	2,350	3,000	700	2,600	3,550
æ	660	1,700	2,400	860	2,050	2,850	1,000	2,300	3,300
ɑ	730	1,100	2,450	850	1,200	2,800	1,030	1,350	3,200
ɔ	570	850	2,400	590	900	2,700	680	1,050	3,200
ʊ	440	1,000	2,250	470	1,150	2,700	560	1,400	3,300
u	300	850	2,250	370	950	2,650	430	1,150	3,250
ʌ	640	1,200	2,400	760	1,400	2,800	850	1,600	3,350
ɚ	490	1,350	1,700	500	1,650	1,950	560	1,650	2,150

turn, have lower frequencies than those of children. This is due to the size of the vocal tract; the larger the vocal tract, the bigger the bodies of air contained. Since larger bodies of air vibrate more slowly, the formants will have lower frequencies. Table 5.2 shows the comparison between men, women, and children (often, the F_3 cannot be seen in children's spectrograms). The frequencies are from Peterson and Barney (1952) data. The F_2 and F_3 values are rounded to the nearest 50.

Although the formant patterns are the first and best markers in identifying vowels, 'duration' is also a very important parameter. As we saw in earlier chapters, several factors such as speaking rate, voicing of the adjacent consonant, utterance position, etc. can influence the duration of vowels. All of these factors will be examined later in this chapter. However, before we do this, let us look at the inherent durational differences among the vowels of English (table 5.3).

As we see, in general, tense vowels and the diphthongs have longer durations than lax vowels. There is, however, a very clear exception to this principle: /æ/, although a lax vowel, has duration greater than some of the tense vowels. The information regarding the vowel duration becomes critical when we have a pair of words in which the different vowel sounds do not present a big difference in F_1 and F_2 frequencies. For example, if we have a pair of words such as bet [bɛt] and bat [bæt], we may have a difference of 100–150 Hz for the first formant frequency between these vowels, which is not very big. As for F_2 minus F_1, which determines the relative backness, the difference may be around 200–250 Hz. In case these differences are not sufficient to distinguish the two vowels in question, the unmistakable difference in duration could be used to make the separation, as /æ/ is significantly longer than /ɛ/.

Table 5.3 Duration of English vowels in stressed and unstressed syllables (in milliseconds)

	Stressed syllable	Unstressed syllable
/i/	118 (119)	75 (78)
/ɪ/	75 (75)	58 (53)
/e/	145 (136)	85 (78)
/ɛ/	103 (106)	73 (60)
/æ/	152 (159)	82 (71)
/ʌ/	99 (103)	—
/ə/	—	55 (49)
/u/	122 (126)	75 (75)
/ʊ/	88 (85)	65 (61)
/o/	156 (162)	92 (96)
/ɔ/	150 (148)	79 (72)
/ɑ/	146 (140)	85 (93)
/aɪ/	178 (172)	120 (114)
/aʊ/	199 (202)	121 (120)
/ɔɪ/	264 (298)	132 (125)

Note: The values given come from the averages of the productions of a list-reading task from three adult native speakers (from Iowa, Ohio, and Florida). The values in parentheses next to those of our three subjects are from Crystal and House (1982). One can easily see the remarkable similarities between the two studies.

5.3 Diphthongs

The diphthongs are different from monophthongal vowels in that the vocal tract changes size and shape because the tongue moves in order to produce one vowel quality followed by another. The changes in the vocal tract shape for diphthongs can be observed from the movements of the first three formants. The diphthong /aɪ/ starts with a low back constriction and ends with a high front constriction. Accordingly, F_2 rises as the constriction moves from back to front, and F_1 falls as the constriction moves from low to high. In /aʊ/, a low back constriction moves to a high back constriction. As the tongue rises, F_1 falls; F_2 also falls because some movement of the tongue occurs farther back for /ʊ/ than /a/; but also due to lip rounding of /ʊ/ all resonance frequencies are lowered. Finally, /ɔɪ/ starts as a low back vowel and ends as a high front vowel. As the tongue moves from back to front F_2 rises; as the tongue moves from low to high F_1 falls. We can observe all the points made above in the spectrogram of the sentence Brian Boitano bowed [braɪn bɔɪtano baʊd] (figure 5.4).

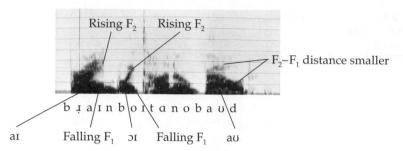

Figure 5.4 Spectrogram of <u>Brian Boitano bowed</u>

5.4 Consonants

5.4.1 Stops

Stops are characterized on a spectrographic display by silence (stop gap) or obvious signal weakening. This is the acoustic interval corresponding to the articulatory occlusion, and it varies in duration depending on the prosodic condition. Because the vocal tract is obstructed, little or no energy is produced. This is followed by a burst of energy, as the closure is released.

There are two dimensions that need to be carefully analyzed in distinguishing stop sounds. One of them is the separation of fortis from lenis (or, as more commonly known, voiceless from voiced). Several indicators can help us to identify the stops with reference to this dimension. These are:

(a) **Duration of the stop gap**, i.e. the silent period during the closure phase. Specifically, /p, t, k/ show longer closure duration than /b, d, g/.

(b) **Presence of a voice bar**, i.e. a dark bar found at low frequencies (generally below 250 Hz) in a spectrogram. Except in intervocalic position, this is one of the least reliable identifying characteristics of the stop sounds. As we saw earlier, voicing is frequently absent in English /b, d, g/ in initial and final positions. Thus, this feature can reliably be used to separate /p, t, k/ from /b, d, g/ only in intervocalic positions; /b, d, g/ will show the voice bar which is indicative of voicing, whereas /p, t, k/ will not show it.

(c) **Release burst** indicated by a strong vertical spike. In general, we observe a stronger spike for /p, t, k/ than /b, d, g/. One qualification is in order here for the final position: as discussed earlier, final stops in English are normally unreleased. In such cases, we will not observe any release burst. Velar stops are said to be more prone to non-release than bilabials or alveolars.

(d) **Duration of the previous vowel:** this refers to positions other than the initial position, where there is no vowel before the stop. In other positions, vowels and/or sonorant consonants are longer before /b, d, g/ than before /p, t, k/.

(e) **Aspiration:** a VOT of more than approximately 30 ms shows up as short frication noise (scattered marks after the release) before vowel formants begin, in initial /p, t, k/ of a stressed syllable.

The other dimension in the identification of stops is the place of articulation. While the above criteria are useful in separating voiced (lenis) from voiceless (fortis), we do not gather much information with respect to the place of articulation. In other words, what should we look for to distinguish a /p/ or a /b/ from a /t/ or a /d/, or from a /k/ or a /g/? The following are helpful in this respect:

(a) **Formant transitions**. Formant transitions (shifts) in CV sequences reflect changes in vocal tract shaping during stop-to-vowel transition. Vowel-to-stop (VC) transition is the opposite of the former. Frequency of the first formant of the vowel increases when stops are at the beginning of a syllable (CV), and falls when they are at the end (VC); this is the case for all stops. While no information for the place of articulation can be gathered from F_1 transitions, F_2 and F_3 transitions can tell us a great deal in this respect. In CV situations, bilabials show upward movement of both F_2 and F_3; the mirror image situation is revealed in a VC sequence. For a velar stop, F_2 and F_3 are close together just after the stop is formed. There will be a downward transition to a vowel with a high F_2. In cases of a VC, there is a narrowing (coming together) of the second and the third formants. The case of alveolar stops is probably the least straightforward; while we observe a flat transition to a vowel with mid or high F_2, there is a downward transition to a vowel with low F_2 in CV. In VC cases, there is very little movement; small downward of the second and small upward of the third is expected.

(b) **Locus** (starting frequency). This is the point of origin to which the transition of the second formant appears to be pointing. For a /b/, this is around 600–800 Hz, for a /d/ it is 1,800 Hz. To identify a /g/, two loci, at 3,000 Hz and 1,300 Hz, are generally noted.

(c) **Release burst**. Bilabials are identified by bursts with a center frequency lower than the F_2 of the vowel (below 2,000 Hz). They show a pattern that is diffuse and weak. Alveolar bursts generally have a center frequency that is higher than the F_2 of the vowel (above 2,000 Hz). The pattern is diffuse and strong. As for velars, they display a compact and strong pattern, and the bursts have a center frequency approximating to the F_2 of the vowel.

(d) **VOT** (/p, t, k/ only). The length of time from the release of a stop until voicing begins for the following segment presents consistent differences depending on the place of articulation of the fortis stop. The time interval includes the spike (the sound that is produced by the separation of the articulators), a short frication noise after the spike, and the aspiration following it. As we move the place of articulation from the front to the back of the mouth, stops tend to have greater VOT. Although this is a rather effective acoustic property for classifying the place of articulation, it should be remembered that it is just a tendency, and that it may be possible to find an alveolar voiceless stop with a longer VOT than a velar voiceless stop. As mentioned in chapter 3, the VOT for a syllable-initial voiceless stop varies somewhat systematically depending on the place of articulation and other segmental context.

If we examine the spectrograms of the words speak, peak, keen, and cake (figures 5.5 and 5.6), we can see these points clearly. In speak, the /p/ is not at the beginning of a stressed syllable, since it is preceded by an /s/, thus we do not have aspiration in the voiceless bilabial stop. The words peak, keen, and cake all have voiceless stops at the beginning of a stressed syllable, and thus are aspirated. However, as one can easily see, the degree of the voice lag (aspiration) is different in each case; shorter in peak, longer in cake, and the longest in keen. The reasons for these differences are as follows. Among the three, peak has the bilabial stop whose expected lag is lower than that of the other two words that start with a velar stop. The difference between the two words that start with velar stops (cake and keen) is due to the type of vowel that follows

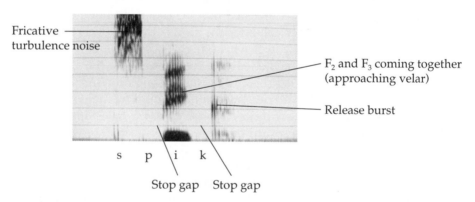

Figure 5.5   Spectrogram of speak

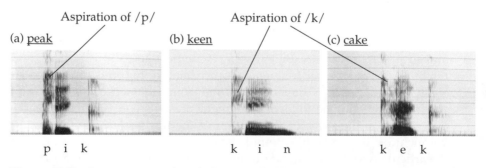

Figure 5.6   Spectrograms of peak, keen, and cake

the voiceless stop. The aspiration in <u>keen</u> is longer than in <u>cake</u>, because in the former /k/ is followed by a high vowel (a vowel with lower sonority), while in the latter the stop is followed by a lower vowel (a vowel with higher sonority). Summarizing all the above, the examples confirm the statements made earlier, that voiceless stops are not aspirated if they are not at the beginning of a stressed syllable; when they are aspirated, the degree of aspiration is greater as we move the place of articulation from front to back (i.e. bilabial, to alveolar, and to velar). When a stop with a given place of articulation is followed by vowels of different height (different degrees of sonority), the amount of lag varies; a stop before a high vowel has greater aspiration than when it is before a low vowel.

5.4.2 Fricatives

Fricatives are produced via a narrow constriction in the vocal tract which creates a turbulent noise (or 'friction'). Such energy appears on a spectrogram as a scribbly pattern, without regular horizontal or vertical lines. The interval of the frication noise is greater in sibilants /s, z, ʃ, ʒ/ than non-sibilants /f, v, θ, ð, h/ and the amplitude for frication noise is 58–68 dB (decibels) for the former, as opposed to 46–52 dB for the latter. The sibilants have places of articulation at or just behind the alveolar ridge. The airstream is funneled smoothly through the groove formed in the surface of the tongue blade and tip. As the air picks up speed it begins to tumble noisily. The tumbling noisy air jet generally strikes the edge of the upper incisor, or edge of the lower lip, and creates additional edge or spoiler turbulence noise. These noises produced by sibilants are long, strong in amplitude, only a few decibels less than that of vowels, and marked by a rich, high-frequency noise spectrum.

The non-sibilant front fricatives are made with labio-dental and interdental constrictions. The tongue tissue held against the teeth for the dental fricatives creates an abrupt narrow constriction that generates a weak turbulence noise whose energy is spread to very high frequencies. The noise is so weak that listeners often derive the acoustic clues for identification not from the noise but from the prominent consonant-to-vowel transitions of these sounds.

If, for example, we make a comparison of /f/ as in <u>fin</u> with /θ/ as in <u>thin</u>, we would expect to find the following. Neither sound would create the frication noise like sibilants (/s/ or /ʃ/). Although the fricative noises are similar in both, the intensity range is lower in the former (3,000–4,000 Hz) than the latter (7,000–8,000 Hz). What may also help to separate them are the formants of the neighboring vowels: F_4 (if visible) is below 4,000 Hz in /f/, and above for /θ/. One additional element may be the greater duration of the labio-dental than the interdental. Finally, one might also find a little higher F_2 locus for the interdental than for the labio-dental. Given all these small differences, it is not surprising that very few languages demonstrate the contrast between these sounds.

Although we must use subtle clues to separate labio-dentals from interdentals, the difference between alveolars and palato-alveolars is rather clear.

If we compare the /s/ of sin, and /ʃ/ of shin, we can easily pinpoint a very clear difference of energy concentration; while the range is something like 4,000–8,000 Hz for the alveolar, it is definitely lower, 2,000–6,500, for the palato-alveolar. The more forward constriction in the vocal tract produces a smaller vibrating body of air in front of the constriction for the alveolar. This smaller mass of air has a higher resonance frequency than the larger air mass in front of the palato-alveolar constriction used in /ʃ/.

Voiceless fricatives have longer noise segment duration, and higher frication noise than their voiced counterparts. The lower frication noise of the voiced fricatives is explained as a result of the total airflow available for producing turbulence at the constriction. Since the glottis opens and closes for vocal cord vibration, the airstream is interrupted, and the friction noise is not as loud in voiced fricatives. Noise that occurs at the beginning of voiceless fricatives is similar to the bursts of /p, t, k/, i.e. aperiodic high-frequency noise during maximal closure.

Voiced fricatives have formants produced by pulses from the vocal cords as well as more random energy, produced by forcing air through a narrow gap. Since the airstream loses some of its kinetic energy to the vocal cord vibration, the frication noise in these sounds is not as loud as in their voiceless counterparts. As a result, they have fainter formants.

The articulatory constriction for a voiced fricative is not as tight as for a voiceless fricative, so as to ensure relatively lower supraglottal air pressure while maintaining a sufficiently high transglottal pressure differential to allow the vocal cords to vibrate. This distinction between the relatively loose articulatory constriction for voiced fricatives and the relatively tight constriction for voiceless fricatives is another variable that reduces the amplitude of the fricative noise component of a voiced fricative in comparison to a voiceless fricative. Whatever the cause of the reduction in amplitude of the noise component, it contributes to the perception of a voiced fricative (whether it is really voiced or not).

Finally, some comments are in order for /h/, because its status is interpreted differently in different publications. The turbulent noise for this sound, generated at the glottis is often accompanied by friction near the vocal tract constriction for the adjacent vowel (/h/ is always a single onset). The constriction of the other fricatives involves the articulators (tongue, teeth, lips); the production of /h/, however, leaves these articulators free. Although it is normally treated as a fricative, /h/ is physically an aspiration. The signal for this turbulent noise is very weak, and tends to be voiced (or breathy) intervocalically, as in ahead or behind.

The spectrograms in figure 5.7 illustrate some of the points made above. Consider the patterns in (a) a fake, (b) sake, and (c) a shake. The difference between (a) and (b) (or (c)) is so obvious that the greater frication noise for sibilants (/s/ or /ʃ/) can be seen effortlessly. When we compare (b) and (c), we observe the frication noise concentrated at different frequencies; approximately 4,000–8,000 Hz for the alveolar /s/, and 2,000–6,000 for the palato-alveolar /ʃ/.

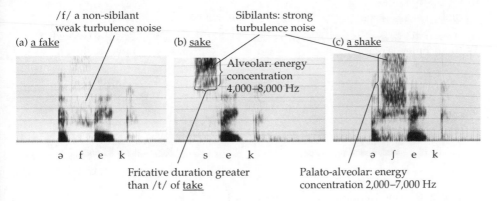

/f/ a non-sibilant
weak turbulence noise

(a) a fake

Sibilants: strong
turbulence noise

(b) sake

(c) a shake

Alveolar: energy
concentration
4,000–8,000 Hz

ə   f   e   k   s   e   k   ə   ʃ   e   k

Fricative duration greater
than /t/ of take

Palato-alveolar: energy
concentration 2,000–7,000 Hz

Figure 5.7   Spectrograms of a fake, sake, and a shake

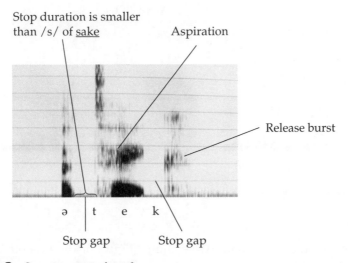

Stop duration is smaller
than /s/ of sake

Aspiration

Release burst

ə   t   e   k

Stop gap   Stop gap

Figure 5.8   Spectrogram of a take

Now, consider the spectrogram for a take (figure 5.8). This is given to show the durational differences between stops and fricatives. If we compare the duration of /t/ in a take with the duration of /s/ in sake, we can verify the greater duration of fricatives than stops.

Finally, if we consider the spectrograms of high and ahead (figure 5.9), we can observe the differences in two different phonetic manifestations of /h/. While it shows as a weak friction in high, it reveals itself as a 'breathy voice' intervocalically in ahead.

5.4.3   Affricates

Like the stop consonants, affricates /tʃ/ and /dʒ/ require a stop-like closure period followed by a quick release into a friction noise. If we look at the

(a) high   (b) ahead

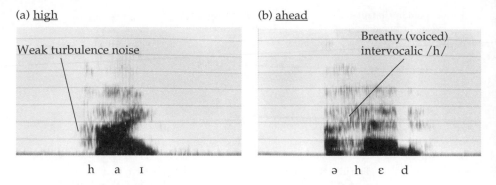

Figure 5.9 Spectrograms of <u>high</u> and <u>ahead</u>

(a) edging   (b) etching

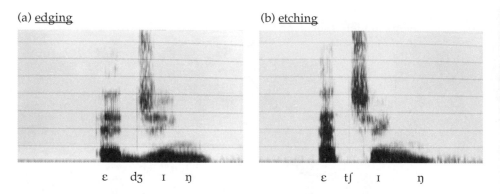

Figure 5.10 Spectrograms of <u>edging</u> and <u>etching</u>

spectrograms of the pair <u>edging</u> vs. <u>etching</u> (figure 5.10), we note the silent period produced by the consonant closures and the noise produced after the release of the consonant closure. Temporal length of the fricative releases is shorter than the closure of the stop portions. Also noteworthy is the difference between the voiceless and voiced members; as expected, the voiceless /tʃ/ is longer than the voiced /dʒ/.

In chapter 3, we stated that affricates, although phonetically a combination of a stop and a fricative, function as single units in the sound system of English. The combined duration of an affricate is shorter than the duration of the corresponding stop plus the fricative. This difference can be seen in the spectrograms of <u>gray chip</u> [gɹe tʃɪp] vs. <u>great ship</u> [gɹet ʃɪp] given in figure 5.11.

5.4.4 Approximants

Liquids and glides form the category of approximants. These sounds are made in such a way that one articulator is close to another without creating enough

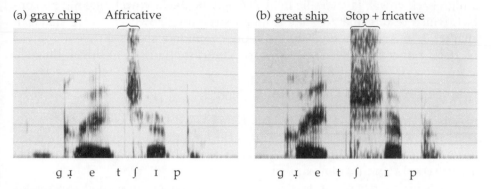

(a) gray chip   Affricative   (b) great ship   Stop + fricative

g ɹ e t ʃ ɪ p   g ɹ e t ʃ ɪ p

Figure 5.11 Spectrograms of gray chip and great ship

narrowing to result in friction. As sonorant consonants, they have formant structures. The shared characteristics in this group include their low F_1, similar durations for the transitions between vowels, and the consonant constrictions.
Glides (or semivowels as they are sometimes known) reveal patterns very similar to, but markedly fainter than, high vowels. In /w/, we see that F_1 and F_2
are very close (like /u/). In /j/, F_1 and F_2 are wide apart, resembling the situation in /i/ (low F_1 and high F_2). A glide starts with a vocal tract configuration similar to the corresponding high vowel, then changes shape for the
vowel which follows it. A glide-to-vowel sequencing is rather different from
a vowel-to-vowel sequencing in that the transition from a glide to a vowel is
faster than from a vowel to a vowel.

Liquids have properties that have similarities to both stops and to glides (especially to /w/). They are quite rapid, like stops, but have resonant quality (low
F_1), and transition speed like glides. They differ from /w/ in frequency of the
third formant; /w/ produces an F_3 that is usually so decreased in intensity that
it is not visible in a spectrogram. The other liquid, /ɹ/, on the other hand, has
a third formant frequency that is relatively low (below 2,000 Hz), strong, and
close to the second formant frequency. While it is relatively easy to separate
/ɹ/ from /w/, /w/ and /l/ may appear quite similar, because they have similar formant values for the first three formants. The following two factors can
be used to discriminate between the two sounds. First, the glide /w/ is
formed with practically no constriction at all; the liquid /l/ is formed with a
constriction of the tongue tip. As a result, the energy around F_3 for /l/ is much
higher than for /w/. Second, because of different degrees of constriction, the
formants in and out of /w/ are continuous, whereas for /l/, the formants at
the vowel junctures show a slight discontinuity. To separate an /l/ from an
/ɹ/, one has to examine the F_3. In /l/, F_3 is much higher. In addition to these
higher frequencies, the higher formants of the lateral are considerably reduced
in intensity. The difference between the 'clear' and the 'dark' /l/ lies in the
timbre of their high front/back vowel. In clear /l/, F_1 and F_2 are farther apart,
as we would expect in a high front vowel, and closer and lower in dark /l/ like

a high back vowel. Postvocalic final /l/ may be like a vowel, making no contact, which results in a /u/-like formant structure. However, as we stated in chapter 3, in American English, /l/ more commonly shows different degrees of 'dark' rather than the 'clear' vs. 'dark' contrast occurring in British English.

5.4.5 Nasals

Nasals are formed by an oral closure accompanied by an open nasal passage. Both airflow and acoustic vibration pass through the open velar port into the nasopharynx and nasal cavities. Formants for nasals are not as dark as they are in vowels (and in approximants).

Nasals have a prominent low-frequency F_1. There are two good reasons for this. Firstly, the nasal cavity is longer than the oral. Secondly, there is a strong attenuation of higher frequencies that are absorbed by the soft mucosal tissue lining the nasal cavities, and consequently, high-frequency energy gets 'damped out'. One of the indicators of a nasal sound is a clear discontinuity between the formants of the nasal and those of adjacent sounds.

All three nasals have a very faint and a very low-frequency F_1 (200–450 Hz). Another visible one is F_3, which is around 2,500 Hz. F_2 is generally not visible. Nasals reveal the abrupt loss of overall energy. The nose is less efficient than the mouth in radiating the energy to the outside.

With respect to place of articulation, formant transitions associated with nasals are very much like stops. For /m/, the bilabial nasal, the second formant has a transition pointing down. For the alveolar /n/, the second formant has a level transition. The transition for the velar points up merging with the third formant.

5.5 Putting It Together

We will review below several characteristics associated with certain sounds that have been discussed by analyzing the spectrograms of eight words: (1) train, (2) kite, (3) pig, (4) happy, (5) basket, (6) ostrich, (7) scar, and (8) chicken.

The eight words are equally divided into two groups in terms of their number of syllables (four monosyllables – scar, train, pig, kite – and four disyllables – ostrich, basket, happy, chicken). Thus, one can separate (1), (2), (3), and (7) for the former (monosyllables) because of their one vocalic nucleus formants, and isolate (4), (5), (6), and (8) for the disyllabics. Among the monosyllabics, scar is the only one that starts with a sibilant. Although all four words show frication noise-like turbulence at the beginning, only (1) and (7) are logical candidates for this target, as the noise patterns of (2) and (3) are generalized to all frequencies (a typical pattern for aspirated stops, thus pig and kite), rather than the expected concentrated pattern for /s/. This suggests that (1) and (7) are train and scar (see figure 5.12). Between the two, (7) is a better candidate for scar, as the frication noise is concentrated between 4,000 and 8,000 Hz, typical for alveolars. There is much other supporting evidence for this identification.

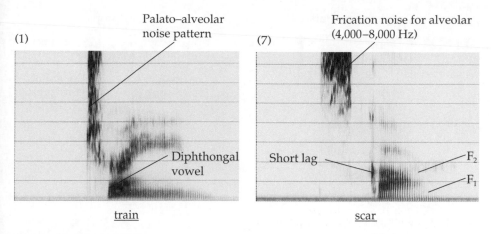

Figure 5.12 Spectrograms of train and scar

The frication noise is followed by a stop gap and the following release, /k/, with a short lag (expected of an unaspirated stop), which in turn is followed by a low back vowel (high F_1, and a narrow space between F_2 and F_1), the r-coloring of the following vowel (the lowering of the third formant). Turning to (1), train, we observe the following: the palato-alveolar nature of the frication noise (i.e. affrication of [tɹ]) is evidenced by the 2,000–8,000 Hz range of the noise pattern. Also, we note the following long and rather diphthongal vowel /e/ (fork-like opening of the formants), and the following faint and very low-frequency F_1 nasal fit the expected pattern.

Words (2) and (3) are kite and pig. How do we know which one is which? While both are CVC words that start with aspirated stops and thus cannot be differentiated via this feature in the spectrograms, the features for the remaining parts make the choices rather clear. First of all, the lengths of the vowel nuclei are quite different. In (3), we see a shorter vowel (/ɪ/ of pig). The nucleus of (2) is longer and diphthongal (/aɪ/ of kite starts with a low vowel followed by a high front vowel, and thus, fork-like opening). To make things further indubitable, one needs to look at the 'coming together' of F_2 and F_3 right before the stop gap for the coda in (3). As discussed earlier, this is typical of velar stops (/g/ of pig). Both words are produced with their final stops released (note the release burst after the stop gaps). This explains the visible voice bar in /g/ of pig. Thus, (2) is kite and (3) is pig (see figure 5.13).

Turning to disyllabics, we again start with the frication noise. The only word that starts with a frication noise is chicken, and (8) is the best candidate for this word, as the noise pattern for /tʃ/ is expectedly dark and goes down to 2,000 Hz, which is typical for palato-alveolars. Word (4) shows some frication noise, but the frequencies and the intensity of it are far less than would be expected of /tʃ/; indeed, it is typical of /h/, which suggests that (4) is happy. There are several other indicators that support the identification of these two words: the vowels in the stressed syllables are of very different length,

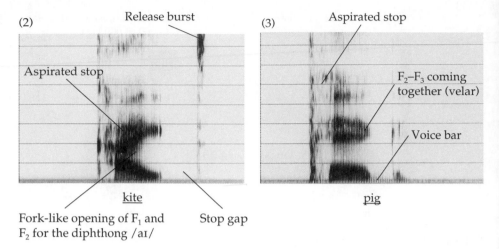

Figure 5.13 Spectrograms of <u>kite</u> and <u>pig</u>

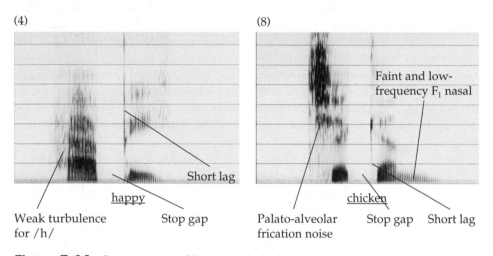

Figure 5.14 Spectrograms of <u>happy</u> and <u>chicken</u>

longer, /æ/ in <u>happy</u>, and short, /ɪ/ in <u>chicken</u>. The portions immediately following the first syllable are expectedly similar (stop gap and short lag release for the unaspirated stops). The differences, however, are clear right after that. The second syllable of (4) has a longer vowel (/i/ of <u>happy</u>), as opposed to the short [ə] of <u>chicken</u> in (8). To add further support to this identification, we can look at the faint and very low-frequency F₁ for the nasal ending of <u>chicken</u> (see figure 5.14).

The two remaining words, <u>basket</u> and <u>ostrich</u>, will have to be matched with spectrograms (5) and (6). This is a rather easy decision for several reasons. Word (6), which has two very obvious frication noises, is <u>ostrich</u>. The first one is /s/ with a typical 4,000–8,000 Hz alveolar pattern, and the second one is /tʃ/ with

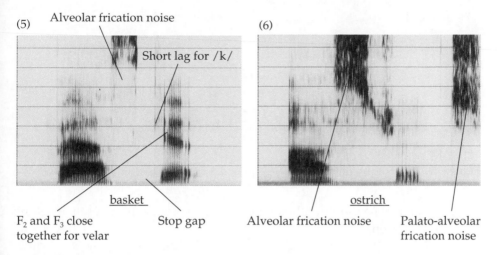

Figure 5.15 Spectrograms of <u>basket</u> and <u>ostrich</u>

a lower push typical of palato-alveolars. The same word shows some affrica-tion for [tɹ] right after /s/. Still in the same word, the stressed first syllable has a longer vowel, which is low, back (note the F_1 and F_2); the second syllable is unstressed (weak intensity and short duration). When we examine (5), <u>basket</u>, we observe the following: unsurprisingly, no visible voice bar for the initial /b/. As discussed in section 5.4.1, except in intervocalic position, this is one of the least reliable identifying characteristics of the stops /b, d, g/. The stressed first vowel, /æ/, is expectedly long, and the frication of /s/, though not as strong as that of <u>ostrich</u>, is still clear. The following sound, /k/, has its stop gap which is followed by an expected short lag release. The formant transitions for the following vowel (F_2 and F_3 are close together just after the stop with a downward transition to a vowel with a high F_2) clearly indicate the velar place of articulation. Finally, we note the second syllable with a rather short vowel followed by a stop coda (see figure 5.15).

5.6 Context

Although we have talked about the characteristics of different sounds in a spectrographic display, as mentioned at the beginning of this chapter, there are no absolute criteria that could uniquely define what a sound /X/ is in all phonetic environments, even for a particular individual. Thus, the lay person's assumption that phonemes exhibit 'invariance' can hardly be justified.

Several factors influence both vowels and consonants. Earlier (see table 5.3), we saw that the duration of vowels is different in stressed and unstressed syllables. Besides this, other variables are important too. One of the frequently mentioned variables is the influence of the following consonant because the

(a) <u>sent</u> – <u>send</u>   (b) <u>kilt</u> – <u>killed</u>

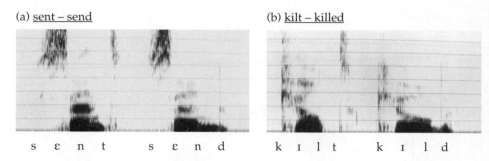

s ɛ n t   s ɛ n d   k ɪ l t   k ɪ l d

Figure 5.16 Spectrograms of <u>sent</u> – <u>send</u> and <u>kilt</u> – <u>killed</u>

same vowel may be significantly longer before a voiced consonant than before a voiceless consonant.

The effect of the following consonant on the duration of the preceding vowel is mentioned above. In fact, as we saw in chapter 3, this effect is also observed in all preceding sonorant segments. If we look at the spectrograms of the pairs <u>sent</u> – <u>send</u>, and <u>kilt</u> – <u>killed</u> (figure 5.16), we can observe the differences in the durations of vowels and the sonorant consonant before voiced and voiceless stops. As we can see, the durations of the vowels and the sonorant consonants are, expectedly, greater before /d/ than /t/.

Fricatives exert an even greater influence over vowels than stops. For example, we get the following readings for the same vowel [ʌ] depending on the nature of the following consonant. We found the following differences with the change in the following segment.

> <u>but</u> [bʌt]   (vowel length before a voiceless stop: 104 ms)
> <u>bud</u> [bʌd]   (vowel length before a voiced stop: 172 ms)
> <u>buzz</u> [bʌz] (vowel length before a voiced fricative: 210 ms)

The length of the word, as well as its number of syllables, seems influential. For example, while we get a reading of 93 ms for the vowel [ɪ] in <u>pick</u>, it goes down to 56 ms in <u>picky</u> and to 37 ms in <u>pickiness</u>.

Position of the word in the phrase or in the sentence, the rate of speaking, the type of word, either topic or comment, all influence the duration significantly. For example, the vowels of the two words <u>dog</u> [ɔ] and <u>man</u> [æ] change their duration by between 20 ms and 65 ms in the following sentences.

> "The /dɔg/ ([ɔ]: 161 ms) bit the /mæn/ ([æ]: 175 ms)"
> "The /mæn/ ([æ]: 155 ms) was bitten by the /dɔg/ ([ɔ]: 226 ms)"

Similarly, in a listing situation, the last item has greater duration. If we compare the following two sentences, we get different durational readings for <u>peaches</u> and <u>oranges </u>in their two locations.

(a) I like apples, oranges, and peaches.
(b) I like apples, peaches, and oranges.

For example, we get an average of 94 ms as the durational reading for the final [z] of <u>oranges</u> in sentence (a), which goes up to a 174 ms reading for the same sound in sentence (b). Pre-pausal (at the end of phrases, clauses, or sentences) stressed vowels seem to have the longest duration; this is diametrically opposed to vowels in function words. As a result, the duration of a vowel in the former position may be up to two or even three times that of the same vowel in the latter.

Consonants also can be influenced by the contexts in which they appear. We saw earlier that the aspiration of the voiceless stops varied according to the following segment. Specifically, there was a longer lag before a sonorant consonant (<u>play</u> [pʰle̥]), than before a vowel (<u>pay</u> [pʰe̥]). As for their duration, fricatives are the consonants that are more consistently affected by the context. For example, we get readings of 196–231 ms for the /s/ of <u>sub</u> [sʌb], which goes up to 309–325 ms in final position in <u>bus</u> [bʌs]. Yet, when we place it at the end of a phrase (<u>take the bus</u>), /s/ gives us a reading of 328–365 ms.

Speakers adapt to various circumstances of communication and adjust their production patterns accordingly. Thus, it is no surprise that the speech style and rate influences the production, and we see a clear difference between slow and careful speech versus fast, colloquial speech. While the former is characterized by a slower tempo, avoidance of reductions and/or deletions, and an attempt to make the production as distinct as possible, the latter is replete with deletions and reductions, and the durations of the components necessarily get smaller. These contrasting phenomena, which are known as *hypospeech* (or "overshooting") versus *hyperspeech* (or "undershooting"), should not be conceived of as a binary split, but rather as a continuum (thus, the terms 'very slow', 'slow', 'normal formal', 'conversational', 'fast', 'very fast'). Consequently, the different speech realizations and different acoustic readings are the results of these varying production patterns.

Example: Colorless green ideas sleep furiously (12-syllable sentence)

very slow	2	syllables per second
slow	2.67	syllables per second
normal formal	4.8	syllables per second
conversational	6	syllables per second
fast	8.0	syllables per second
very fast	12	syllables per second

5.7 Practical Applications: Some Examples

As we noted at the beginning of the chapter, spectrographic analysis is a very useful tool in applied disciplines. The increasingly affordable software on the market has made its use very viable in a clinical context and in foreign language teaching. The utility of spectrographic analysis comes from the fact that it provides quantitative and objective data on a wide range of speech parameters (e.g. nasalization, vowel quality, segmental duration, place and manner of articulation, voice onset time) and greatly enhances the scope of auditory-based perceptual judgments of speech. It is particularly helpful in monitoring changes during remediation (clinical and/or classroom context).

Real-time spectrographic displays have been used in speech training with individuals who have severe and profound hearing impairments. Although some have expressed concerns about the usefulness of spectrograms in speech training, citing their complex and abstract nature, several investigators have pointed out their successful use with hearing-impaired adults (Maki 1980, 1983; Maki et al. 1981) and children (Ertmer and Stark 1995; Ertmer et al. 1996) with respect to contrasts such as voiced–voiceless, durational differences, tongue position for vowels, and differences in manner of consonant production. Recently, Ertmer (2004) examined how well children with normal hearing and children with impaired hearing can recognize spectrographic cues for vowels and consonants, and the ages at which these visual cues are distinguished. Subjects' training activities involved instruction, highlighting of target spectrographic cues, matching of spectrograms by the children, and feedback on correctness. Results showed that a variety of spectrographic cues were recognized with greater-than-chance accuracy at each age level and across both hearing statuses. On average, formant cues were recognized with greater accuracy than consonant manner features, making vowels, diphthongs and vowel-like approximants easier to recognize. This saliency, Ertmer suggests, may be the result of a combination of greater duration, darker energy traces, and distinctive visual patterns.

For another example, we can consider problems related to VOT, which may be of concern for a variety of populations. Individuals who are suffering from *aphasia* (language deficit due to damage to certain regions of the brain, in this case Broca's area) seem to be unable to control the timing between the release of a stop and the onset of voicing. Individuals with *apraxia* (neurological disorder of motor programming for speech) tend to have problems in areas such as timing and coordination that might lead to troubles in VOT production. In several studies *dysarthria* (a group of speech disorders resulting from a disease or damage to neural mechanisms that regulate speech movements) patients have been reported to show increased variability in their VOT productions. VOT deficiencies have also been reported in relation to *hearing impairment.*

The significance of VOT deficiencies is not restricted to the clinical context and is very important in foreign language teaching and accent reduction contexts. As mentioned earlier in this chapter, and in chapter 3, the difference between English /p, t, k/ and /b, d, g/ is not voiced/voiceless in initial position, as /b, d, g/ also may have no voicing before the release of the stop closure. Thus, the aspiration of /p, t, k/ is very important for a segment to be perceived as /p/ rather than /b/ (similar situation for /t/ vs. /d/, and /k/ vs. /g/). Learners of English coming from Romance languages with unaspirated /p, t, k/ (e.g. Spanish, Portuguese) face a big challenge in learning the English patterns, because their productions may be (and indeed, in many cases, are) perceived as /b, d, g/ by native speakers of English. While aspiration of /p, t, k/ is perceived by the hearer in a binary fashion (i.e. all or none occurrence), studies on first and second language acquisition production data show that delay of the onset of voicing is typically gradual in the case of voice lag. Thus, the value of acoustic data becomes ever more important during the remediation process. In considering the productions of the client (learner/patient), their progress needs to be constantly evaluated via instrumentation. Monitoring the changes and making the learners/patients aware of this progress, however incomplete, would encourage them and thus accelerate the remediation process.

It is frequently pointed out that transcribing vowels accurately is more difficult than doing the same for consonants. This task is made harder when we deal with different vowel sounds that are not part of our native inventory, or different vowel sounds we might encounter in disordered speech. The key here is to identify the differences between the system to be remedied and the target system. Although the cardinal vowel system discussed in chapter 1 may be helpful, this requires a very strong phonetic training if one is to rely on it. Acoustic analysis provides a viable alternative here. As mentioned earlier, vowels can be accurately described by the frequencies of their first three (in most cases, two) formants. Thus, with the help of spectrographic analysis, the practitioner will be in a position to identify the nature and the extent of the mismatches between the target system and the system of the patient/student, and plan the remediation.

Apart from its utility in identifying different vowel qualities, acoustic analysis is also a powerful tool for vowel durations, an issue which may be crucial in both clinical context and foreign language teaching. For example, as we saw earlier, voicing is frequently absent during closure of final /b, d, g/. Because vowels preceding voiced obstruents are lengthened, the final consonant will be perceived as voiced even though no specific evidence of voicing is present. When the learner/patient fails to implement this expected lengthening, the practitioner can identify this unambiguously via spectrographic analysis. Also, during remediation s/he can carefully monitor changes via spectrographic data in the vowel durations. This can help measure the progress by accurately describing the productions that may not be evident perceptually.

Failure to implement voicing contrasts among obstruents is not uncommon in some aphasic patients. For example, a 63-year-old female Broca's patient (Code and Ball 1982) did not have the voicing contrast involving fricatives (e.g. proofing vs. proving, pence vs. pens). Analyzing her data spectrographically, however, the investigators were able to find out that her productions for such pairs were not homophonous, and that although she did not have the voiced/voiceless distinctions in target fricatives, she did maintain the contrasts via the length of the vowel before target fricatives; that is, vowels were (just like in normal speech) longer before voiced (lenis) targets than before voiceless (fortis) targets.

The same subject's data were also instructive with respect to the duration of target fricatives. As pointed out earlier, duration of frication of voiceless targets is longer that that of voiced ones. The subject in the above-mentioned study did also make a difference (somewhat smaller than in normal speech) in the duration between voiceless and voiced targets. Thus, out of three parameters that are available to contrast /f/ vs. /v/, /s/ vs. /z/, and so on (voicing of the target, vowel length before the target, duration of frication) the patient was able to utilize the last two. Without the use of spectrographic data, the investigators would not have been able to find out that the patient was making the phonemic distinctions and that the disability was phonetic.

All the above point to a conclusion that spectrographic analysis allows a quantification of mismatches between the normative data and the client's productions. In addition to the fact that such quantification is indispensable for the diagnosis of the trouble spots, it greatly enhances, by monitoring changes, the ability of the professional who deals with the remediation.

Finally, we can also mention that spectrographic data can help professionals dealing with voice disorders, training of the singing voice, speaker identification, and identification of the correlates of speech in stressful conditions, and intoxicated speech.

SUMMARY

In this chapter, we examined spectrographic characteristics of speech. Although precise acoustic makeup of each sound will differ for each individual speaker, there are core features that would enable us to identify general patterns. In the investigation of vowels and diphthongs, the formant patterns are the cues for recognition. In stops, fricatives, and affricates, which form the group of obstruents, the different degrees of obstruction reveal clear acoustic patterns: a gap for stops, frication noise for fricatives, and a stop gap followed by a frication noise for affricates. Sonorant consonants behave rather like vowels in that they exhibit a voice bar along with formant-like structures. We also saw that the context in which a particular sound occurs (e.g. adjacent sounds, word positions, suprasegmentals, speech style and rate, etc.) influences the acoustic characteristics. Finally, we briefly looked at some practical applications of spectrographic analysis in remedial contexts.

APPENDIX

Tips on what to look for for certain sound classes on a spectrographic display:

Stops

Voiced (lenis) vs. voiceless (fortis)

	#___	V__V	___#
Duration of stop gap		voiceless longer	
Voice bar (/b, d, g/)	?	Yes	?
Release burst		stronger for voiceless	
		(if released)	
Duration of previous V	NA	longer before /b, d, g/	

Aspiration (VOT of more than 30 ms in initial /p, t, k/ of a stressed syllable)

Place of articulation

- F$_2$ and F$_3$ transitions (CV) (VC formant transition is the opposite of CV transition): /b/ both upward, /d/ third falls and second has only a small movement, /g/ second and third close together.
- Locus (starting frequency): /b/ 600–800 Hz, /d/ 1,800 Hz, /g/ (2 loci) 300 Hz and 1,300 Hz (F$_2$–F$_3$ relationship is important for velars).
- Release burst:

  Bilabials: burst with a center frequency lower than the F$_2$ of the V (diffuse and weak)
  Alveolars: burst with a center frequency higher than the F$_2$ of the V (diffuse and strong)
  Velars: burst with a center frequency approximating to the F$_2$ of the V (compact and strong)

- Aspiration: velars have greater VOT than alveolars, which in turn have greater VOT than bilabials.

Fricatives

- An interval of frication noise (greater in sibilants than non-sibilants). Voiceless fricatives have greater frication noise than the voiced counterparts.
- Have longer duration (longer than 130 ms) than stops (less than 75 ms) and affricates (75–130 ms).
- Voiced fricatives have shorter noise segment duration.

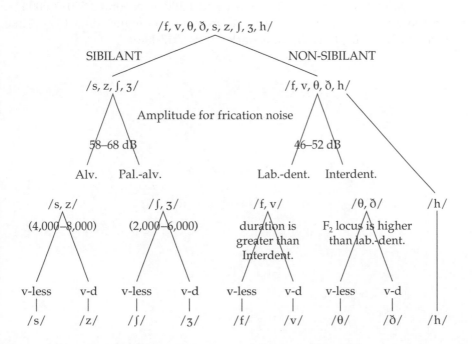

Affricates

Stop gap followed by noise segment (frication).

Nasals

- Formants are not as loud as they are in vowels (and in approximants).
- A very faint and a very low-frequency F_1 (200–300 Hz).
- F_2 around 2,500 Hz, F_3 around 3,200 Hz (if visible).
- Formant transitions associated with nasals (re: place of articulation) are very much like stops.

Glides

- Similar to high vowels: /w/ F_1 and F_2 very close (like /u/); /j/ F_1 and F_2 apart.
- The transition from a glide to a vowel is faster than from a vowel to a vowel, but slower than from a stop to a vowel. Stop + V (shorter than 50 ms); glide + V (60–100 ms); V + V (more than 100 ms).

Liquids

- Properties like stops (quite rapid), and glides (resonant quality – low F_1 and F_2, transition speed); differ from glides in F_3 frequency.
- /r/: lowered F_3 (narrowly separated from F_2); lowers the F_3 of surrounding Vs. F_1 around 320; F_2 around 1,100; F_3 around 1,600 Hz.
- /l/: F_2 is higher, F_3 is much higher (higher formants considerably reduced in intensity). F_1 around 300–360; F_2 around 1,300; F_3 around 2,500–3,000 Hz.
- Postvocalic final /l/ may be like a V, making no tongue contact (/u/-like formants), (clear /l/ is /i/-like, dark /l/ is /u/-like).

1. What differences do you expect to find in the spectrograms of the
    following pairs?

    Example: (a) court – (b) scored

    •   Initial frication noise of /s/ in (b)
    •   Initial aspiration of /k/ in (a)
    •   longer vowel before /d/ in (b)
    •   longer duration for final /t/ in (a)
    •   ?? voice bar in final /d/ in (b)

    (i)   (a) sip   (b) zip

    (ii)   (a) britches   (b) bridges

    (iii)   (a) hat   (b) ahead

    (iv)   (a) parade   (b) pilot

    (v)   (a) name   (b) mine

2. Match the following spectrograms with the targets open, tiger, pack-
    age, camel, apple, table. Explain your rationale.

    (a)

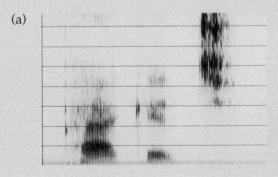

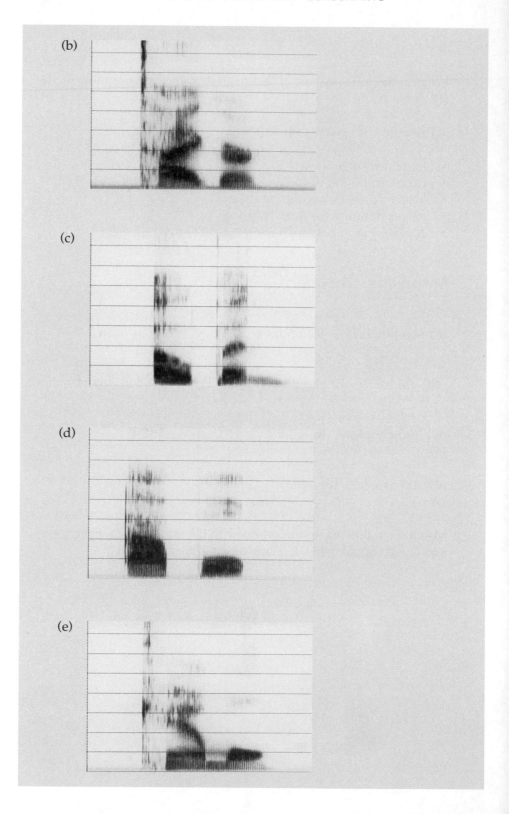

(f)

3. Transcribe the following (about 'second language varieties of English'). Based on P. Trudgill and J. Hannah, *International English* (London: Edward Arnold, 2002).

English is a language which has more non-native speakers than

....

native speakers. Besides the fact that it is learned by millions of people

....

around the world as a foreign language, there are millions of speakers

....

of English as a second language in many countries. In the Americas,

....

English is an important second language in Puerto Rico, and also has

....

some second-language presence in Panama. In Europe, it has official

....

status in Gibraltar and Malta and is also widely spoken as a second

....

language in Cyprus. In Africa, there are large communities of native

....

speakers of English in Liberia, South Africa, Zimbabwe and Kenya,

....

but there are even larger communities in these countries of second-

....

language speakers. Elsewhere in Africa, English has official status, and

....

is therefore widely used as a second language lingua franca in

....

Gambia, Sierra Leone, Ghana, Nigeria, Cameroon, Namibia,

....

Botswana, Lesotho, Swaziland, Zambia, Malawi and Uganda. It is also

....

widely used in education and for government purposes in Tanzania

and Kenya. In the Indian Ocean, Asian and Pacific Ocean areas,

English is an official language in Mauritius, the Seychelles, Pakistan,

India, Singapore, Brunei, Hong Kong, the Philippines, Papua New

Guinea, the Solomon Islands, Vanuatu, Fiji, Tonga, Western Samoa,

American Samoa, the Cook Islands, Guam and elsewhere in

American administered Micronesia. It is also very widely used as a

second language in Malaysia, Bangladesh, Sri Lanka, the Maldives,

Nepal and Nauru.

Syllables

6.1 Introduction

The patterns of vowels and consonants we have reviewed thus far have, frequently, made references to the phonological unit of syllable. Rules about the allophonic variations regarding aspiration (i.e. voiceless stops are aspirated at the beginning of stressed syllables); glottalization or glottal stop replacement of /t/ (i.e. /t/ may be optionally glottalized or totally replaced by a glottal stop in syllable-final position); lowering of /ɔ/ to /ɑ/ before /ɹ/ (i.e. /ɔ/ can be optionally replaced by /ɑ/ before /ɹ/, if the vowel and /ɹ/ belong to different syllables); as well as distribution of some sounds, as in the case of /h/ and /ŋ/ (i.e. /h/ is always syllable-initial and never syllable-final, and /ŋ/ is always syllable-final and never syllable-initial), show the relevance of the unit of syllable in phonological description.

Beyond its relevance for the phonological rules, syllable has an important role with respect to the phonotactic constraints in languages. This refers to the system of arrangement of sounds and sound sequences. It is on this basis that a speaker of English can judge some new form as a possible/impossible word. For example, both [blɪt] and [bmɪt] are non-existing as English words. If asked to choose between the two, a native speaker of English, without a moment's hesitation, would go for [blɪt]. The reason for this is that [bl] is a possible onset cluster in English, whereas [bm] is not. This is not to say that no English word can have [bm] sequence. Words such as <u>submarine</u> [sʌbməɹin], <u>submission</u> [sʌbmɪʃən] are clear demonstrations of the fact that we can have /m/ after /b/ in English. This, however, is possible only if these two sounds are in different syllables. So, the rejection of a word such as [bmɪt] is strictly based on syllable-related generalization.

Although we have made numerous references to syllables and syllable position up until this point, we have not dealt with the definition of syllable, nor have we dealt with the question of syllabification. Before we do these, we will look at the hierarchical internal structure of syllable. Earlier (in chapter 1), we suggested a binary split between the onset and the rhyme for syllables. Thus, a monosyllabic word such as <u>dog</u> [dɔg] has the following structure:

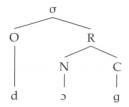

σ = syllable
O = onset
R = rhyme
N = nucleus
C = coda

The justification of onset–rhyme separation is not hard to find. First of all, rhyming (whether two words rhyme) is totally based on the vowel/diphthong and anything that follows it (nucleus + optional coda = rhyme); onset has no relevance in this. If, on the other hand, we look at the device of alliteration (i.e. the repetition of the same consonant sound(s) at the onset position in two words as in stem [stɛm] and stern [stɛɹn]), we see that, here, it is the onset that counts and the rhyme is irrelevant. More strong evidence that rhyme is a constituent comes from the stress rules. In several languages (English included) in which the stress is sensitive to the structure of syllables, the structure of the rhyme is the determining factor; onsets do not count. Also, restrictions between syllabic elements are, overwhelmingly, either within the onset or within the rhyme. For example, as mentioned above, the restriction that a stop cannot be followed by a nasal is valid in the onset (across syllables, this is allowed, e.g. batman, admonish). Similarly, the statement that English does not allow non-homorganic nasal + stop is valid for coda clusters, because while a form such as [lɪmk] is impossible, we can get such non-homorganic sequences across syllables (e.g. kumquat, pumpkin). Another example for a similar phenomenon comes from the sequences of two obstruents with respect to voicing. While it is not difficult to find examples such as cubs [kʌbz] and cups [kʌps], where the sequences of bilabial stops and alveolar fricatives agree in voicing, we do not find words such as [kʌpz] and [kʌbs] with disagreement in voicing. This does not mean that there are no words in English where we put two obstruents with opposite voicing. Examples such as absurd [æbsəˑd], obsolete [absəlit], and Hudson [hʌdsən] can be easily multiplied. The difference between these two groups of words lies in the tautosyllabic (i.e. in the same syllable) nature of the two obstruents in the former, and the split of the sequence of stop and the fricative by a syllable boundary in the latter. Also, further attesting the existence of rhyme as a constituent, dependencies between nuclei and codas are commonly found. To give an example from English, we can look at the /aʊ/ nucleus and its relationship with its coda:

brown	[bɹaʊn]	But	* [bɹaʊŋ] / [bɹaʊm]
spouse	[spaʊs]		* [spaʊf]
trout	[tɹaʊt]		* [tɹaʊp] / [tɹaʊk]
rouse	[ɹaʊz]		* [ɹaʊv]
crowd	[kɹaʊd]		* [kɹaʊg] / [kɹaʊb]

What these examples demonstrate is that the coda that follows /aʊ/ has to be alveolar; this nucleus cannot be followed by labial or velar consonants.

Having made the point that onsets and rhymes should be seen as auto-nomous units, each with their own constraints on their internal structure, we are now ready to look at the details (for a different view, which argues against the necessity of the rhyme as a unit, see Davis 1988). In the word dog above, the final units of the syllable each contained one segment. However, as we will see shortly in greater detail, there are several other possibilities in English. To give some examples, let us look at the words blue, side, wind, and ground.

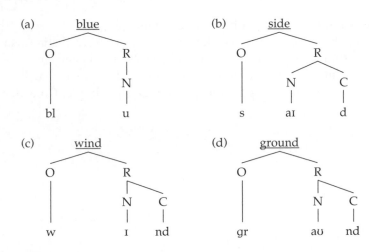

When we look at these representations, we see that several positions are taken by sequences of two segments and that would make it obvious, for example, that the onset cluster of (a), /bl/, will be longer than the single onset of (b), /s/. While this is true, the representation, as it is, is not sufficient to make any distinction between the nucleus of (a) (/u/, a long vowel) and the nucleus of (c) (/ɪ/, a short vowel). To remedy this situation, we introduce the skeletal tier (i.e. 'X') that would reveal the timing slots for each unit. Thus, we represent the difference between (a) and (c) in the following manner:

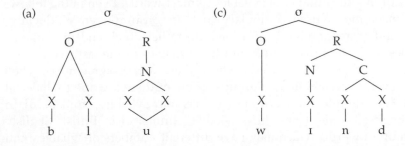

In this revised representation, long vowels and diphthongs will have two timing slots (branching), whereas short vowels will have one (non-branching). Multiple onsets/codas will also be branching. Finally, we give the revised tree of the CVC word dog,

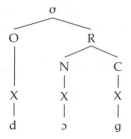

that has a non-branching onset, and a branching rhyme, [ɔg].

The advantage of the design with skeletal tiers is not only to distinguish branching from non-branching, which, as we will see shortly, is very important in stress assignment rules. It also helps us to deal with segments such as affricates that are phonetically complex but phonologically simple. Consider the following:

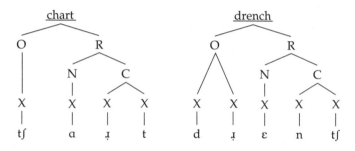

whereby the clusters are branching (two timing slots) but the phonetically complex affricates are non-branching (one timing slot).

6.2 Number of Syllables

It is generally agreed that speakers of English do not have a great deal of difficulty in identifying the number of syllables in most words. Even in the following rather uncommonly used vocabulary such as consumptiveness, docility, divinatory, and cosmographical, decisions are rather quick and unanimous; four syllables in the first two words, and five syllables in the last two.

There are, of course, some words where there are disagreements. They belong, however, to certain limited groups. Some of these are due to dialectal differences. For example, the word military has four syllables, [mɪ.lə.tɛ.ɹi], in American English, while it has three syllables, [mɪ.lə.tɹi] in British English. Another group of words, which may have different numbers of syllables, can result from the [ə] deletion, as exemplified in veteran [vɛ.tə.ɹən] (three syllables) or [vɛ.tɹən] (two syllables). Similarly, management could have three syllables, [mæ.nədʒ.mənt], or two, [mændʒ.mənt]. The remaining disputable items, generally, all relate to sonorant consonants. In some of these, the number of syllables will vary depending on whether the nasal consonant is syllabic or not. For example, chasm may be said to have one or two syllables depending on the status of the final nasal. Similarly, <u>Catholicism</u> may be judged as having four or five syllables. As with nasals, we can cite words with laterals following non-low front vowels. Items such as <u>real</u>, <u>male</u>, and <u>feel</u> may be judged as having one or two syllables. Finally, /ɹ/ may be the source of disagreement in words such as <u>fire</u>, <u>hire</u>; these words are monosyllabic for some, but disyllabic for others.

The cases with disagreement are clearly limited and should not distract us further from the more important question regarding the definition of the unit syllable. Unfortunately, there is no unanimous decision among scholars regarding the question as to where the unit syllable belongs; whether it should be defined acoustically, articulatorily, or auditorily. Our approach in this book will be based on sonority and the syllables will be described on the basis of peaks of sonority; that is, the suggestion is that the number of syllables in a word will be equal to the number of sonority peaks in that word.

6.3 Sonority

Before we start using the concept, we need to define what sonority is. This, in itself, is not an easy task, as it is also far from being uncontroversial. For pedagogical purposes, we will keep it as straightforward as possible. The sonority of a sound is primarily related to the degree of opening of the vocal tract during its articulation. The more open the vocal tract is for a sound, the higher its sonority will be. Thus vowels, which are produced with greater degree of opening, will be higher in sonority scale than fricatives or stops, which are produced either with a narrow opening or with a complete closure of the articulators. The second, and relatively secondary (ancillary) dimension is the sound's propensity for voicing. This becomes relevant when the stricture (degree of opening) is the same for two given sounds; the sound that has voicing (e.g. voiced fricative) will have a higher degree of sonority than its voiceless counterpart (voiceless fricative). Putting all these together, we can say that low vowels (/æ, ɑ/), which have the maximum degree of opening, will have the highest, and voiceless stops, which have no opening and no voicing, will have the lowest sonority. The remaining sounds will be in between. One does find different hierarchies of sonority in different books and manuals. However, the differences are in details rather than the basic relative ordering. In this book, we adopt the following 10-point scale suggested by Hogg and McCully (1987):

Sounds	Sonority values	Examples
Low vowels	10	/ɑ, æ/
Mid vowels	9	/e, o/
High vowels (and glides)	8	/i, u/
Flaps	7	/r/
Laterals	6	/l/
Nasals	5	/m, n, ŋ/
Voiced fricatives	4	/v, ð, z/
Voiceless fricatives	3	/f, θ, s/
Voiced stops	2	/b, d, ɡ/
Voiceless stops	1	/p, t, k/

Having stated the relative sonority of sounds, we are now ready to look at the number of syllables in words as peaks of sonority. In auditory terms, the sonority peak is more prominent than the surrounding segments. Since vowels and diphthongs are higher in sonority than other segments, they, typically, occupy the peak positions in syllables. We show this with the following displays for publicity and condemnation:

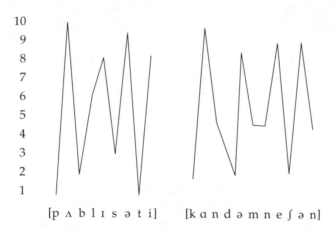

[p ʌ b l ɪ s ə t i]   [k ɑ n d ə m n e ʃ ə n]

The principle of peaks of sonority correctly identifies the number of syllables, 4, in these two cases.

As we saw earlier, in English we can have syllables that do not contain a vowel. In these cases, the most sonorant consonant will be the syllable peak (i.e. syllabic consonant):

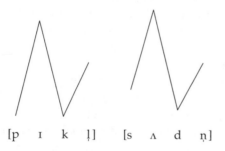

[p   ɪ   k   l̩]   [s   ʌ   d   n̩]

Since the existence of the syllabic consonants is due to the deletion of the reduced vowel, [ə], they are confined to unstressed syllables. In stressed syllables, we always have full vowels that will assume the syllabic peaks; this leaves no chance for the consonant to be syllabic.

Although the principle of equating the sonority peaks to the number of syllables would hold for thousands of English words, it does not mean that it is without exceptions. We must acknowledge the fact that some English onset clusters with /s/ as the first consonant (e.g. stop [stɑp]), and coda clusters with /s/ as the last consonant (e.g. box [bɑks]) do violate this principle. These cases will be discussed in greater detail later in this chapter. Before we deal with them, however, we will look at the issue of syllabification.

6.4 Syllabification

Although finding the peaks of sonority aids us greatly in identifying the number of syllables in a word, it does not tell us much about the syllabification, that is, where the syllable boundaries lie. For example, where do the intervocalic consonants belong in publicity? How do we assign /b/ and /l/ between the first and the second syllables? What about the /s/? Is it the coda of the second syllable or the onset of the third?

The principle that makes the decision in these cases, which is known as the 'maximal onset principle', simply assigns any series of intervocalic consonants to the syllable on the right as long as it does not violate the language-specific onset patterns. To demonstrate this, let us look at the word publicity again. This word, unambiguously, has four syllables and the nuclei are clearly identifiable vowels. First, we need to phonetically transcribe the word and identify the syllable nuclei.

[p ʌ b l ɪ s ə t i]

The next step is to go to the end of the word and start connecting the nucleus of each syllable with the surrounding consonants. The last syllable has no coda, and the nucleus will be attached to the preceding /t/, because [ti] is an acceptable sequence in English. After this, we move to the nucleus of the preceding (third) syllable, which is an [ə]; the lack of any coda in this syllable and the acceptability of a [sə] sequence in English tell us that this will be the third syllable of the word. There are two consonants to the left of the nucleus of the second syllable /ɪ/. Connecting /ɪ/ to the immediately preceding /l/ is no problem, as [lɪ] is perfectly normal sequence in English. The next consonant to the left, /b/, is also going to be connected with the second syllable, because the resulting [bl] is an acceptable onset in the language (e.g. blue [blu], block [blɔk]). Thus, the resulting syllabification of this word will be:

[p ʌ . b l ɪ . s ə . t i]

Sometimes, we see the same sequences of sounds syllabified differently in different words. We will illustrate this phenomenon in the following two words, temptation and complain. The syllabifications of these two words are given in the following:

[k ə m . p l e n]   [t ɛ m p . t e . ʃ ə n]

Our focus will be the [mp] sequence the two words share. As the syllabifications above make clear, the same sequence behaves differently in the two words. While in temptation [tɛmp.te.ʃən] the [mp] sequence is the double coda of the first syllable, in <u>complain</u> [kəm.plen], the two sounds fall into separate syllables; [m] belongs to the coda of the first syllable, and [p] is part of the double onset of the second syllable. The reason for this difference is what is allowed as a maximal onset in English. Since [pt] is not a possible onset, [p] has to stay in the first syllable of <u>temptation</u>. In <u>complain</u>, however, [p] is part of the onset of the second syllable because [pl] is a permissible onset in English.

Dividing the word <u>complain</u> as [kəmp.len] would not have resulted in any violation of English onsets or codas, because both [kəmp] and [len] are permissible in the language. However, doing this would have meant maximizing the coda. The observed syllabification [kəm.plen], on the other hand, follows the maximization of allowed onset in English. Assigning intervocalic consonants as onsets of the following syllable rather than coda of the preceding syllable forms the basis of the 'maximal onset principle', and this is derived from the fact that onsets are more basic than codas in languages. All languages, without a single exception, have CV (open) syllables, whereas many languages may lack VC (closed) syllables. To summarize what has been said so far, we can say that the principle that guides spoken syllabification assigns the maximum allowable number of consonants to the syllable on the right.

Before we leave this section, we should emphasize the importance of the language-specific nature of syllabification, as the same sequence of sounds may be divided differently in different languages. To illustrate this point, let us look at the following two cases, /bl/ and /sl/, and compare the situation in English with two other languages. In Turkish there are no onset clusters, although the sequence [bl] may be found across syllables. For example, the word <u>abla</u> "older sister" would invariably be divided as [ab.la]. This is very different from the [bl] sequence of English in [pʌ.blɪ.sə.ti]. As for [sl], we can compare English with Spanish. Although Spanish has onset clusters, these are not allowed with /s/ as the first member. This does not mean that there are no [sl] sequences in the language. The word [isla] "island" shows that this is possible with the following syllabification [is.la]. In English, however, since [sl] is a possible onset, the syllabification of a word such as <u>asleep</u> is [ə.slip]. These two examples demonstrate that how a given sequence of sounds may behave is strictly dependent on language-specific patterns. Finally, if we can state the obvious from the examples above, we can predict that a native speaker of Turkish will attempt the syllabification of <u>publicity</u> as [pʌb.lɪ.sə.ti], and a native speaker of Spanish would reveal [əs.lip] for <u>asleep</u> in their attempts to acquire English as a foreign language.

6.5 English Syllable Phonotactics

While we were talking about the syllabification of words which involve the use of two or more consonants in a row between vowels, the determination regarding which syllable they should belong to was made with reference to language-specific facts. For example, a word such as <u>acne</u> [ækni] will have the first consonant as the coda of the first syllable, and the second consonant as the onset of the second syllable. The obvious reason is that English does not allow /kn/ as an onset cluster. This will not be the case if we are talking about Norwegian (e.g. Knut), Hebrew (e.g. Knesset), Russian (e.g. kniga), or German (e.g. Knabe). It is time now to deal with the specifics of English syllable structure. We start from the general formula, which can be stated as:

(C) (C) (C) V (C) (C) (C) {C}

What this characterization says is that a V (vowel or diphthong), which is the nucleus, is the only obligatory element in an English syllable (e.g. 'a' [e]). The surrounding consonants in parentheses are optional elements. Thus, we can have a V with one, two, or three consonants before it as single, double, or triple onsets:

CV (e.g. say [se])
CCV (e.g. pray [pɹe])
CCCV (e.g. spray [spɹe])

Just like adding the consonants as onsets, we can add them as codas after the nucleus:

VC (e.g. at [æt])
VCC (e.g. act [ækt])
VCCC (e.g. busts [bʌsts])

In the general formula given at the outset, there is also a fourth consonant in the coda, given in brackets. This is different than the others, because it is possible only if it belongs to a suffix, that is, coming from the following morpheme, as in bursts [bɝsts]. Single and multiple onsets can also be combined with single and multiple codas and create further possibilities:

CVC (e.g. beat [bit])
CCVC (e.g. break [bɹek])
CCCVC (e.g. strike [stɹaɪk])
CVCC (e.g. binge [bɪndʒ])
CVCCC (e.g. text [tɛkst])
CCVCC (e.g. print [pɹɪnt])
CCVCCC (e.g. sphinx [sfɪnks])
CCCVCC (e.g. sprint [spɹɪnt])

Beyond these, the following are possible if we include the suffixes:

CCCVCCC (e.g. sprints [spɹɪnts])
CVCCCC (e.g. worlds [wɝldz])
CCVCCCC (e.g. twelfths [twɛlfθs])

CCCVCCCC is a logical possibility with no commonly found vocabulary.

The picture given above is still a very general one and does not include the numerous restrictions we have on onsets and codas.

6.5.1 Single onsets

As stated in sections 3.2 and 3.4, the only consonant that is not allowed to take this position in English is /ŋ/. Another sound, /ʒ/, does not start an English word (save for items such as genre, as well as some foreign names such as Zhivago) but is capable of occurring in non-word-initial onsets, as in vision [vɪ.ʒən], measure [mɛ.ʒɚ]. Finally, /ð/ deserves a mention for its restricted occurrence in word-initial position; this sound is found only in grammatical (function) words (the, then, there, etc.) word-initially.

6.5.2 Double onsets

Table 6.1 shows the occurring double onsets of English. We can make the following observations: Affricates are the only class of consonants that do not appear in onset clusters. Besides this general statement, there are several other restrictions for two-member onset clusters.

- No voiced fricatives can serve as C_2, and only /v/ can be a C_1 and can combine only with /j/ (e.g. view).
- No non-lateral approximant (/ɹ, w, j/) can serve as C_1; the lateral can only precede /j/ (only for some speakers).
- No voiced stop can serve as C_2.
- No fricative other than /f/ can serve as C_2, and this can only be preceded by a /s/ in rarely found vocabulary (e.g. sphere).
- No stops or nasals are allowed as C_2, except after /s/ (e.g. speak, small).
- /s/ and /ʃ/ are complementary: /s/ does not occur before /ɹ/, and /ʃ/ occurs only before /ɹ/ (e.g. shrimp).
- /h/ and /m/ can only occur before /j/ (e.g. huge, music).
- /θ/ can precede only /ɹ/ and /w/ (e.g. three, thwart).
- Labials (C_1) do not cluster with a labial approximant.
- No geminates (i.e. doubled consonant sounds) are allowed.
- Alveolar stops (C_1) do not cluster with /l/.

We can summarize the situation in the following manner. In general, English double onsets are either (a) /s/ + C (where C = any consonant that can assume the position of C_2 except /ɹ/; /ʃ/ appears before /ɹ/), and (b) Obstruent + approximant, with the limitations cited above.

While the pattern of C_1 as an obstruent and C_2 as a sonorant is very common, we do not have any double onset in which the reverse (C_1 = sonorant and C_2 = obstruent) is true. This pattern that we observe for English is also commonly found in many other languages, and can be accounted for by the principle known as 'sonority sequencing'. We referred to sonority earlier for

Table 6.1 English double onsets

	p	t	k	f	m	n	l	ɹ	w	j
p	■						✔	✔		✔
b							✔	✔		✔
t		■						✔	✔	(✔)
d								✔	✔	(✔)
k			■				✔	✔	✔	✔
g							✔	✔	✔	
f				■			✔	✔		✔
v										✔
θ								✔	✔	
s	✔	✔	✔	✔	✔	✔	✔		✔	(✔)
ʃ								✔		
h										✔
m					■					✔
n						■				(✔)
l							■			(✔)

Note:
✔ Double onsets that are allowed in English.
(✔) For most speakers of American English, these are not found.
■ Impossible combination.

the syllable peaks, and now we make reference to it for the sequencing of sounds with respect to a syllable peak. As stated by Selkirk (1984: 116),

> In any syllable, there is a segment constituting a sonority peak that is preceded and/or followed by a sequence of segments with progressively decreasing sonority values.

Thus, the expected pattern is that, going from C_1 to C_2, the sonority level will rise. Such is the case in the overwhelming majority of English double onsets (e.g. play [ple], cry [kɹaɪ], quick [kwɪk]). The violations of this principle are s + stop clusters (/sp, st, sk/) in which the sonority level drops, instead of rises, going from C_1 to C_2. As we will see with the triple onsets as well as with double and triple codas, /s/ behaves exceptionally. To account for such cases, several scholars have suggested a special 'adjunct' status for /s/ clusters. We will not go into the details of such a proposal, but suffice it to state that this exceptional behavior of /s/ is also found in several other languages.

6.5.3 Triple onsets

Triple onsets can be described as an addition of /s/ as C_1 to voiceless stop + approximant double onsets. Thus, we have: C_1 = /s/, C_2 = voiceless stop, C_3 = approximant. Although the combinations can give us 12 logical possibilities, only 7 of these are occurring:

s p
- ɹ   e.g. spring
- l   e.g. splash
- j   e.g. spew
- w   e.g. * (excluded because /w/ cannot occur after labials)

s t
- ɹ   e.g. string
- l   e.g. * (excluded because no lateral after an alveolar stop)
- j   e.g. * (/tj/ non-existent for most speakers)
- w   e.g. *

s k
- ɹ   e.g. scrape
- l   e.g. * (very rare, sclerosis)
- j   e.g. skewer
- w   e.g. squeeze

6.5.4 Codas

The only sound that cannot occur in English codas is /h/. Also, /ʒ/ is somewhat less solid than other consonants; although it is firm for several speakers, we still can hear the [dʒ] realizations in garage [gəɹɑdʒ], massage [məsɑdʒ] from some speakers. Two other sounds, /j, w/, are also frequently included in the list of consonants that cannot occur in codas. While this is true, the existence of diphthongs /aɪ, ɔɪ/, and /aʊ/ weakens the case, as the endings of these diphthongs are very similar, if not identical, to /j/ and /w/ respectively. (This can be attested in alternative phonetic symbols used ([aj, aw, ɔj]) in some systems).

6.5.5 Double codas

Double non-suffixed English codas can be generalized in the following fashion:

(1) C_1 is a nasal and C_2 is an obstruent (no voiced obstruent permitted except /d, z, dʒ/). Also excluded are /mb/, /ŋg/, /mv/, /nð/.

(2) C_1 is /s/ and C_2 is a voiceless stop.
(3) C_1 is a liquid (/l, ɹ/) and C_2 any consonant except for /z, ʒ, ð/. Also non-existent is the /lg/ cluster.
(4) C_1 is a voiceless non-alveolar stop (/p, k/) and C_2 is a voiceless alveolar obstruent (/t, s/). Also permitted is the /ft/ cluster.

Possibilities increase considerably if we add to these the clusters created by the suffixes with /t, d, s, z, θ/ (past tense, plural, possessive, ordinals, etc.). Table 6.2 gives the actually occurring double codas.

As stated earlier, the sonority sequencing principle dictates the opposite of onset sequencing for codas. This means that optimal codas should have the sonority level dropping as we move from C_1 to C_2. Indeed, as table 6.2 shows, this is the case for the double codas we find in non-suffixed (monomorphemic) forms in English (e.g. arm [aɹm], sharp [ʃaɹp], belt [bɛlt]). Exceptions are (a) two-stop sequences, which are never homorganic (e.g. apt [æpt], act [ækt]), (b) stop + /s/, which always agree in voicing (lapse [læps], tax [tæks]).

6.5.6   Triple codas

The triple codas of English do not lend themselves to the similar and rather simple formula we gave for the triple onsets. We can say, in more general terms, that with the exception of (1), below, which has three obstruents, all the other combinations consist of a liquid or a nasal (sonorant) followed by two voiceless obstruents. The following combinations are found in non-suffixed forms:

		C_1	C_2	C_3	Examples
1		stop	fricative	stop	/dst/ midst, /kst/ next
2	(a)	nasal	stop	stop	/mpt/ exempt, /ŋkt/ sacrosanct
	(b)	nasal	stop	fricative	/mps/ mumps, /ŋks/ jinx
	(c)	nasal	fricative	stop	/nst/ against, /ŋst/ amongst
3	(a)	l	stop	stop	/lpt/ sculpt
	(b)	l	stop	fricative	/lts/ waltz
	(c)	l	fricative	stop	/lst/ whilst
4	(a)	ɹ	stop	stop	/ɹkt/ infarct, /ɹpt/ excerpt
	(b)	ɹ	stop	fricative	/ɹps/ corpse, /ɹts/ quartz
	(c)	ɹ	fricative	stop	/ɹst/ first
	(d)	ɹ	l	stop	/ɹld/ world
	(e)	ɹ	l	fricative	/ɹlz/ Charles

We have to acknowledge the fact that midst in (1), against in (2c), and whilst in (3c) are controversial and may be included in the suffixed category, as we encounter in some publications. Exactly how relevant these historical reasons are (midst as the superlative form of mid) for the synchronic (i.e. present-day) description of English is the question to be answered here.

In addition to these, a multiplicity of other triple codas is created via suffixation, the great majority of which are provided by /t, d/ of simple past tense,

Table 6.2　English double codas

	p	b	t	d	k	g	tʃ	dʒ	f	v	θ	s	z	ʃ	m	n	l
p	■		✔								X	✔					
b		■	X										X				
t			■								X						
d				■							X		X				
k		✔			■							✔					
g			X			■							X				
tʃ			X				■										
dʒ			X					■									
f		✔							■		X	X					
v			X							■			X				
θ			X								■	X					
ð			X										X				
s	✔		✔		✔							■					
z			X										■				
ʃ			X											■			
ʒ			X														
m	✔		X	X						✔			X		■		
n		✔	✔				✔	✔			✔	✔	X			■	
ŋ			X	✔								X	X				
l	✔	✔	✔	✔	✔		✔	✔	✔	✔	✔	✔	X	✔	✔	✔	■
ɹ	✔	✔	✔	✔	✔	✔	✔	✔	✔	✔	✔	✔	X	✔	✔	✔	✔

Note:
✔ Non-suffixed double codas.
X Suffixed double codas.
■ Impossible combination.

and /s, z/ of the plural, the possessive, and the third person singular of simple present. Also noteworthy are the possibilities created by /θ/ of 'ordinal number morpheme' (sixth [sɪksθ]), and the ending deriving nouns from adjectives (denominal morpheme) (warmth [wɔɹmθ]). The following list gives the possibilities of triple codas via suffixation in terms of general classes; thus, actually occurring clusters have many more combinations than the examples cited here:

		C₁	C₂	C₃	Examples
1		nasal	obstruent	/t, d, s, z/	laments
2		/s/	stop	/t, d, s, z/	lisped
3	(a)	/l/	obstruent	/t, d, s, z/	gulped
	(b)	/l/	nasal	/d, z/	filmed
4	(a)	/ɹ/	obstruent	/t, d, s, z/	wharfs
	(b)	/ɹ/	/l/	/d, z/	curls
	(c)	/ɹ/	nasal	/d, z/	turned
5		obstruent	obstruent	obstruent (only /pts, kts, fts, pst, kst/)	lifts

It is important to point out that while nasals and liquids serve frequently as C₁ in triple codas, and the sequences of /lk, mp, sk/ freely occur as double codas in English, triple codas combining these elements are very restricted. Thus, it is a noteworthy fact that English lacks /ɹlk, ɹmp, ɹsk, lmp, nsk/ as triple codas. Similar to double codas, clusters of obstruents in triple codas always agree in voicing (e.g. /spt/ lisped).

Before we leave this section, it would be appropriate to point out some modifications that are commonly observed with respect to deletions in final clusters. When the word ending in a cluster is followed by a word that begins *with a consonant*, the final member of the cluster is deleted, as shown below:

/nd/	hand made	[hæn med]	(cf. hand out)
/st/	next class	[nɛks klæs]	(cf. next hour)
/ft/	left street	[lɛf stɹit]	(cf. left arm)

This pattern repeats itself in words with suffixes and in compounds, as in the following:

/nd/	handsome	[hænsəm]
/st/	textless	[tɛksləs]
/ft/	softness	[safnəs]

However, if clusters are created by the addition of grammatical endings, this simplification is much less likely, if at all, to occur. Thus, we normally get the following non-reduced forms:

/nd/	planned trip	[plænd tɹɪp]
/st/	fixed game	[fɪkst gem]
/ft/	autographed book	[ɔtəgɹæft bʊk]

Finally, mention should also be made to the creation of normally impermissible clusters because of reduced vowel deletions in connected speech:

	Slow speech	Fast speech
Topeka	[təpikə]	[tpikə]
Canadian	[kənediən]	[knediən]
marina	[məɹinə]	[mɹinə]
photography	[fətagɹəfi]	[ftagɹəfi]
potato	[pəteto]	[pteto]
malaria	[məlɛɹiə]	[mlɛɹiə]
fanatics	[fənætɪks]	[fnætɪks]
tomorrow	[təmaɹo]	[tmaɹo]

Dialectal variations

The following are commonly found in AAVE.

Word-final consonant clusters ending in a stop may delete the final member when both members of the cluster are either voiced (e.g. send [sɛn], gold [gol]) or voiceless (e.g. act [æk], fist [fɪs]). This process is not restricted to a single morpheme and may apply across morpheme boundaries (e.g. sipped [sɪp], dressed [dɹɛs]). Also, the sequencing of final 's + stop' may be transposed as in ask [æks], grasp [gɹæps]. Finally, the /t/ of initial /stɹ/ clusters may move back to /k/ (e.g. street [skɹit]). In the deep south, this process may be extended to initial /tɹ/ clusters (e.g. tree [kɹi]).

6.6 Written Syllabification

People who wrote term papers, theses, or dissertations before the advent of computers, and thus of word processing programs, had to deal with the problem of written syllabification frequently because it was not possible to arrange words on a given line ending perfectly at the right margin. The decisions as to where to break the words were not always easy, as the writer could not simply follow the breaks that s/he would make in the spoken language. Thus, one had two choices: (a) have a page full of written lines with uneven right margin appearance, or (b) consult a dictionary and break up the word according to the dictionary suggestions. This appears to be a non-issue today due to the availability of the 'justified margin' option in word processors. By the use of this option, we do not have to break any words at the end of a line. If, towards the end of a line, a word is too long or too short, the program would either expand or contract the spacing between letters without causing any breaks. However, as the following examples from printed media demonstrate, the problem is still with us.

In the past weeks, **boat-**
ers have reported several
whale carcasses floating in the
waters off Big Pine Key.　　　　　　　　　　　　(*Miami Herald*, May 24, 2003)

... Monetary Fund and the Arab
Fund for social and Economic **Devel-
opment**, will have a seat on ...   (*New York Times*, May 23, 2003)

Hypocrisy often is waist-deep in **Washington**. But the spectacle of people **defend-
ing** ...   (*Newsweek*, May 12, 2003)

... According to Perry, **dur-
ing** the trip Venezia announced ...   (*Atlantic Monthly*, April 2003)

... never has the Conservative
party that he joined as a youth needed **sav-
ing** more.   (*The Economist*, December 21, 2002)

... one of the weirdest and least **rep-
utable** landscapes on Earth: the New Jersey
Meadowlands.   (*National Geographic*, February 2001)

... diplomatic campaign by
Saddam Hussein's **gov-
ernment** – one that, up till now, has
continued to score success.   (*World Press Review*, February 2003)

... New homes
also are dictated by what we pay for the **prop-
erty**.   (*Miami Herald*, May 24, 2003)

... Cover each breast with **anoth-
er** duck breast, skin side up.   (*Food and Wine*, October 2001)

As you might have easily detected, as hundreds of native speakers I have
tested have, there are obvious discrepancies between the breaks that are in
print and the syllable breaks we use in the spoken language for the words
underlined.

Written breaks	**Spoken syllabifications**
boat.ers	[bo/tɚz]
sav.ing	[se/vɪŋ]
de.fend.ing	[di/fɛn/dɪŋ]
prop.er.ty	[pɹɑ/pɚ/ti]
dur.ing	[du/ɹɪŋ]
de.vel.op.ment	[dɪ/vɛ/ləp/mənt]
an.oth.er	[ə/nʌ/ðɚ]
gov.ern.ment	[gʌ/vɚn/mənt]
rep.u.ta.ble	[ɹɛ/pju/tə/bəl]

To make matters worse, we find some morphologically related words with the
following:

gra.di.ent	grad.u.al	[gɹe/di/ənt]	[gɹæ/dʒu/əl]
pe.nal	pen.al.ty	[pi/nəl]	[pɛ/nəl/ti]
mi.ner	min.er.al	[maɪ/nɚ]	[mɪ/nə/ɹəl]
pu.ni.tive	pun.ish	[pju/nɪ/tɪv]	[pʌ/nɪʃ]

While the native speakers' spoken syllabifications are in complete agreement with the written breaks suggested by the dictionaries for words in the left column (gradient, penal, miner, and punitive), they are in total disagreement for the words in the right column. We hear [gɹæ/dʒu/əl] (*not* [gɹædʒ/u/əl]), [mɪ/nə/ɹəl] (*not* [mɪn/ɚ/əl]), etc.

What is really unfortunate is that dictionary representations are not simple suggestions for the breaks for written language, but also are claims, in phonetic transcription, for the spoken syllabifications of the words. For this reason, and the reason that this system is taught to elementary schoolchildren, we would like to make the difference very clear and make the practitioners aware of the entirely different principles used in written syllabification. This is an important issue, because, as we will see in the next chapter, several stress rules of English are sensitive to syllable structures, and these are entirely based on spoken syllables and have nothing to do with the conventions of written breaks.

Written syllabification seems to follow two principles:

(1) if a word has prefixes and/or suffixes, these cannot be divided; and
(2) if the orthographic letter a, e, i, o, u, or y represents long or short vowel sound. When one of these letters in the written form stands for a long vowel or a diphthong /i, e, u, o, aɪ, aʊ, ɔɪ/, the next letter representing the consonant in the orthography goes in the following syllable in written language. If, on the other hand, these orthographic letters stand for a short vowel sound, then the next letter goes with the preceding syllable. To verify these, we can look at pairs such as penal – penalty and miner – mineral. In the first word of the first pair, the letter e represents the long vowel /i/ and the written syllabification is pe.nal (which happens to correspond to the spoken syllabification [pi/nəl]). In the second word of the same pair, the same letter e stands for a short vowel, /ɛ/, and thus the written syllabification is pen.al.ty. Similarly, in the second pair (miner – mineral), the letter i stands for the diphthong /aɪ/ in the first word (thus, the syllabification mi.ner, which corresponds to the spoken [maɪ.nɚ]), and the short vowel /ɪ/ in the second (thus, the syllabification min.er.al).

We should also point out that the first principle is the stronger one in that even if the orthographic letter stands for a long vowel or a diphthong, the integrity of a prefix or a suffix is maintained. This will be clear if we look at the word boaters, which is syllabified as boat.ers in the written language. Although the orthographic representation of the first syllable stands for a long

vowel in speech [o], the following letter, t, does not go into the following syllable in the written representation, and the only reason for this is the suffixation
that this word has. Similarly, in the word saving, the written break is given
as sav.ing, which, despite its total conflict with the spoken version ([se.vɪŋ]),
has to follow the integrity of the suffix -ing. As for an example of a conflict
created by the integrity of a prefix, we can cite the written syllabification of
un.able, as opposed to its preferred spoken syllabification [ʌ.ne.bəl].

6.7 Syllable Weight and Ambisyllabicity

Although the first principle of written syllabification (the integrity of prefixes/
suffixes) creates severe clashes between the written and spoken syllabifications,
and will not be commented on further, the second principle that relates to some
orthographic letters and the vowel sounds they stand for may have some
relevance to speakers' responses to some indeterminate spoken syllabifications.
If we ask for the spoken syllabification of the following words,

medicine	federal
origin	positive
happen	Canada
finish	river
funny	punish

it is possible that we receive different reactions from the native speakers of
English.

While several speakers go along with the syllabifications based on the
maximum onset principle and give [mɛ/də/sən], [hæ/pən], [pɑ/zə/təv], etc.,
some others may not feel very comfortable with such divisions and may
suggest the inclusion of the consonants after the vowel in the first syllable as
the coda of that syllable. There are some obvious similarities between these
words and the ones we discussed in relation to written syllabification above.
This is related to the kind of vowel sounds that are represented by the orthographic letters a, e, i, o, u. In all these words, the vowel sounds/æ, ɛ, ɪ, ɔ, ʌ/
(from top to bottom respectively), represented by the orthographic letters in
question, are in the stressed syllables and the problem is related to what happens to the consonant following that vowel. This issue is directly related to
stress and syllable weight. Although stress will be treated in detail in the next
chapter, we will briefly deal with some points here that are relevant to the issue
we are focusing on.

Syllable weight is an important factor in stress assignment in languages. The
weight of a syllable is determined by its rhyme structure. In English, a syllable
is light if it has a non-branching rhyme (a short vowel and no coda in its rhyme,
as in the first syllable of around); it is heavy if it has a branching rhyme (has
a short vowel followed by a coda (simple or complex), or has a long vowel

or a diphthong with or without a following coda. These can be shown in the following.

Rhyme of a light syllable
short vowel: <u>a</u>.mong

Rhyme of a heavy syllable
short v + coda: <u>net</u>, <u>nest</u>
long v/dipht. + (coda): <u>seed</u>, <u>sea</u>, <u>side</u>

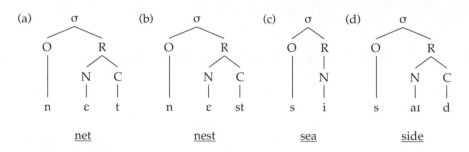

net   nest   sea   side

In (a), (b), and (d), the branching rhymes are obvious; in (c), we achieve this via branching nucleus.

Having made this digression to explain the syllable weight, we can conclude that heavy syllables attract stress, and essentially, in English, no stressed syllable may be light. With this information, we are now ready to go back to the problematic cases we considered above. In <u>medicine</u>, <u>happen</u>, <u>finish</u>, etc., we have a conflict between the maximal onset principle and stress. While the maximal onset principle dictates that the first syllables of each of these words be light, the stress which falls on this very syllable is in contradiction with the principle that light syllables cannot receive stress. This is the reason why some speakers are not comfortable with the syllabic divisions in these words. In such cases, linguists invoke the concept of ambisyllabicity whereby the consonant in question is treated as behaving both as the coda of the preceding and the onset of the following syllables at the same time. To put it succinctly, we can say that a consonant that is (part of) a permissible onset (cluster) is ambi-syllabic if it occurs immediately after a short vowel /ɪ, ɛ, æ, ʌ, ʊ, ɔ/ɑ/ (i.e. lax vowels plus [ɔ/ɑ]), that is, the nucleus of a stressed syllable. We can represent this in the following.

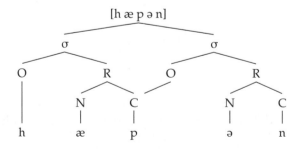

This is a consequence of the tendency for a stressed rhyme to be heavy (i.e. branching).

6.8 Practical Applications

The constraints we have examined in relation to the sequencing of sounds in syllables via sonority have far-reaching implications in many applied situations such as in normal phonological development, in clinical populations, and in foreign language learning. For example, the process of consonant cluster reduction, which is commonly observed in all three populations mentioned above, is far from being haphazard. A target such as <u>play</u> [ple] is much more likely to be reduced to [pe] than the alternative [le]. The reason for this is that the former is the more unmarked (more expected) one because it provides a higher jump in sonority from the single onset to the nucleus ([pe] the sonority index of /p/ = 1, the sonority index of /e/ = 9; thus the resulting sequence is a change from 1 to 9; [le], on the other hand would result in a change from 6 to 9 in sonority indices). Since a CV sequence is more natural when the contrast between the C and the V is greater, [pe] is the more valuable one of the two logical alternatives. The support for the validity of such a constraint is not hard to find in developing phonologies. Chin (1996) observed several children with phonological disorders whose modification of target onset clusters was governed by the principle reviewed above. In one instance, the subject applied consonant cluster reduction for all targets with #sC (e.g. <u>stove</u> [sov], <u>snow</u> [so], etc.) while not reducing other target clusters (e.g. <u>play</u> [ple], <u>brush</u> [bwʌs], etc.). Looking at several examples, Chin concluded that the child applied the reduction process for those targets where the sonority difference between C_1 and C_2 was less than 3 (i.e. <u>stove</u> 3 to 1 = –2, <u>snow</u> 3 to 5 = 2). Targets that had a difference of 3 in sonority from C_1 to C_2 (<u>play</u> 1 to 7 = 6, <u>sleep</u> 3 to 6 = 3, <u>brush</u> 2 to 7 = 5) were not subject to reduction.

   Another subject revealed the following patterns:

(a) stop + approximant → stop (<u>twin</u> [dɪn], <u>drum</u> [dʌm], <u>play</u> [pe])
(b) fricative + sonorant → fricative (<u>few</u> [fu], <u>swim</u> [sɪm], <u>shrub</u> [ʃʌb])
(c) fricative + stop → stop (<u>spoon</u> [bun], <u>stove</u> [dov], <u>sky</u> [daɪ])

The modification patterns by the child do not allow us to make a statement if C_1 or C_2 of the cluster is deleted, as C_1 is deleted in (a) and (b), but C_2 is the one that is deleted in (c). If, however, we analyze the results in terms of sonority rises, we see that the behavior of the subject is very regular in that he follows the path resulting in the greatest jump in sonority from the resulting C to the nucleus V. Thus, while the observed simplification of the target <u>drum</u> is [dʌm] with a movement from 2 to 10 in sonority, the alternative, [ɹʌm] would have resulted in 7 to 10, which is a much smaller jump. Similarly, in <u>sky</u> becoming [daɪ], we have a jump from 2 to 10, while the alternative [saɪ] would have given a smaller (3 to 10) jump.

   Sonority-driven modification of onset clusters has also been observed in aphasic patients. Blumstein (1978), invoking the concept of sonority for the erroneous cluster formation in paraphasias, notes that the addition of, for example, a liquid in an erroneous production goes to the right of a vowel, thus forming the sequence 'obstruent + liquid + vowel', which is in accordance with the sonority sequencing principle. Beland, Caplan, and Nespoulos (1990) noted that their patient's deletion of one member of the sequence 'obstruent + liquid + V' was always the liquid, resulting in the maximum jump to 'obstruent + V'. Christman (1992) also found sonority to be influential in the syllable production patterns of jargon aphasics. More recently, Romani and Calabrese (1998) provided further support for sonority-driven patterns by showing their 40-year-old Italian aphasic patient's modification of #CCV sequences. By producing 'obstruent + liquid + V' targets as 'obstruent + V', 'obstruent + j + V' targets as 'obstruent + V', and 'nasal + j + V' targets as 'nasal + V', the patient deletes the segment of higher sonority in the target cluster and produces a sequence with a maximum rise in sonority from the onset to the nucleus. Telugu-speaking children with prelingual hearing loss have been reported to have greater difficulty in CV syllables in which the sonority jump is small (e.g. 'glide + V') than those in which the sonority jump is bigger (e.g. 'obstruent + V') (Duggirala Vasanta, personal communication).

That such principles are firmly grounded can also be shown in normally developing children. Ohala (1999) examined the productions of CCVC targets with 16 children ages 1;9–3;2. The prediction was that when the CCVC targets were reduced to CVC sequences, the deleted member of the double onset would be the one that had a higher sonority index, because its deletion could provide the remaining sequence of the single onset to the nucleus with the maximal rise in sonority. The overall results confirm the predictions in that children preserved the least sonorous consonant member of the onset cluster and created the maximal rise in sonority. Yavaş and Someillan (in press) tested the same hypothesis with a group of Spanish–English bilingual children with target #sC sequences. It was hypothesized that among the possible sequences of English #sC clusters ('s + stop' sky, 's + nasal' snail, 's + l' sleep, 's + w' swim), subjects' success rates would be higher for the targets in which the sonority jump from C_1 to C_2 was higher. The results confirmed the hypothesis overwhelmingly, at least when C_2 was a continuant, that the easiest target was 's + w' (sonority jump from 3 to 8), which is followed by 's + l' (sonority jump from 3 to 6). The difference between the clusters in which the C_2 was a non-continuant (i.e. 's + stop' and 's + nasal') did not reveal any significance.

The ease/difficulty of acquisition of onset clusters invoking sonority indices has also been shown in foreign language phonology. Broselow and Finer (1991) examined the data from 24 native speakers of Korean and 8 native speakers of Japanese with respect to their productions of the target English /pɹ, bɹ, fɹ/, /pj, bj, fj/. The hypothesis was that clusters with a greater sonority jump from C_1 to C_2 (e.g. /pj/ from 1 to 8) would be less problematic than clusters with a smaller sonority difference (e.g. /fɹ/ from 3 to 7). In general, the error rates of the subjects supported the predictions (for more on this in foreign language phonology, see section 8.4).

If maximum rise in sonority is the most unmarked (expected) sequencing from the onset to the nucleus, minimum descent in sonority is the most unmarked (expected) sequencing for a movement from the nucleus to the coda. The reason for this is that the most common (natural, unmarked) syllable type is codaless (CV) where there is no descent in sonority. Thus, when we have a coda, the smaller the descent from the nucleus the more valuable it is. That this principle is at work can be seen in developing phonologies. Ohala (1999) examined the coda cluster modifications of children (ages 1;9–3;2) whereby CVCC targets were modified to CVC. She hypothesized that the member of the coda cluster to be deleted would be the one which is lower in sonority so that the remaining higher-sonority item would provide the minimum descent from the nucleus. Thus, for example, a sequence such as [maɹp] was expected to reduce to [maɹ] (sonority shift of 10 to 7 from the nucleus to the coda), and not as [map] (from 10 to 1). The results were supportive of the hypothesis in that the expected reductions were higher than 50 percent of the time, and the unexpected modifications were only around 16 percent.

Evidence for behavior governed by the principles of sonority also comes from second language phonology data. Hansen (2001) examined the acquisition of English codas by Mandarin speakers. In dealing with three-member target English codas, the learners have the greatest difficulty with clusters that violate the requirement of gradual lowering in sonority from the nucleus to the members of the cluster. Triple codas such as 'liquid + stop + fricative' (e.g. /lps/ <u>alps</u>, /ɹdz/ <u>words</u>) and 'nasal + stop + fricative' (e.g. /nts/ <u>prints</u>, /ndz/ <u>bands</u>) have sonority descending from V to C_1 to C_2, but rising from C_2 to C_3. Learners modified such targets much more frequently than the unmarked codas that follow gradual sonority fall (e.g. /ɹst/ <u>first</u>, /ɹld/ <u>world</u>). Also significant were the resulting two-member codas when subjects reduced the target CCC# by deleting one of the consonants; all resulting two-member codas obeyed the demands of the sonority sequencing principle in that C_1 was higher in sonority than C_2 (for more on this in foreign language phonology, see section 8.4).

SUMMARY

In this chapter, we looked at the syllable structure of English. First we examined the hierarchical internal structure of the unit, which has the constituents of 'onset' and 'rhyme', the latter of which can be examined with its components 'nucleus' and 'coda'. We also looked at the syllabification rules of the spoken and written languages, which can be very different in certain cases. In syllable phonotactics, we dealt with the sequencing restrictions in English and pointed out various onset and coda consonant cluster patterns. Finally, we looked at syllable weight, which is determined by the rhyme structure, and ambisyllabicity whereby the same consonant behaves both as a coda of the preceding syllable and the onset of the following syllable at the same time.

1. In section 6.5.6, several patterns for non-suffixed triple codas are dis-
    cussed. Which ones of these (if any) violate(s) the sonority sequencing
    principle? State the example(s) and your rationale.

2. Do the same as above for the suffixed triple codas.

3. Which of the following would qualify for ambisyllabicity? Circle the
    word(s), state your rationale, and give the tree diagram(s).

    metric, regime, anecdote, camera, integrity, person, panic, majesty,
    Africa, rival

4. Consider the following:

Short V + CC	Long V/diph. + C	Long V/diph. + CC
(a) pimp	(b) wipe	(c) mind BUT * [maɪmb]
lint	light	grind * [maɪŋg]
sink	bike	* [gɹaɪmb]
	weep	* [gɹaɪŋg]
	seed	
	beak	

    While certain combinations are possible, certain others (in c) are not
    allowed. State the generalization.

5. In section 6.5.6, we saw that, because of reduced vowel deletions,
    several normally impermissible consonant clusters can be created
    (e.g. photography [ftɑgɹəfi]). Find five examples of such clusters.

6. English final consonant clusters are simplified by deleting the final
    member of the cluster in certain contexts (e.g. /nd/ in sand piles
    [sæn paɪlz], /st/ in first class [fɚs klæs]). The same is not possible in
    other contexts (e.g. /nd/ in canned vegetables [kænd vɛ ...], /st/
    in missed goals [mɪst golz]). State the generalization and give three
    examples for each possibility.

7. Transcribe the following (about 'English in America') *from* J. Jenkins, *World Englishes* (London: Routledge, 2002).

Walter Raleigh's expedition of 1584 to America was the earliest from
....
the British Isles to the New World, though it did not result in a
....
permanent settlement. The voyagers landed on the coast of North
....
Carolina near Roanoke Island, but fell into conflict with the native
....
Indian population and then mysteriously disappeared altogether. In
....
1607, the first permanent colonist arrived and settled in Jamestown,
....
Virginia, to be followed in 1620 by a group of Puritans and others on
....
the Mayflower. The latter group landed further north, settling at what
....
is now Plymouth, Massachusetts, in New England. Both settlements
....
spread rapidly and attracted further migrants during the years that
....
followed. Because of their different linguistic backgrounds, there
....
were immediately certain differences in the accents of the two groups
....
of settlers. Those in Virginia came mainly from the West of England
....
and brought with them their characteristic rhotic /r/ and voiced /s/
....
sounds. On the other hand, those who settled in New England were
....
mainly from the east of England, where these features were not a part
....
of the local accent.
....

Stress and Intonation

7.1 Introduction

Stress is a cover term for the prosodic features of *duration*, *intensity*, and *pitch*; thus, the prominence of stressed syllables is generally manifested by their characteristics of being longer, louder, and higher in pitch than unstressed syllables. From the speaker's point of view, this corresponds to the amount of effort expended, while it is the perceptual prominence from the hearer's point of view.

As mentioned in chapter 1, English has variable stress. It is characteristic of Germanic languages for any syllable in a polysyllabic word to be able to carry the stress. For example, in the following trisyllabic nouns, <u>article</u>, <u>tomato</u>, and <u>kangaroo</u>, the stress moves from the first to the second and then to the third syllable, respectively ([ɑ́ɹtɪkl̩], [təméDo], [kæŋgəɹú]).

In addition to variability, English stress is said to be *mobile*. This can be shown in the morphologically related words in which the stress shifts on to different syllables:

<u>origin</u> [ɔ́ɹədʒən]	<u>original</u> [ɔɹídʒənəl]	<u>originality</u> [ɔɹədʒənǽləDi]
<u>constitution</u>	<u>constitutional</u>	<u>constitutionality</u>
[kɑ́nstətuʃən]	[kɑnstətúʃn̩]	[kɑnstətuʃənǽləDi]
<u>photograph</u> [fótəgɹæf]	<u>photography</u> [fətágɹəfi]	<u>photographic</u> [fotəgɹǽfɪk]
<u>diplomat</u> [dípləmæt]	<u>diplomacy</u> [dɪplóməsi]	<u>diplomatic</u> [dɪpləmǽtɪk]

Although the above discussion may suggest a highly variable and unpredictable situation, this does not mean that there are no rules or principles underlying stress patterns of English. It should be noted, however, that these regularities are tendencies rather than airtight rules. It is a characteristic of English that the grammatical category or morphological structure of words frequently affects the stress patterns. The topic under discussion has been treated differently in different books and manuals. Some have detailed formulations to cover several exceptions, others present more practically oriented descriptions that are more general in nature. Some do count syllables and do not make any distinctions among word classes, such as nouns and verbs, others do separate word classes but don't count syllables. Each one of these approaches has certain benefits and drawbacks. The approach followed in this book will resemble several of the above descriptions in different respects.

We will first look at simple words and then examine the forms with affixes. There are many difficulties regarding the description of stress patterns because many exceptions are the results of events in the history of English. While many words retain their Germanic stress patterns, many others have been acquired through historical events; one such event is the Norman Conquest, which is responsible for the plethora of French vocabulary and Romance stress patterns. In addition, religion and scholarship have had significant influence in securing the original stress patterns of vocabulary from Greek and Latin.

In some books, in order to deal with certain exceptions, descriptions invoke some morphological parsing which will not be followed here. This is especially true for some so-called 'prefixes'. For example, one might encounter the underlined portions of the following words, _award_, _surprise_, _proposal_, _forget_, _obtain_, _admit_, _intend_, _compel_, treated as prefixes. Some of these prefixes are of Germanic origin and others are of Latin origin. However, if we are interested in the description of present-day English, it would be very difficult, if not impossible, to think that such separations are real for the users of the language because the non-prefix portions of the above (a)_ward_, (sur)_prise_, etc., are not to be treated as existing roots. Thus, in this book, these forms will be treated as one morpheme.

Before we start our account of English stress, it will be useful to remember the conditions of a stressable syllable. As we stated in chapter 6, syllable weight is an important factor in stress assignment in that heavy syllables attract stress. The weight of a syllable is determined by its rhyme structure. If the rhyme is non-branching (a short vowel, and no coda), the syllable is light. If, on the other hand, the rhyme is branching (has a short vowel, except [ə] which is weightless and cannot carry stress, followed by a coda (simple or complex), or has a long vowel or a diphthong with or without a following coda), the syllable is heavy. Also useful is to define the terms _ult_ (the last syllable), _penult_ (the syllable before the ult), and _antepenult_ (the syllable before the penult), which will be used for the location of the syllables in a word. These can be shown in the following word, probability:

[p ɹ ɑ . b ə . b   ɪ . l   ə . t i]
         ante-   _penult_ _ult_
         penult

7.2 Noun and Adjective Stress

There seem to be sufficient commonalities between the stress patterns of nouns and adjectives that they would warrant a single grouping. In disyllabics, the default stress is on the penult. In a 20,000 monomorphemic word sample reported by Hammond (1999: 194), both disyllabic nouns and adjectives reveal penult stress over 80 percent. More precisely, 81.7 percent (2,986 out of 3,652) nouns and 81 percent (1,047 out of 1,294) disyllabic adjectives followed this pattern. Below are some examples from both categories:

Noun	Adjective
ágent	ábsent
bálance	árid
bállad	cómmon
bóttom	flúent
cábbage	pérfect
cóuntry	hónest
émpire	réady
dímple	súdden
fáther	búsy
húsband	ámple
spínach	vúlgar

The exceptions to the penult rule fall into two groups. The first contains examples with weightless (unstressable) penults, because they have [ə] nuclei, and thus are stressed on the final (ult) by default; for this reason, they might be considered exceptions:

Noun	Adjective
appéal	banál
ballóon	corrúpt
canóe	enoúgh
Brazíl	remóte
machíne	secúre
paráde	sincére

The second group constitutes the real exceptions because they are stressed on the final (ult) despite the fact that they have stressable penults with branching rhymes:

respéct	mundáne
sardíne	obscúre
shampóo	imménse
antíque	robúst
typhóon	okáy

In trisyllabic and longer nouns, we formulate the following: stress penult if stressable (heavy/branching rhyme); if not stressable, then stress the next left heavy syllable. We show this with the following examples:

Three syllables		**More than three syllables**
tomáto	ábdomen	barracúda
aróma	álgebra	aspáragus
diplóma	ánimal	apócalypse
horízon	búffalo	basílica
enígma	cómedy	hippopótamus
bonánza	vítamin	

The words in the leftmost group are stressed on the penult because their penults are stressable (the first four qualify for their long vowel or diphthong nuclei, and the last two because of the closed rhyme). The words in the second tri-syllabic group receive their stresses on the antepenult because their penults are not stressable (all with [ə] nuclei). The rightmost group consists of words that have more than three syllables, but the stress rule remains the same. The first word, <u>barracuda</u>, is stressed on the penult, as it contains a stressable penult, [u]. The remaining words (three with four syllables, and the last one with five syllables) all have unstressable penults ([ə] nuclei) and thus are stressed on the antepenult. As for the frequency of such patterns, Hammond reports that this regularity accounts for over 90 percent of nouns (42 percent or 859 out of 2,074 trisyllabics have penult stress, and 49.5 percent, or 1,027 out of 2,074 are antepenult-stressed because of unstressable penult). The exceptions, exem-plified by the following, are below 10 percent:

clarinét
cavalíer
kangaróo
chimpanzée
serenáde
gasolíne
cigarétte
magazíne
mayonnáise

These examples, mostly borrowings from French, retain the original final stresses. Most of these exceptional words have unstressable penults, and thus the rule predicts that the stress would go on the antepenult instead of the ult, a tendency revealed by several native speakers for the last 3–5 words on the list.

Some other trisyllabic exceptions, on the other hand, receive antepenult stress despite the fact that they have stressable penults, as shown in

álien
mánia
périod

There is another group of words, trisyllabic or longer, that deserves atten-tion. The words in this group, overwhelmingly coming from place-names, are stressed on the penult, despite the fact that it is not heavy, as exemplified below:

(a)	Yokoháma	(b)	vendétta	(c)	Calcútta	(d)	Louisiána
	Milwáukee		Viénna		Kentúcky		Montána
	Granáda		Venezuéla				Indiána
							Seáttle
							Tallahássee

The stressed penults of these words (a)–(d) do not have branching rhymes (the rhymes are /ɑ/, /ɛ/, /ʌ/, and /æ/ respectively).

There are some other words, again mostly place-names, which also carry the stress on their non-heavy penult:

(e) Morócco   (f) Cincinnáti
     Osáka   Havána
     Chicágo   Carácas
     Guatemála   Nicarágua
     tomórrow   Savánnah
     cantáta   banána

The penults in words (e) and (f), /ɑ/ and /æ/ respectively, do not constitute heavy syllables, but are stressed, nevertheless. However, these words are somewhat different than the violations observed in words (a)–(d), because words in (e) and (f) do not have any other heavy syllable to the left of the penult (they all have [ə] nuclei). In other words, the stress is on the penult by default.

Trisyllabic adjectives, of which there are far fewer, also show a similar pattern to that of nouns. Hammond reports that over 90 percent of trisyllabic adjectives follow the expected path: 75.3 percent (502 out of 666) with penult stress, and 15 percent (100 out of 666) with antepenult stress because of un-stressable penult.

7.3 Verb Stress

If nouns and adjectives have the penult as their pivot, verb focus is on the ult. The general tendency is as follows: stress ult if heavy (branching rhyme); if not, go to the next left heavy syllable, as shown in the following:

Heavy ult stressed	Unstressable ult, thus penult stressed
achíeve	bálance
admít	blóssom
agrée	bóther
annoúnce	dístance
confíne	fúrnish
digést	hárvest
impórt	súrface
predíct	vísit
replý	díffer

With the above generalization, we can account for over 99 percent of the stresses of disyllabic words (Hammond reports 47.6 percent, or 987 out of 2,072, with heavy ult stressed, and 52.3 percent, or 1,085 out of 2,072 as penult-stressed because of unstressable ult). The few exceptions to the general tendency can be exemplified by the following, where penult is stressed despite the fact that the verb has a heavy ult:

cópy
réscue

There are not many trisyllabic verbs; they generally are predictable by the above rule. Hammond's data state the following distribution: 39.5 percent (151 out of 378) heavy ult-stressed, 40 percent (157 out of 378) penult-stressed because of unstressable ult, and 18.5 percent (70 out of 378) antepenult-stressed because of unstressable ult and unstressable penult.

Before we conclude this section, it is worth noting that English has dozens of orthographically identical word-pairs differentiated by stress as nouns (penult stress) or verbs (ult stress), as exemplified in the following:

abstract
address
ally
combat
convict
export
import
insert
insult
permit
protest
refuse
survey

Although noun–verb shift is accomplished by a shift in stressed syllable in some of these (e.g. import, insult), in many others, the difference of stress is also accompanied by the vowel reduction in the unstressed syllable, and thus these noun–verb pairs, although homographs, are not homophonous. For example:

abstract	N	[ǽbstɹækt],	V	[əbstɹǽkt]
convict	N	[kánvɪkt]	V	[kənvíkt]
protest	N	[pɹótɛst]	V	[pɹətést]
refuse	N	[ɹɛ́fus]	V	[ɹəfúz]

7.4 Secondary Stress

So far our discussion has been around the primary stress (or 'strong stress'). In texts describing the sound patterns of English, it is commonplace to see mention made of a secondary stressed (or 'lightly stressed') syllable. This refers to situations where, in many words (especially longer words), there is prominence of more than one syllable. For example, if we consider the words photography and photographic, we see different patterns; while in the first word [fətɑgɹəfi], we have one prominent syllable (second, or 'antepenult' syllable), we have two prominent syllables in the morphologically related word [fotəgɹǽfɪk] (first and third, or 'pre-antepenult' and 'penult'). When we have more than one prominent syllable in a word, we speak of a secondary stress, which is exemplified by the first syllable of the word photographic.

In agreement with Ladefoged's (2001a) account of stress patterns, this book will likewise treat the difference between the primary stress and the secondary stress as a difference in pitch instead of stress. In other words, both syllables (primary and secondary stressed) have prominence, and their difference results from the superimposition of the pitch pattern; the syllable which is commonly known as the primary stressed is the one with the major pitch change. Thus, both the first and the third syllables of <u>photographic</u> have prominences, but only the third will show the major pitch change, which is called the *tonic accent*. Thus, we can say that (a) an English syllable is either stressed (+stress) or unstressed (−stress), (b) if there is only one prominent syllable in the word, then it necessarily is the stressed syllable and has the tonic accent; if there is more than one prominent (stressed) syllable, then only one of them will have the major pitch-changing 'tonic accent', and (c) a stressed syllable necessarily has a full vowel (no vowel reduction can take place in a stressed syllable); thus, the vowel reduction is a question relevant only for unstressed syllables. We can illustrate these dependencies in the following diagram:

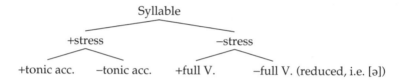

Thus, we have the following combinatory possibilities for English syllables:

Primary stressed syllable : +stress, +tonic accent, +full V.
Secondary stressed syllable: +stress, −tonic accent, +full V.
Unstressed syllable: −stress, −tonic accent, +/−full V.

Let us now look at the two words we have been discussing:

	[fə. tá. gɹə. fi]				[fò. tə. gɹǽ. fɪk]			
Stress	−	+	−	−	+	−	+	−
Ton. ac.	−	+	−	−	−	−	+	−
Full V.	−	+	−	+	+	−	+	−

In <u>photography</u>, we have one prominent syllable, which necessarily carries the tonic accent. Since it is the stressed syllable, it will also have a full vowel. Among the remaining three unstressed syllables, only the last one has a full vowel; the others have reduced vowels. In the second word, <u>photographic</u>, we have two prominent syllables, the second of which carries the major pitch change (i.e. tonic accent). As suggested by Ladefoged, this system can easily be converted into the traditional numerical system. A syllable with three pluses will get 1, two pluses will get 2, one plus will get 3, and the syllable with no plus will get 4. Thus, the numbers for <u>photography</u> will be 4 1 4 3, and for <u>photographic</u> 2 4 1 4.

Some students, while not having any problem in detecting the syllable with the primary stress (syllable with the tonic accent), do have difficulties in identifying the ones with secondary stress. The following generalizations, some more consistent than others, are usually helpful in detecting the secondary stress.

(1)   The longest sequence of reduced vowels in an English word is two.
(2)   A full vowel will have stress
      unless
      (a)   it is in final open syllable;
      (b)   the word has *two* other more prominent syllables;
      (c)   it is one of the alternating cases of /i, o, u/ with [ə] (see section 4.7).
(3)   In general, secondary stress comes before the primary stress (major pitch change tends to be on the last stressed syllable).

If there is only one syllable before the primary stress, this is usually unaccented (so as not to place two stressed syllables next to one another) (e.g. divinity [də.ví.nə.ti], urbanity [ɚ.bǽ.nə.ti]). However, there are exceptions (e.g. martini [màɹ.tí.ni], cucumber [kjú.kʌm.bɚ]).

When there are more than two syllables before the primary stress, a secondary accent will fall two or three syllables back according to the presence of a full vowel (e.g. gratification [gɹæ̀.tə.fə.ke.ʃən], bibliography [bɪ.bli.ɑ.gɹə̀.fi]).

We can now analyze the word pronunciation in light of what has been said so far.

	[pɹə.	nʌn.	si.	e.	ʃən]
Stress	−	+	−	+	−
Tonic accent	−	−	−	+	−
Full V.	−	+	+	+	−

The second and the fourth syllables are the prominent ones and receive +stress and consequently +full V; all others receive −stress. The fourth syllable, in addition, is the major pitch-changing syllable and receives +tonic accent. All others are − for this feature. Two of the −stress syllables (the first and the last) have reduced vowels, [ə], and get − for 'full V', whereas the third syllable has a + for full V because of /i/. The word is quite typical in many respects: a long, five-syllable word with two prominent syllables, the primary and the secondary stresses are not next to one another, and the first syllable, even if uttered by a full vowel /o/, will not be eligible for the secondary stress because it is alternating with [ə].

In some long words (four syllables or more), we may encounter two syllables with secondary stresses (e.g. Afghanistan [æ̀f.gǽ.nə.stæn], reconciliation [ɹè.kən.sɪ̀.li.é.ʃən], excommunicate [èk.skə.mjú.nə.kèt], expugnatory [èk.spʌ́g.nə.tɔ̀.ɹi].

Finally, mention should be made of another group of words in relation to secondary stress. While we generally see secondary stresses in longer words (three syllables and longer), there are some disyllabic words with both syllables stressed. As shown below, both logical possibilities are entertained.

Primary–secondary: (post-tonic secondary stress) cáshèw, cráyòn, própàne, cýclòne, fránchìse, émpìre, áspèct, áccènt
Secondary–primary: (pre-tonic secondary stress) bàmbóo, sàrdíne, hòtél, tỳphóon, càffeíne, tràpéze, sùpréme, ràccóon

7.5 Affixes

If the basic rules of stress looked rather untidy and replete with exceptions, the rules accompanying affixes can easily be said to overshadow the mono-morphemic roots. Since the addition of prefixes does not change word stress, our presentation will be on the varying effects of suffixes on word stress. We can classify the suffixes as:

(1)   stress-bearing (-attracting) suffixes
(2)   stress-shifting (fixing) suffixes
(3)   stress-neutral suffixes

The common element between groups (1) and (2), when added to a root, is that they change the location of the stress from its original position. Stress-bearing suffixes attract the stress to themselves, while stress-shifting suffixes move the stress to some other syllable. Groups (2) and (3) have the common element of not carrying stress.

7.5.1   Stress-bearing (-attracting) suffixes

As stated above, these suffixes attract the stress. Below are common deriva-tional suffixes.

-ade	lémon – lemonáde
-aire	míllion – millionaíre
-ation	réalize – realizátion
-ee	ábsent – absentée (exception: commíttee)
-eer	móuntain – mountainéer
-ese	Japán – Japanése
-esque	pícture – picturésque
-ette	kítchen – kitchenétte
-itis	lárynx – laryngítis

Expectedly, these stress-bearing suffixes always constitute heavy syllables. The items above with suffixes should not be confused with the same/similar-looking monomorphemic forms such as *brigade, jamboree, grotesque, brunette, bursitis,* etc.

7.5.2   Stress-neutral suffixes

These suffixes never make any difference to the stress pattern of the resulting word. Such suffixes include all eight inflectional suffixes (plural; possessive; 3rd person singular present tense '-s'; progressive '-ing'; past '-ed'; past participle '-en'/'-ed'; comparative '-er'; and superlative '-est'), and several derivational ones:

-al	arríve – arríval
-cy	célibate – célibacy
-dom	frée – fréedom
-er	pláy – pláyer
-ess	líon – líoness
-ful	gráce – gráceful
-hood	nátion – nátionhood
-ish	gréen – gréenish
-ism	álcohol – álcoholism
-ist	húman – húmanist
-ive	submít – submíssive
-less	bóttom – bóttomless
-ly	fríend – fríendly
-ness	fránk – fránkness
-ship	fríend – fríendship
-some	búrden – búrdensome
-wise	clóck – clóckwise
-th	grów – grówth
-ty	cértain – cértainty
-y	sílk – sílky

We should point out that the last item, adjective-forming suffix -y, should not be treated in the same way as the noun-forming -y, which shifts the stress to antepenultimate, as in homophone – homophony, photograph – photography, etc.

   While the above-listed suffixes do not normally change the location of the stress, when several unstressed syllables are piled up to the right of the stress, we see that the stress moves to the antepenult.

   móment – mómentary *but* momentárily

7.5.3   Stress-shifting (fixing) suffixes

A multiplicity of derivational suffixes, when added to a root, shift the stress from its original position to the syllable immediately preceding the suffix. Below are some of the common ones in this group:

-ean	Áristotle – Aristotélian
-ial	súbstance – substántial

-ian	líbrary – librárian
-ical	geómetry – geométrical
-icide	ínsect – insécticide
-ic	périod – periódic (exceptions: Arabic, lunatic)
-ify	pérson – persónify
-ious	lábor – labórious
-ity	húmid – humídity
-ometer	spéed – speedómeter
-ual	cóntext – contéxtual
-ous	móment – moméntous
-y	hómonym – homónymy

We need to point out that if the original stress is on the last syllable of the root (the syllable immediately before the suffix), no change in location of the stress will result, because it is already where it should be (e.g. divérse – divérsify, absúrd – absúrdity, obése – obésity).

There is also a group of suffixes that put the stress on the syllable immediately before them if that syllable is heavy (i.e. has branching rhyme). The suffix -al in refusal, recital, and accidental is an example of this phenomenon. The stress falls on the syllable that is immediately before the suffix, because that syllable is heavy (long vowel, diphthong, and closed syllable, respectively). However, if the syllable in question is not heavy, then the stress moves one more syllable to the left (e.g. séasonal, práctical). The same is observable in the suffix -ency of emérgency and consístency on the one hand, and présidency and cómpetency on the other. While in the first two words the stress is on the syllable immediately before the suffix (closed syllable), it falls on the syllable one more position to the left in the last two words because the syllable before the suffix is light.

It is worth pointing out that there are some other endings that seem to vacillate between the different suffix types, of which -able is a good example. This suffix behaves like stress-neutral in most cases, as in quéstion – quéstionable, adóre – adórable, mánage – mánageable. However, in several disyllabic stems with final stress, it shifts the stress one syllable left (to stem-initial), as in admíre – ádmirable, compáre – cómparable, prefér – préferable (however, note the more recent tendency for stress-neutral behavior, e.g. compárable, admírable). To complicate things further, -able may also shift the stress one syllable to the right, as in démonstrate – demónstrable.

Another interesting case is the -ive suffix. When added to a monosyllabic root, the stress, expectedly, is on the root (-ive cannot bear stress) as in áct – áctive. However, in words with three or more syllables, we may see the stress falling on the syllable before it (e.g. decísive, offénsive), or moving one more to the left (e.g. négative, sédative), or even to one further left (e.g. génerative, méditative). There are attempts to separate cases such as decisive, offensive, etc. from others by stating that in these the roots are preceded by prefixes. Such explanations, although historically justifiable, are very dubious synchronically, and will not be followed here.

We can also point out that the classification has nothing to do with the morphological division of inflectional and derivational suffixes. While the eight inflectional suffixes:

-s (3rd person singular present)	e.g.: she looks here	(cf. 'you look here')
-s (plural)	two cats	(cf. 'one cat')
-s (possessive)	cat's tail	(cf. 'a cat tail')
-ed (past tense)	she looked here	(cf. 'you look here')
-en, -ed (past participle)	she has eaten	(cf. 'eat your food')
-ing (progressive)	she is eating	(cf. 'eat your food')
-er (comparative)	she is shorter than you	(cf. 'a short book')
-est (superlative)	she is the shortest	(cf. 'a short book')

do not have any effect on the stress (i.e. the addition of these suffixes does not change the location of the stress), derivational suffixes have no such predictability. As we saw in several examples above, while they may stay neutral to the stress, e.g. bottom – bottomless [bɑDəm] – [bɑDəmləs], they can shift the stress, e.g. geography – geographic [dʒiɑgɹəfi] – [dʒiəgɹæfək], or even carry the stress themselves, lemon – lemonade [lɛmən] – [lɛməned].

7.6 Stress in Compounds

A compound is composed of more than one root morpheme (mostly two free morphemes) but functions like a single word in syntactic and semantic terms. The practice in the written language is not consistent; a compound can be written as a single word (e.g. 'blueprint'), or with a hyphen in between (e.g. 'fail-safe'), or with a space between the elements (e.g. 'flower girl'). Although there are no consistent rules of choice among these, there seems to be a tendency that the ones with a primary stress on the first element will be written as one word or with a hyphen in between, and the ones that receive the main stress on the second element will be written with a space in between.

Noun compounds: Compounds that function as nouns are by far the most common, and account for 90 percent of all compounds. In this category, the most common formulation is the 'noun + noun' (e.g. 'phónecard', 'mátchbox', 'téapot', 'póstman'). Other noun compounds may have one of the following combinations:

'adjective + noun' (e.g. 'whíte house')
'verb + noun' (e.g. 'stóp watch')
'particle/adverb + noun' (e.g. 'óverdose', 'únderwear')

All noun compounds receive the stress on their first element. Exceptions to this rule almost always involve names (e.g. Lake Érie, Mount Sínai, Great Brítain).

Adjective compounds: The stress, as in the previous group, is on the first element. We find the following combinations:

'noun + adjective' (e.g. 'natíonwide', 'séasick', 'bédridden')
'adjective + adjective' (e.g. 'réd hot')
'preposition + adjective' (e.g. 'óverripe')

Verb compounds: The following combinations can give us compounds that function like verbs:

'noun + verb' (e.g. 'báby-sit', 'bád-mouth', spóon-feed', 'cár wash')
'adjective + verb' (e.g. 'drý-clean')
'particle/adverb + verb' (e.g. 'undertáke', 'oversléep')
'verb + verb' (e.g. 'drop-kíck')

While the stress patterns of the first two combinations in this group of compounds are like those of the previous groups (stress on the first element), it shifts to the second element for the last two combinations.

Compounds with more than two elements are almost always stressed on the first element (e.g. 'flý-by-night', 'forgét-me-not', 'jáck-in-the-box', 'móther-in-law').

Complex compounds, which are formed by joining a noun compound to another noun, have the stress on the first element.

(a) 'noun + noun'   'assémbly line worker'
                         N   N
                     ‹————————————›
                          noun

(b) 'adjective + noun'   'hígh school student'
                           adj.   N
                       ‹————————————›
                            noun

(c) 'verb + noun'   'píck up truck'
                      V   N
                   ‹————————›
                      noun

A complex compound can itself join a noun to create a longer complex compound, keeping the stress on the first element (e.g. 'hígh school student essay', 'assémbly line worker dispute').

7.7 Differences between American and British English

There are several words that receive different stresses between American and British English, which lend themselves to some groupings.

(a)   The first group consists of two-syllable nouns of French origin. These words are stressed on the final syllable in American English, while they receive the stress on the first (penult) syllable in British English:

    brochúre
    ballét
    café
    chatéau
    cliché
    cornét
    crochét
    debrís
    fillét
    frontíer
    garáge
    plateáu
    premíer
    salón
    soufflé
    toupée
    vermóuth
    valét

(b)   Another group of nouns do exactly the reverse (final stress in BE, initial stress in AE):

    wéekend
    pótluck
    fínance
    príncess
    récess
    résearch
    áddress
    ínquiry
    móustache

There are also some other nouns that are longer and receive initial stress in AE, but final stress in BE:

    ártisan
    Pórtuguese
    cígarette
    mágazine
    cóntroversy (second-syllable stress in BE: 'contróversy')

(c)   Two-syllable verbs ending in -ate are generally stressed initially in AE, but finally in BE:

    cástrate
    crémate

díctate
dónate
frústrate
gýrate
mígrate
púlsate
rótate
tránslate
stágnate
vácate
víbrate
phónate
lócate
mútate

However, in <u>confláte</u>, <u>creáte</u>, <u>debáte</u>, <u>defláte</u>, <u>eláte</u>, <u>reláte</u>, <u>abáte</u>, <u>infláte</u>, <u>negáte</u>, AE, like BE, places the stress on the final syllable.

The following two groups of words have one thing in common in that one variety has, in addition to the primary stress, a secondary stress while the other variety has a reduced vowel in the equivalent syllable.

(d)   Forms ending in [εɹi] (spelt <u>-ary</u>/<u>-ery</u>) and [ɔɹi] (spelt <u>-ory</u>) receive a secondary stress on the penult in AE, whereas the same syllable has a reduced vowel in BE. For example, the word <u>secondary</u> is [sékəndèɹi] in AE, but [sékəndəɹi] in BE, which can turn into [sékəndɹi] by way of deleting the reduced vowel, and thus reducing the number of syllables to three. The following list consists of such items:

nécessàry	cémetèry	állegòry
árbitràry	conféctionèry	cátegòry
díctionàry	dýsentèry	dórmitèry
Fébruàry	mónastèry	excúlpatòry
imáginàry	státionèry	mándatòry
líteràry		obsérvatòry
mílitàry		térritòry
órdinàry		* láboratòry
prímàry		prómissòry
sécretàry		inhíbitòry
témporàry		antícipatòry
* córollàry		refórmatòry
mómentàry		compénsatòry
légendàry		explóratòry
sédentàry		consérvatòry
córonàry		
sánitàry		
vísionàry		
mónetàry		
contémporàry		

* = In addition to not having the secondary stress, these items have the primary stress on the second (not first) syllable in BE.

However, if the primary stress is immediately before -ary/-ery/-ory, as in salary, bravery, ivory, lottery, elementary, anniversary, documentary, complimentary, and infirmary, there is no secondary stress in AE either.

A similar pattern to the above list (secondary in AE, reduced vowel in BE) is obtained in words ending in -mony:

ácrimòny   [ǽkɹɪmɔ̀ni] (AE)   [ǽkɹɪməni] (BE)
álimòny
céremòny
mátrimòny
téstimòny

(e)   The other group of words (all ending in -ile) that behaves differently in the two varieties shows the reverse, i.e. reduced vowel in AE, but secondary stress in BE:

ágile   [ǽdʒəl] (AE)   [ǽdʒàɪl] (BE)
dócile
fértile
frágile
fútile
hóstile
móbile
míssile
stérile
vérsatile
vírile

However, prófìle, réptìle, sénìle with [aɪ] have secondary stress in both AE and BE.

The above-mentioned differences between AE and BE do not mean that other varieties have to choose between these two; they may differ in their stress patterns without necessarily copying either of them. For example, words ending in -ate, -ize are stressed on the final syllable in Indian English, Hong Kong English and Singapore English. Thus, we get alternáte, educáte, homogeníze, terroríze (Wells 1982). Non-reduced vowels and non-initial stress on words of more than one syllable (e.g. economic, faculty, necessary) are found in Indian English and Singapore English (Wells 1982). Suffixes tend to be stressed and function words, which are reduced (e.g. of [əv]) in other varieties, are not reduced in Indian English (Trudgill and Hannah 2002). Also noteworthy is the general tendency towards fewer vowel reductions in varieties of English spoken in Hawaii, Hong Kong, Singapore, and India, as well as in the Caribbean and African varieties, which results in more of a 'syllable-timed' rhythm.

7.8 Intonation

Earlier, in chapter 1, we defined intonation as pitch variations that occur over a phrase/sentence. Intonation contours can be described in terms of tone groups or intonational phrases. A tone group is the part of a sentence over which an intonation contour extends. Within a tone group, each stressed syllable has a minor pitch increase, but there is one syllable in which this pitch increase is more significant. The syllable which carries the major pitch change is called the tonic syllable. For example, in the following sentence

    (1)   The ˋboy ´gave the ˋbook to his *teacher

the elements marked with a ´ are stressed, but the major pitch increase is on 'teacher', which is marked with an asterisk. Since in the usual cases in English, the utterance-initial position is reserved for shared (old) information, and the new information is placed in utterance-final position, the most common pattern is to put the tonic accent on the last stressed lexical item (noun, verb, adjective, adverb).

    One should note, however, that this is merely a tendency, as we may easily find cases where the tonic accent is brought forward.

    (2a) He was somewhat *discouraged

    (2b) He was *somewhat discouraged

In (2b) the tonic accent on <u>somewhat</u> is a result of emphasis (contrast). Not all cases of placing the tonic accent earlier than the last stressed lexical item involve contrast/emphasis, as exemplified in (3):

    (3)   I have *a party to plan
                *letters to write

It is important to note that a tone group is a unit of information rather than a syntactically definable unit. Thus, the way the speaker shapes his/her utterance(s) depends on what s/he considers to be the important point(s) in the sentence. In (3), the speaker has the lexical item 'letters/exams' that has the greater importance. Likewise, while the neutral expression of (4a) will assign the tonic accent to the last lexical word 'vegetable' (talking about the category/characterization of 'spinach'),

    (4a) Spinach is a *vegetable,

we would be likely to bring the tonic accent on to 'spinach' in a discussion of vegetables and considering what would fit into that group.

    (4b) *Spinach is a vegetable.

Before we leave this issue, it will be useful to mention some other cases that are also exceptions to the tonic accent falling on the last lexical item. The first one of these relates to the tone group that has an intransitive verb or verb phrase whose subject is non-human.

(5a)   Our *town is on an upswing
(5b)   The *bird flew away (cf.: the man *swore)

The second involves certain types of adverbials in final position. Sentential adverbials (i.e. those which modify the whole sentence) and adverbials of time usually do not take the tonic accent.

(6a)   I don't watch *TV typically (cf. contrastive: I don't watch TV *typically)
(6b)   It wasn't a very nice *day unfortunately

The sentences we have considered so far (1)–(6) all are examples of 'falling intonation contour', which is quite typical for utterances that express finality. It may be useful, however, to make a distinction between 'full' (or 'long') *fall* versus 'low' (or 'short') *fall*. A *full fall* is unmarked for declaratives where there is clear finality in the statement (i.e. there is nothing more to be said).

(7)   I am leaving the house right now.

This pattern is common in expressing emotional involvement:

(8)   I'm so glad.   (with genuine enthusiasm)

A falling contour is also typical for <u>wh</u>-questions (questions that start with a <u>wh</u>- word (<u>what</u>, <u>which</u>, <u>where</u>, and so on):

(9)   Which way did she go?

While a full (or long) fall shows a definitive, involved mood, a short (or 'low') fall is, generally, an indication of a detached mood by the speaker. It displays a rather neutral, perfunctory attitude:

(10)   Whatever you say. (i.e. 'I agree with it')

If falling contour is indicative of 'finality' or 'completion', *rising* intonation represents 'non-definiteness', 'lack of assurance', or 'incompletion'. This pitch pattern is addressee-oriented, and the degree of 'rise' is gauged to the degree of uncertainty/incompleteness. Accordingly, we can describe this pattern as

(a)   'high' (or 'long') rise, or
(b)   'low' (or 'short') rise.

High (or '*long*') *rise* is a more marked pattern, which is indicative of an attitude of puzzlement or unbelieving.

- In yes–no questions (typical order, or with statement order), such as

    (11a)   Is this a joke?

    (11b)   This is a joke?

    The speaker has the attitude of asking "are you sure you know what you are saying?" or "this is hard to believe."

A *low rise*, on the other hand, is more common and is used in a variety of situations.

- In yes–no questions (typical order or with statement order), such as

    (12a)   Has your uncle left already?

    (12b)   Your uncle has left already?

- Echo questions, such as

    (13)   Where will I work? I haven't thought of that yet.

- Repetition questions, such as

    (14)   What are you doing? (I haven't heard you)

    Note that this is different from (9), where the question is information-seeking.
- Open-choice alternative questions, such as

    (15)   Would you like a paper or magazine? (something to read?)

Note the falling contour for the 'closed choice' alternative

"paper or magazine ?"
- Certain tag questions that signal uncertainty, such as

    (16)   She usually comes at ten, doesn't she?

display rising intonation. However, if the sentence is uttered in eliciting agreement/confirmation, then it will end in a falling contour. In this case it is indeed a rhetorical question, as no answer is sought.

- Items in a list prior to the last item, such as

(17)   I need to buy a shirt, a jacket, and a tie.

- Questions that display readiness to present some new information, such as

(18)   Do you know when the first kidney transplant was?

If this is uttered as a neutral 'information-seeking' question, it will end in a falling pitch.

Other than the falling and rising intonation discussed thus far, there are two other patterns that are combinatory. A *falling–rising* intonation is indicative of an agreement with reservation:

(19)   You can do it that way.

The speaker accepts that it can be done the way the speaker suggested and at the same time expresses some reservation or hesitation (i.e. "I don't think you should").

The opposite, a *rising–falling* intonation, which is the dramatic equivalent of a simple 'fall', reveals strong feelings of approval/disapproval:

(20a)   That's wonderful. (cf. "That's wonderful" with simple fall)

(20b)   You can't do that. (cf. "You can't do that" with simple fall)

Finally, mention should be made of a level intonation, which marks the 'bored' or 'sarcastic' attitude:

(21)   A: John will be at the party.

       B: Great.

Putting all these together, we can clearly attend the message intended by the speaker:

(22a)   All right   (short fall)   "I agree with it" (factual)

(22b)   All right   (long fall)   enthusiastic acceptance

(22c)   All right   (sharp rise)   "No, that is not acceptable"

(22d)   All right   (low rise)   "I am listening, go on" "Is it all right?"

(22e) All right (fall–rise)   "Yes, but I am doubtful"
                                  (with reservation)

(22f) All right (rise–fall)   more dramatic than (22b), great
                                  enthusiasm, emphatic

(22g) All right (level)   "how uninspiring!"

7.9 Variations among the Varieties

Finally, a brief mention should be made of some variations among the varieties of English. Among the more significant patterns, we can cite the following. In Hawaii, the typical terminal high rise of yes–no questions is replaced
by an earlier rise followed by a fall (e.g. "Would you like some tea?"). In Welsh
English, question tags are manifested with a 'rise–fall' pattern that gives a more
emphatic impression.

A noteworthy difference within American English is the frequency of rising
pitches in Southern AE, as in (pitch going up at the accent marks)

> We played gámes and went for híkes and had the most wónderful tíme.
> (Bolinger 1998: 55)

Such rises are indicative of the speaker asking for reassurances that he is being
paid attention to. This pattern is even extended to more routine utterances, such
as answering "where are you from?" as "from Texas" (Bolinger 1998: 55). The
same tendency has also been noted for Australian English.

The main difference between American English and British English is the
latter's less frequent use of high initial pitches and a more frequent use of final
ones in yes–no questions. While in AE the following is expected:

"Would you like some coffee?"

In BE, we encounter

"Would you like some coffee?"

or with no final rise

"Would you like some coffee?"

Since intonation conveys affect and attitude, differences among the varieties
may result in misimpressions. For example, the typical AE rising intonation in
yes–no questions may be interpreted by the British as too businesslike, while,
on the other hand, Americans may find the British version 'over-cordial' and
'unduly concerned' (Bolinger 1998).

Bailey (1983: 16–17) gives the following example to contrast four varieties of English:

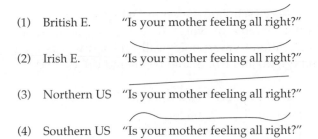

(1) British E.   "Is your mother feeling all right?"

(2) Irish E.   "Is your mother feeling all right?"

(3) Northern US "Is your mother feeling all right?"

(4) Southern US "Is your mother feeling all right?"

And he labels each one for the impression it creates on an outsider as (1) condescending, (2) insultingly incredulous, (3) repetitive, (4) unaccountably surprised. (For a detailed study of intonation in English and comparisons with several languages, the reader is referred to Bolinger 1989.)

Summary

In this chapter, we looked at some basic patterns in English stress and intonation. Although English stress is variable and mobile, there appear to be some significant generalizations about its predictability. The so-called 'front weight', i.e. stressing the penultimate syllable, seems to be the norm in disyllabic nouns and adjectives (over 80 percent of the cases). In nouns and adjectives of three or more syllables, the focus still remains the penult. However, if the penult contains less than two timing units, then the stress falls on the next left that has two timing units. For verbs (regardless of the number of syllables) the stress focus is the ultima. However, if the ult has less than two timing units, then the stress falls on the next left that has two timing units. In complex forms, affixes have varying effects on the stress; some attract the stress to themselves, some cause the stress to shift, while the third group is neutral to stress. In longer words, it is also common to find a lightly stressed (secondary stressed) syllable. Such syllables are prominent like the main stressed syllables without an effect of major pitch change, and their existence is in large part predictable.

We also considered intonation, which is the pitch variation over a phrase or a sentence. We noted that the arrangements of tone groups or intonational phrases have a lot to do with what the intentions of the speaker are, and can vary accordingly. At the same time, however, we stated certain general principles regarding different intonation patterns. Falling intonation patterns (including the rising–falling) are assertive, conclusive, and the degree of finality varies with the degree of the fall (i.e. sharper, fuller fall indicating more rigorous degree). On the other hand, the rising contours (including the falling–rising) are continuative, non-definitive. Finally, we looked at some significant differences between the stress patterns in American English and British English, as well as the intonational variations among different varieties of English.

EXERCISES

1. In the following we observe schwa deletion in fast speech for words
   (a)–(k); the same is not possible in words (l)–(v). State the generalization. Pay special attention to morphologically related words such
   as (f) and (s), (g) and (v), (h) and (u), (i) and (t), (j) and (q), (k) and (r).

		Careful Speech	Fast Speech
(a)	camera	[kæməɹə]	[kæmɹə]
(b)	veteran	[vɛtəɹən]	[vɛtɹən]
(c)	aspirin	[æspəɹən]	[æspɹən]
(d)	temperature	[tɛmpəɹətʃɚ]	[tɛmpɹətʃɚ]
(e)	reasonable	[ɹizənəbl̩]	[ɹiznəbl̩]
(f)	imaginative	[ɪmædʒənətɪv]	[ɪmædʒnətɪv]
(g)	principal	[pɹɪnsəpəl]	[pɹɪnspəl]
(h)	management	[mænədʒmənt]	[mændʒmənt]
(i)	testament	[tɛstəmənt]	[tɛstmənt]
(j)	general	[dʒɛnəɹəl]	[dʒɛnɹəl]
(k)	opera	[ɑpəɹə]	[ɑpɹə]
(l)	famous	[feməs]	[feməs] not [fems]
(m)	vegetarian	[vɛdʒətɛɹiən]	[vɛdʒətɛɹiən] not [vɛdʒtɛɹiən]
(n)	motivate	[motəvet]	[motəvet] not [motvet]
(o)	pathology	[pæθalədʒi]	[pæθalədʒi] not [pæθaldʒi]
(p)	facilitate	[fəsɪlətet]	[fəsɪlətet] not [fəsɪltet]
(q)	generality	[dʒɛnəɹæləti]	[dʒɛnəɹæləti] not [dʒɛnɹæləti]
(r)	operatic	[ɑpəɹætɪk]	[ɑpəɹætɪk] not [ɑpɹætɪk]
(s)	imagination	[əmædʒəneʃən]	[əmædʒəneʃən] not [əmædʒneʃən]
(t)	testimony	[tɛstəmoni]	[tɛstəmoni] not [tɛstmoni]
(u)	managerial	[mænədʒɛɹiəl]	[mænədʒɛɹiəl] not [mændʒɛɹiəl]
(v)	principality	[pɹɪnsəpæləti]	[pɹɪnsəpæləti] not [pɹɪnspæləti]

2. Analyze the stress patterns of the following words by using the three
   parameters (stress, tonic accent, and full vowel), and give the traditional numbers.

   Example: mineralogy

   [mɪ.nə.ɹɑ.lə.dʒi]

Stress	+	−	+	−	−
Tonic accent	−	−	+	−	−
Full vowel	+	−	+	−	+

   2 4 1 4 3

(a) choreography   (b) discretional   (c) mythical
    [   ]   [   ]   [   ]
    St.
    T.a.
    F.v.
(d) gratification   (e) autograph   (f) modality

(g) conciliation   (h) punishable   (i) phonological

(j) profundity   (k) consumptiveness   (l) resumption

(m) diagnosis   (n) neutralize   (o) resignation

(p) eccentricity   (q) recessional   (r) protestation

3. In light of what you have seen regarding the intonation patterns in section 7.8, determine where the tonic accent will be in the following (in their neutral, non-contrastive readings).

   (a) A: Are you coming to the movie?
       B: I have exams to grade.
   (b) The dog barked.
   (c) The building's falling down.
   (d) I go to Boston, usually.

4. Match the intonation patterns of the following with the six types indicated below.

   (a) low rise, (b) high (long) rise, (c) low fall, (d) long (full) fall, (e) fall–rise, (f) rise–fall

(i)   I am so happy for you. ____
(ii)   Would you like to have coffee or tea? (open choice reading)
         ____
(iii)   Would you like to have coffee or tea? (closed choice) ____
(iv)   Where will the meeting be held? (information seeking) ____
(v)   Where will the meeting be held? (I couldn't hear you) ____
(vi)   What am I doing? I am trying to fix the TV. ____
(vii)   Her predictions came true. (clear finality) ____
(viii)   Who was at the meeting? ____
(ix)   Whatever you say. ____
(x)   We should look for him, shouldn't we? ____
(xi)   You can take the old route. (agree with reservation) ____
(xii)   Are you out of your mind? ____
(xiii)   Did you wash the car yet? ____
(xiv)   I would have done it the same way, wouldn't you? ____

5. Transcribe the following (about 'English in America', cont.) *from* J. Jenkins, *World Englishes* (London: Routledge, 2002).

During the seventeenth century, English spread to southern parts of
....
America and the Caribbean as a result of the slave trade. Slaves were
....
transported from West Africa and exchanged, on the American coast
....
and in the Caribbean, for sugar and rum. The Englishes which
....
developed among the slaves and between them and their captors were
....
initially contact pidgin languages but, with their use as mother tongues
....
following the birth of the next generation, they developed into creoles.
....
Then, in the eighteenth century, there was large-scale immigration
....
from Northern Ireland, initially to the coastal area around Philadelphia,
....
but quickly moving south and west. After the Declaration of
....
American Independence in 1776, many loyalists (the British settlers
....
who had supported the British government) left for Canada.
....

Structural Factors in Second Language Phonology

8.1 Introduction

A foreign accent is created when there are phonological mismatches between the learner's native language (L₁) and the target language (L₂) that is acquired. People with different native languages have remarkably different productions in their pronunciations in a given foreign language. It is common to hear comments such as 'Spanish speakers say it as ____, but Japanese speakers say it as ____', and so on. Such clear differences are not restricted to languages that are unrelated to one another such as Spanish and Japanese, but also are observable between speakers of languages that are closely related. For example, as will be clear later in this chapter, it is a rather simple task to differentiate between a speaker of Portuguese and a speaker of Spanish by their pronunciations of English. The reason for this is that the mismatches existing between Spanish (L₁) and English (L₂) are very different from the ones existing between Portuguese (L₁) and English (L₂), and result in different resolutions of the conflicts, which create different foreign accents.

Learners' renditions of English targets are governed by their native language sound patterns. The terms 'interference' or 'transfer' have long been used to designate the influence of the native language over the target patterns. Mismatches between the target and the native language may take different forms. One of the common situations is represented by the lack of the target sound in the native language. For example, the interdental fricatives of English, /θ/ and /ð/, are absent in many of the world's languages; these are usually substituted by /s, z/ or /t, d/ respectively. Another frequently attested mismatch between L₁ and L₂ is created by under-differentiation of phonemic distinctions of the target language. For example, as noted earlier, the English contrast between /tʃ/ and /t/ (e.g. <u>chip</u> – <u>tip</u>), is not patterned in the same way in Portuguese; rather, these two sounds are the allophones of the one and the same phoneme, /t/. The Portuguese production of the phoneme /t/ is [tʃ] before /i/. Thus, it is only to be expected that speakers of Portuguese pronounce the target word <u>teacher</u> [titʃɚ] as [tʃitʃɚ] via a Portuguese filter.

The foreign accent is not always due to a complete lack of the target phoneme, nor is it because of the under-differentiation of target phonemic distinctions. Rather, the culprit is the phonetic differences between identically defined targets and native sounds. For example, liquids present a good case for this. The phonetic quality of the non-lateral liquid of American English is very different than other r-sounds (taps, trills) found in a great many languages. Another such example is provided by the lateral liquids across languages. Differences between the so-called 'clear' and 'dark' laterals are easily observable, as shown by the following cognate word <u>animal</u> in English [ænɪməl] (with a final 'dark-l') and Spanish [animal] (with final 'clear-l'). While the substitutions of these phonetically different sounds between the native and the target languages may not create a breakdown in communication by changing the word meaning (e.g. tip – <u>chip</u>), they create a *very recognizable* foreign accent.

Mismatches in phonotactic (sequential) patterns also create significant problems. For example, while English allows up to triple onsets and triple codas, a language such as Japanese has no clusters. Such a mismatch between these two languages expectedly creates tremendous problems for Japanese speakers learning English. In addition, the number of onset or coda members is not the only problem; often the problem is created because of the type(s) of sound(s) and/or combinations demanded by the L_2 not matching what is allowed by the L_1. For example, while double onsets are allowed both in English and Spanish, the variety of the combinations in English is much larger. Predictably, such a situation creates difficulties for the speakers of Spanish. Specific examples regarding the above points will be given in the following section on contrastive patterns.

Besides the segmental and sequential mismatches discussed above, there may be suprasegmental (prosodic) mismatches that obviate visible foreign accent. Rhythmic differences between the two languages considered, involving stress and intonation, are well known. Also worth mentioning, the stress-timed versus syllable-timed nature of the two languages produces noticeable non-native productions.

The observation of such clashes between L_1 and L_2 resulting in foreign accent created a huge industry of contrastive phonological studies in the 1950s and 1960s, which provided invaluable material for teachers and remediators.

In the following section, we will present a number of mini contrastive phonological structures between English as the target language and different languages as native languages, and point to the insights that can be gained from such analyses. It is important to stress the 'mini' character of these analyses, as each of these comparisons could be a book-length project that can be dealt with in a semester. Our aim here is simply to make the case in a thought-provoking manner and to stimulate the student and/or practitioner to make more detailed investigations.

The status of contrastive phonologies, as opposed to contrastive analyses in other domains (e.g. syntax), differs in a speaker's ability to communicate. While it is common to observe the native language interference in syntax (e.g. 'I have twenty-five years', instead of the native English 'I am twenty-five years old', uttered by a Spanish or Portuguese speaker, is clearly a direct translation from L_1), problems of several aspects in the syntactic domain may not be apparent all the time. For example, if a learner does not have sufficient knowledge of the differences in the uses of the 'simple past' and the 'past perfect', s/he can paraphrase things and get by with the use of 'simple past' alone. To give another example, we can look at the modal verbs of 'obligation'. While English possesses a plethora of forms (e.g. 'must', 'have to', 'should', 'ought to') with certain nuances, several other languages deal with the corresponding situations with one or, at the most, two forms. Thus, when speakers of such languages learn English, they encounter a problem. A learner who does not dominate the nuances among multiple English forms (let us say that s/he has limited competence for 'ought to') can get by perfectly without using 'ought to' once; nobody will stop and remind him/her that 'ought to' was required in one of the utterances s/he made and that otherwise s/he sounded non-native. When we look at the phonology of L_2, however, we realize that such evasions are not possible. A learner who has a problem with the interdental fricatives of English cannot simply utilize a strategy to avoid in his/her speech words containing /θ/ or /ð/. The frequency of /ð/ in grammatical morphemes such as the definite article, the, the demonstrative pronouns (e.g. this, that, etc.), the case forms of the personal pronouns (e.g. them, thou), and in some common adverbs (e.g. then, thus) is more than enough to create a disastrous situation.

All the above make a special case for contrastive phonology in that, unlike in other domains of language, in interlanguage phonology the learner is in an exposed state, with nowhere to hide the limitations. Thus, the mismatches that exist between the native and the target languages are very relevant for professionals who deal with remediation. Such factors are especially relevant when we deal with post-pubescent learners for whom the effects of foreign accent are much more obvious and more lasting. I will not go into details of the age factor in L_2 phonology learning, but simply present a display (figure 8.1) from Scovel (1988), which reveals the difference between pre-pubescent and post-pubescent learners unambiguously.

8.2 Mini Contrastive Analyses

In this section we will look at some contrastive situations that exist between the target language (i.e. English) and ten different first languages. As stated earlier, these are not exhaustive descriptions but rather summary statements. To clarify the purpose of the section, our first example, Spanish–English, will be a little more detailed; the remaining examples from nine other languages will be presented in a briefer manner.

8.2.1 Spanish–English

We start our description by giving the phonemic inventory of the L_1 consonants and vowels.

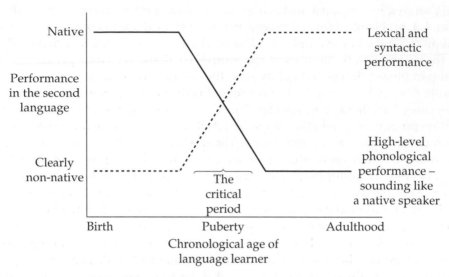

Figure 8.1 Contrasts in success between phonological learning and other linguistic skills, viewed chronologically
(*Source*: from T. Scovel (1988) *A Time to Speak: A Psycholinguistic Inquiry into Critical Period for Human Speech*. Reproduced by permission of the author.)

Consonants of Spanish

	Bilabial	Labiodental	Dental	Alveolar	Palatal	Velar	Glottal
Stop	p b		t d			k g	
Fricative		f		s		x	h
Affricate					tʃ		
Nasal	m			n	ɲ		
Liquid				l r ɾ	ʎ		
Glide					j	w	

Vowels of Spanish

	Front	Central	Back
High	i		u
Mid	e		o
Low		a	

Before we go into the mismatches, we should mention some facts about Spanish. While the status of the vowels is rather consistent across varieties of Spanish, consonants show considerable variation. For example, /θ/, which is not included in the above table, is used only in dialects in Spain. Voiceless velar and glottal fricatives are encircled to indicate that either one or the other, not both, occur in a given variety. Also noteworthy is the fact that the palatal lateral liquid /ʎ/, which is in contrast with the alveolar lateral /l/ in some varieties, is gradually being lost.

The inventory of the L₁ (Spanish) given above is useful to depict the target English phonemes that are entirely missing. Accordingly, we can easily see that the targets /v, θ, ð, z, ʃ, ʒ, dʒ/ will be problematic for the learners, as Spanish does not have these. That these predictions are correct can be shown by the following frequently attested examples, where the missing targets are replaced by the closest sounds that are available in the native L₁ inventory, resulting in several phonemic violations.

/θ/ → [t/s] (e.g. <u>thin</u>/<u>tin</u> → [tɪn], or [sɪn]),
/ð/ → [d/z] (e.g. <u>they</u>/<u>day</u> → [de]),
/v/ → [b] (e.g. <u>vowel</u>/<u>bowel</u> → [baʊl]),
/z/ → [s] (e.g. <u>zeal</u>/<u>seal</u> → [sil]),
/ʃ/ → [tʃ] (e.g. <u>shop</u>/<u>chop</u> → [tʃɑp]).

It should be mentioned that one of the sounds above, [ð], is different from the others; this sound is phonetically present in both languages but has different phonemic mappings. As mentioned earlier (chapter 2), it is a separate phoneme in English and contrasts with /d/ (e.g. <u>they</u> vs. <u>day</u>); in Spanish, however, [d] and [ð] are allophones of the same phoneme.

Although the inventory is capable of telling us the above-mentioned problems, it is rather limited in scope, as different allophonic rules of the identically described phonemes in two languages are also responsible for foreign accents. For example, despite the fact that the two languages in question have the same number of stop phonemes, they are far from being problem-free. Voiceless stops are always unaspirated in Spanish, whereas they are contextually (at the beginning of a stressed syllable) aspirated in English. Thus, in their production of English, Spanish speakers are expected to produce unaspirated stops in, for example, <u>ton</u>, <u>pay</u>, <u>car</u>. Also, voiced stops, /b, d, g/, of Spanish have fricative allophones [β, ð, ɣ] respectively. Stop variants occur after pauses, after nasals and /l/; the fricative variants occur in other environments. Thus, Spanish speakers may produce fricatives for target voiced stops in <u>adore</u>, <u>aboard</u>, and so on.

Distributional restrictions are also the cause of problems in L₂ phonology. Spanish has rather severe restrictions with respect to final consonants. Since the language allows only /s, n, r, l/ (and maybe /d/) to occur in final position, we might encounter several instances of final consonant deletion because English can demand that all consonants (except /h/) occur in this position. Similarly, since the only nasal that can occur finally is /n/ in Spanish, a target such as <u>from</u> with a bilabial nasal may be realized with a final [n] instead.

Another source of a foreign accent is the salient phonetic dissimilarities in certain sounds between the two languages. This is nowhere more obvious than with the comparison of the liquids. While both languages have lateral and non-lateral liquids and can employ them in the same word positions, their clearly identifiable phonetic differences in the two languages produce easily detectable foreign accents. The alveolar lateral is always realized as 'clear-l' (i.e. non-velarized) in Spanish, whereas the American English counterpart is produced mostly as shades of 'dark-l' (i.e. velarized). The non-lateral liquids (i.e. r-sounds) of the two languages also exemplify considerable phonetic dissimilarity.

The American English r̠ is a retroflex approximant, while the two r-sounds of Spanish are a trill and a flap. Thus, we have the following mismatch:

Spanish		English
	[ɹ] ———————	/ɻ/
/ɾ/ ———————	[ɾ]	
/r/ ———————	[r]	

We can summarize the above in the following overlay of the L₁ inventory over the target English inventory (Spanish phonemes that have no relevance to the mismatches, such as /ʎ, x, ɲ/ are not considered here).

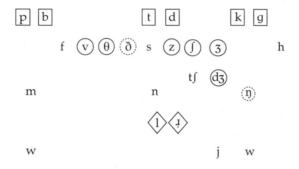

The following symbolizations are used throughout the comparisons between the target language (English) and the various first languages:

○ Missing target phoneme in L₁
◌ Sound existing only as an allophone of another phoneme in L₁
☐ Different allophonic/distributional patterns in L₁ and L₂
◇ Salient phonetic difference between the target and the L₁ counterpart.

The comparison of the vowel systems also makes certain problematic aspects rather obvious. Although there are no distributional problems in vowels (Spanish vowels can occur in all word positions), Spanish has a far smaller number (5) of vowels than English, and this proves to be an important and frequent source of insufficient separation (i.e. under-differentiation) of target phonemic distinctions. The frequently attested lack of contrasts (i.e. homophonies) that result include /i/ – /ɪ/ (e.g. grid – greed), /u/ – /ʊ/ (e.g. fool – full), /ʌ/ – /ɑ/ (e.g. buddy – body), /ɛ/ – /æ/ (e.g. mess – mass). The following chart summarizes these potential confusions:

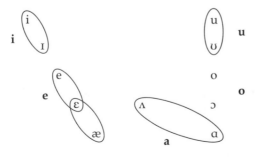

The following conventions are used throughout the comparisons with vowel systems of L_1 and L_2.

○   Circling of vowels indicates that these target contrasts are overlooked by learners coming from a specific L_1.

i a ɛ   Bold-type vowel symbols indicate the expected native language vowels used in the rendition of targets.

It should be pointed out that the use of identical phonetic symbols for the bold-type L_1 vowel does not imply that it is phonetically identical to any of the L_2 (English) targets. For example, we use /i/ and /ɪ/ for the English high front vowels. Spanish speakers' rendition of /i/ does not mean that they are successful for English /i/ and unsuccessful for /ɪ/. Spanish substitution of /i/ is not identical to either English vowel. In almost all the languages we compare, the symbols /i, e, o, u/ indicate phonetically simple (not long and diphthongized) vowels. Similarly, the use of other symbols (e.g. /ɛ, ɔ/) does not make a claim that the phonetic qualities of these vowels are identical to those of English. The reader should keep these facts in mind when examining the vowel charts throughout.

The diphthongs are not expected to create problems for Spanish speakers as the language has a wide variety of diphthongs including all of those occurring in English.

Phonotactics (i.e. sequential patterns) is another aspect to consider in the comparison. In the present case, we see a rather disparate situation between Spanish and English.

Syllable structure

(L₁) Spanish   (L₂) English

(C) (C) V (C) (C*)   (C) (C) (C) V (C) (C) (C) (C**)

  * possible only if syllable-final within word as 'stop/sonorant + /s/'
** possible only if an affix

While English allows triple onsets and triple codas, the maximum number of consonants in Spanish in these positions is two. The number of consonants in clusters can tell only part of the whole story. The disparities are greater once we examine the other relevant dimension, namely the possible combinations. For example, English has a wide variety of double codas (see chapter 6), whereas Spanish has very limited combinations (stop/sonorant + /s/) only in word-internal position. There are differences for the double onsets too. The variety of combinations Spanish allows is limited to 'stop//f/ + liquid'; any English target cluster other than these (there are a multiplicity of cases) can create significant trouble for Spanish speakers learning English.

Finally, mention should be made of the suprasegmental effects. Firstly, we can mention the stress-timed (English) versus syllable-timed (Spanish) difference. A rather obvious consequence of this difference is seen in the rhythm because of the lack of vowel reductions, which are mandatory in English. Another aspect of the prosodic differences is related to the different stress patterns. Such mismatches are especially dangerous in the case of cognates. Learners may (and indeed do) fall into the 'same/similar form and meaning' trap between the two languages. This is especially true when Spanish words have the stress on the final syllable, which English avoids. Here are some examples of such conflicts:

- **Disyllabics:**   ult in Spanish vs. penult in English: <u>color</u>, <u>labor</u>, <u>honor</u>, <u>fatal</u>, <u>accion/action</u>
- **trisyllabics:**   ult in Spanish vs. antepenult in English: <u>animal</u>, <u>general</u>, <u>cultural</u>, <u>natural</u>
    ult in Spanish vs. penult in English: <u>decision</u>, <u>informal</u>, <u>profesor/professor</u>
- **four syllables:**   ult in Spanish vs. penult in English: <u>artificial</u>, <u>horizontal</u>, <u>education/educacion</u>
    ult in Spanish vs. antepenult in English: <u>particular</u>, <u>original</u>, <u>opinion</u> (or on pre-antepenult in English because the antepenult has an [ə], which is unstressable: <u>calculator</u>, <u>operador/operator</u>, <u>navegador/navigator</u>).

The following summarizes the major trouble spots:

- entirely missing targets: /v/ → [b], /θ/ → [t], /ð/ → [d], /ʃ/ → [tʃ], /z/ → [s]
- distribution: only /s, n, l, ɾ/ occur finally in L_1
- aspiration of target /p, t, k/
- fricative variants of L_1 voiced stops intervocalically (e.g. <u>adore</u> → [aðɔɾ])
- significant phonetic violations: liquids
- consonant clusters
- insufficient separation of several target vowel contrasts
- stress
- rhythm

8.2.2 Turkish–English

The overlay of the native language consonantal system on the target English inventory results in the following:

From the consonantal inventory, we can easily see potential troubles for the missing English targets /θ, ð, w, ŋ/, which manifest themselves in <u>thin</u> → [tin], they → [de]. Although there is also no /ŋ/ in the consonantal inventory of Turkish, [ŋ] is phonetically present in Turkish before velar stops, as in Ankara [aŋkaɾa], banka 'bank' [baŋka]. Also, while [v] is used for the missing target /w/ (e.g. well → [vɛl]) this problem is not present intervocalically, as /v/ has a [w] allophone in this position.

Non-continuant obstruents (i.e. stops and affricates) have voicing contrasts in initial and medial positions; in final position, however, we find only the voice-less members of these pairs. This is the source of substitutions, for example, in bag → [bɛk], bid → [bit]. The progressive ending -ing [ɪŋ] creates a problem, which can be accounted for in two steps. Since [ŋ] in Turkish requires the pres-ence of a following velar stop, and the velar stop in final position cannot be anything other than the voiceless variant, the rendition of -ing [ɪŋ] is [ɪŋk] as in going [goɪŋk].

Significant phonetic differences are relevant to liquids, especially for the non-lateral target retroflex approximant. Turkish r-sound is an alveolar tap /ɾ/. In addition, it is produced voiceless (and with friction) in final position (e.g. [kaɾ] "snow"). The alveolar lateral has both the 'clear' and the 'dark' variants, although their distributions are different from those of English and create mis-matches. All word-initial laterals and all coda laterals after front vowels are 'clear' (cf. English 'dark' realizations in lawn and sell).

The conflicts in vowels involve several insufficient separations of contrast-ing English pairs /i/ – /ɪ/ (e.g. peach – pitch), /ɛ/ – /æ/ (e.g. mess – mass), /ʌ/ – /ɑ/ (e.g. buddy – body), /u/ – /ʊ/ (e.g. fool – full), which are sum-marized in the following chart:

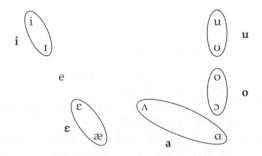

Other Turkish vowels not relevant for the mismatches: /y, ø, ɯ/

The syllable structure of Turkish can be described as (C) V (C) (C). There are no initial clusters. The language does allow certain double codas, which can be described as 'C₁ = sonorant and C₂ = obstruent, or C₁ = fricative and C₂ = stop'. Because of great differences between these clusters and those of English, all target onset clusters, all triple codas, and several double codas expectedly create problems.

Coming from a syllable-timed language, Turkish speakers are expected to have difficulties with English vowel reductions and with rhythm. In addition, the stress patterns of the two languages are significantly different and prove to be sources of difficulty.

The following summarizes the major trouble spots:

- missing target phonemes: /θ/ → [t], /ð/ → [d], /w/ → [v] (except in V—V), /ŋ/→ [n] (except before a velar stop)
- final devoicing of non-continuant obstruents /b, d, g, dʒ/
- significant phonetic differences: liquids, especially the non-lateral
- under-differentiation of certain target vowel contrasts
- onset and coda clusters
- stress
- rhythm

8.2.3 Greek–English

The overlay of the L₁ consonants over the English targets results in the following picture:

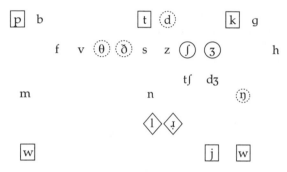

Other Greek phonemes not relevant for mismatches: /x, ɣ/

Starting with the targets missing in the L₁ inventory, we note the lack of palato-alveolar fricatives /ʃ/ and /ʒ/; these tend to be replaced by the alveolar fricatives with their combinations with [j] as [sj] and [zj] respectively. Also lacking in Greek are the palato-alveolar affricates /tʃ/ and /dʒ/, which are replaced by the closest native alveolars /ts/ and /dz/, respectively.

Although circled as a missing target phoneme, /ŋ/ is a little different from the others, because [ŋ] is an allophone of /n/ in Greek occurring before velar obstruents. Thus, problems are expected only in its occurrences in English with no adjacent velar stops.

Voiceless stops in Greek are always unaspirated. Thus, problems are expected for the English targets in the beginning of stressed syllables.

As far as the salient phonetic differences are concerned, we need to highlight the liquids. The Greek alveolar lateral is always 'clear' and exemplifies a salient phonetic difference; the r-sound in Greek is also noticeably different, as it is an alveolar flap/trill. A minor difference can be cited between the /t/ and /d/ phonemes in the two languages; while these two are alveolars in English, they are dentals in Greek.

Positional/distributional restrictions are also sources of difficulty. All Greek consonants can occur initially and medially, and all except /d, θ, ð/ (among the relevant ones) occur finally. Thus, English targets with the above three in final position may cause problems.

Glides /w, j/ can create problems between the two languages, as Greek learners of English tend to hear and pronounce these glides as high vowels /u/ and /i/ respectively. While there is sufficient phonetic similarity between the glides and the corresponding high vowels, pronouncing them as vowels will give the impression to the English native speaker that there are separate syllables.

Vowel mismatches create the following insufficient separations for the target distinctions:

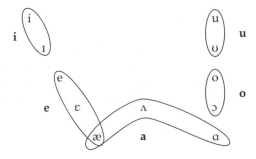

Greek has no diphthongs, but two vowel sounds can occur in sequence, and thus learners can handle the target English diphthongs.

Major problems with the phonotactics are associated with the final clusters, which are non-existent in Greek. Thus, in addition to some simple codas pointed out earlier, Greek speakers will have problems with all the complex codas of English.

Greek is another syllable-timed language in our list, and expectedly has no vowel reduction. This results in considerable difficulties in learning the rhythm of English. In addition, different lexical stresses in the two languages are sources of problems.

The following summarizes the major trouble spots:

- missing target phonemes: /ʃ, ʒ, tʃ, dʒ/
- aspiration
- distributional restrictions: /θ, ð, d/
- salient phonetic differences: approximants
- insufficient separation of target vowels
- stress
- rhythm

8.2.4 French–English

The overlay of the native phonemes on the target English inventory gives us the following picture:

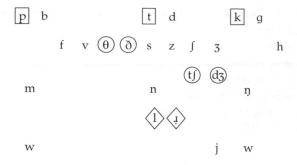

French consonants that are not relevant for the discussion: /ɲ, ɥ/

Missing target phonemes include the interdentals /θ/ and /ð/ (which are rendered as [s] and [z] respectively, giving rise to mispronunciations such as think [sɪŋk], that [zæt]), and affricates /tʃ/ and /dʒ/ (which are rendered as [ʃ] and [ʒ] respectively). The status of /ŋ/ is different in that while it does not occur in native French words, one does find it in final position in borrowed words.

Allophonic differences may be observed in /p, t, k/ regarding aspiration. As in other Romance languages, voiceless stops are unaspirated in French, leading to mispronunciations of English targets.

Salient phonetic differences belong, once again, to the realm of liquids. The lateral in French is always 'clear', and the non-lateral is either an alveolar trill, /r/, or the uvular fricative/approximant, /ʁ/, and these are consistently used to substitute the English liquid targets. The sounds /t, d/ present minor phonetic differences, as these are dental in French.

The mismatches and the under-differentiations regarding the target vowel contrasts are highlighted in the following diagram:

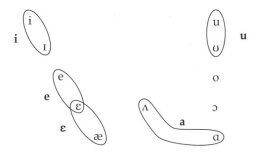

French vowels that are not relevant: /y, ø, œ/ and the nasal vowels /ɛ̃, ã, ɔ̃, œ̃/.

The syllable structure of French, which can be described as (C) (C) V (C) (C), allows a maximum of double onsets and codas. In addition, the combinations allowed by these double onsets (basically, C_1 = /f, v/ or stop, C_2 = liquid), and codas (basically C_1 = liquid, C_2 = stop) are more limited than those of English. Thus, some problems are expected in these mismatches.

Although French is classified as a syllable-timed language, it does not have the typical 'staccato' (or 'machine gun') rhythm, and has reduced vowels. Despite this, the rhythm is quite different than that of English. In an English rhythm group, the first syllable is stressed and its pitch is higher than the other unstressed syllables. In French, on the other hand, the final syllable of each rhythmic group is lengthened and its pitch is leveled to half way before it is lowered. Thus, learners have considerable problems with English stress and rhythm.

The following summarizes the major trouble spots:

- missing target phonemes: /θ, ð, tʃ, dʒ, (ŋ)/
- aspiration
- salient phonetic differences: liquids
- certain onset and coda clusters
- insufficient separation of several target vowel contrasts
- stress
- rhythm

8.2.5 German–English

The overlay of the native phonemes on the target English inventory reveals the following:

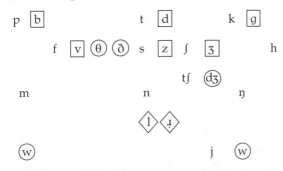

Other German consonants: /χ, ç, tˢ, pᶠ/

Missing targets include /θ, ð, dʒ, w/, which are commonly rendered as [s, z, tʃ, v] respectively.

Voiced obstruents /b, d, g, v, z, ʒ/, although shared by the two languages, do present problems in final position, as they are rendered voiceless in German.

Salient phonetic differences, once again, are related to the liquids. The German lateral is 'clear', and the r-sound is a uvular fricative. It is also worth mentioning that, /ʁ/ is normally an approximant intervocalically; after voiceless obstruents it is voiceless (e.g. trat [tχat] "kicked"); postvocalically before a consonant or word-finally, it is vocalized to [ɐ]. All these variations are sources of the problems learners face when dealing with the target English retroflex approximant /ɹ/. It may also be worth mentioning a slightly different phonetic realization of German /j/ in that it is produced with a friction.

Vowel mismatches are depicted in the following chart:

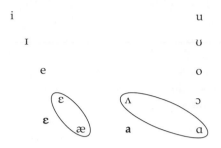

Other German vowels: /y, ʏ, ø, œ, ɛ:, a:/

The tense vowels in German /i, e, o, u/ have just length in German and lack the diphthongal characteristics of the ones in English. This presents slight phonetic mismatch.

German syllable structure, which can be described as (C) (C) (C) V (C) (C) (C), is as complex as that of English, although the specific combinations allowed may not be identical. Thus, any difficulty that may be observed will not be due to the number of consonants but rather to mismatches of the combinations of the types of sounds.

Being stress-timed languages, English and German share many characteristics in stress and rhythm. Thus, these areas are not expected to create problems for learners.

The following summarizes the major trouble spots:

- missing target phonemes: /θ, ð, dʒ, w/
- distributional restrictions: voiced obstruents
- salient phonetic differences: liquids
- insufficient separation of target vowel distinctions

8.2.6 Arabic–English

The overlay of the Arabic consonantal phonemes on the target English inventory reveals the following:

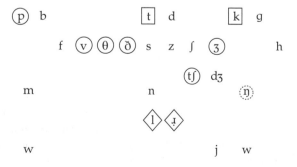

Other Arabic consonants: /x, ɣ, ħ, ʕ/ and the pharyngealized (emphatic) consonants /tˤ, dˤ, sˤ, lˤ, ðˤ/

Missing target phonemes /p, g, v, θ, ð, ʒ, tʃ/ are responsible for the following phonemic clashes:

/p/ → [b] <u>pan</u> – <u>ban</u>,
/f/ → [v] <u>fan</u> – <u>van</u>,
/θ/ → [s]/[t] <u>thin</u> – <u>sin</u>, <u>tin</u>,
/ð/ → [z]/[d] <u>breathe</u> – <u>breeze</u> – <u>breed</u>,
/tʃ/ → [ʃ] <u>chin</u> – <u>shin</u>.

The occurrence of /θ/ and /ð/ in classical Arabic complicates the problem, giving the impression that the learner should not have problems with these targets in English, because s/he has been exposed to these sounds in the study of Arabic. This, however, does not translate into reality and learners have serious problems with respect to English interdentals.

The sound /dʒ/, although present in some dialects of Arabic, was lost in Egyptian Arabic; also noteworthy is the questionable status of /ʒ/.

The case of /ŋ/ is similar to those of Turkish and Greek, in that this sound occurs as an allophone of /n/ before a velar stop, but cannot stand alone. Thus, while <u>finger</u> [fɪŋgɚ] may not be problematic, because [ŋ] is followed by a velar stop, <u>sing</u> [sɪŋ] and <u>singer</u> [sɪŋɚ] will be (i.e. the expected productions are [sɪŋg] and [sɪŋgɚ]).

The two voiceless stops of Arabic /t, k/ are unaspirated and are expected to be problematic.

Salient phonetic differences are related to liquids once again. The Arabic lateral is 'clear', and the r-sound is an alveolar apical trill. In addition, both liquids of Arabic have voiceless allophones prepausally following voiceless obstruents. All these result in obvious foreign accents in their English productions. Slight phonetic differences are observed in /t, d/ because they are dental in Arabic.

Mismatches and the resulting insufficient separation of English vowel contrasts are depicted in the following:

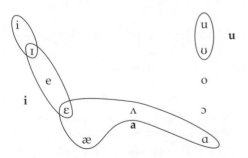

Arabic syllable structure, (C) V (C) (C), is in considerable clash with that of English. Having no onset clusters and allowing only very limited double codas result in an epenthetic vowel to break up complex English targets.

Although Arabic is a stress-timed language, vowel reductions do not follow English patterns, and this results in some differences in rhythm.

Word stress is fairly regular in Arabic; it falls on the final heavy syllable (one with either a long vowel or a VCC rhyme) of a morpheme. This is responsible for the commonly observed errors (stress on the final syllable as opposed to the native English pattern of initial stress) in <u>difficult</u>, <u>expert</u>, <u>narrowest</u>, <u>insti-tute</u>, where the first three words have VCC rhymes, and the last word has a long vowel in the final syllable.

The following is a summary of the major trouble spots:

- missing target phonemes: /p, f, θ, ð, tʃ, (dʒ), (ŋ)/
- aspiration
- salient phonetic differences: liquids
- insufficient separation of several target vowel contrasts
- onset and coda clusters
- stress
- rhythm

8.2.7 Russian–English

The overlay of the native language phonemes on the target English inventory reveals the following:

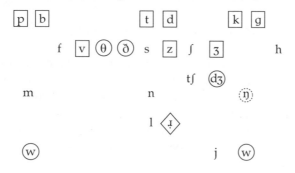

Other Russian consonants: /pʲ, bʲ, tʲ, dʲ, kʲ, gʲ, fʲ, vʲ, sʲ, zʲ, x, xʲ, ts, mʲ, nʲ, rʲ, lʲ/

Missing target phonemes in L₁ include /θ, ð, dʒ, ŋ, w/, which have the sub-stitutes [t, d, tʃ, ŋ, v], respectively.

Notable distributional and/or allophonic mismatches concern the following:

- All voiced obstruents are devoiced in final position, resulting in commonly observed homophonies neutralizing the target contrasts such as <u>bag</u> – <u>back</u>, <u>cab</u> – <u>cap</u>, <u>bed</u> – <u>bet</u>, <u>save</u> – <u>safe</u> in favor of the voiceless member.
- Voiceless stops, /p, t, k/, unlike in English, are unaspirated and provide another source for observable foreign accent.
- While the lateral liquid is quite similar to that of English (i.e. 'dark'), we have a different situation with the non-lateral. The Russian r-sound is an alveolar trill and this gives rise to a distinct foreign accent. There are some cases that provide minor phonetic differences. Among these are /t, d, n/ which are dental in Russian, and /tʃ/ which is slightly more palatalized in Russian.

As the list of Russian phonemes below the diagram demonstrates, Russian has several palatalized consonants, and learners may use the palatalized sound when English targets occur in environments conducive to palatalization, such as before a high front vowel or /j/.

Similar to the situation mentioned for Turkish, /ŋ/ targets in final position undergo a two-step process. First is the insertion of the velar support, /g/, and then the subsequent devoicing of it to [k], yielding productions such as going [goɪŋk].

The clashes in the vowel systems of L₁ and L₂ result in the following under-differentiations of the target distinctions.

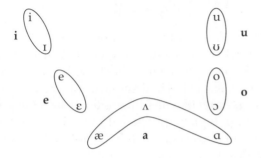

The limited five-vowel system of Russian is reduced to three, [i, a, ə] in unstressed syllables. Although both English and Russian are stress-timed languages, vowel reductions work differently; in Russian, [ə] never occurs immediately before the stressed vowel, and this results in non-reduction in many pretonic syllables of English target words. Also, Russian words contain only one stress, thus learners will tend to stress only the syllable with the tonic accent.

The syllable structure of Russian, which can be described as (C) (C) (C) V (C) (C) (C), is comparable in its complexity to that of English, and thus, this area is not expected to be problematic for the learners.

The following summarizes the major trouble spots:

* missing target phonemes: /θ, ð, dʒ, ŋ, w/
* aspiration
* final devoicing of the obstruents
* salient phonetic differences: non-lateral liquid
* insufficient separation of target vowel contrasts
* stress
* rhythm

8.2.8 Korean–English

The overlay of the L₁ consonant phonemes on the target English inventory results in the following:

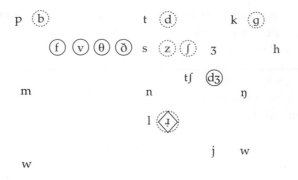

w

Other Korean phonemes: /pʰ, p', tʰ, t', kʰ, k', tʃʰ, tʃ', s'/

Target phonemes that are missing in L₁ completely include /f, v, θ, ð, dʒ/, and they are rendered as [p, b, t, d, tʃ] respectively in target English words. Although /b, d, g/ are not in the Korean phonemic inventory, [b, d, g] are present as allophones of /p, t, k/ between two voiced sounds. As a result, we expect difficulties in English /b, d, g/ targets when they are not in between two voiced sounds (e.g. <u>book</u>, <u>cab</u>, <u>dog</u>). Equally problematic are the /p, t, k/ targets when between two voiced sounds, as exemplified in the following erroneous productions: <u>apart</u> [əbaɹt], <u>attack</u> [ədæk], <u>mocha</u> [mogə].

As mentioned in chapter 2, [z] and [ʃ] exist in Korean as allophones of /s/. We repeat the distributional requirements here for convenience:

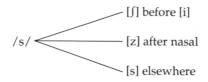

[ʃ] before [i]

/s/   [z] after nasal

[s] elsewhere

Consequently, we expect the target <u>sea shells</u> [si ʃɛlz] to be rendered as [ʃi sɛls].

Liquids present both phonemic and phonetic problems. The Korean r-sound is a flap and is in complementary distribution with the lateral; [ɾ] occurs intervocalically and [l] elsewhere, thus giving rise to failures to distinguish between target pairs such as <u>feeling</u> – <u>fearing</u>, <u>soul</u> – <u>sore</u>.

The mismatches between the vowel systems of L₁ and L₂ result in the following under-differentiations.

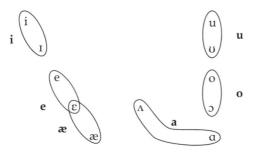

Other Korean vowels: /y, ø, ɯ/

The syllable structure of Korean, which is described as (C) V (C) (C), is much simpler than that of English. Although the above formulation allows double codas, the actual combinations are very limited. As a result, the wide variety of double and triple onsets and codas in target English words are broken by vowel insertions.

Korean stress patterns are quite different from those of English, mainly manifested as the rise in pitch on the initial syllable of the word or phrase. In addition to the mismatches in stress, Korean, as a typical syllable-timed language, does not have vowel reductions and this results in a clearly different rhythm.

The following summarizes the major trouble spots:

- missing target phonemes
- sounds existing as allophones
- salient phonetic differences
- insufficient separation of target vowel contrasts
- onset and coda clusters
- stress
- rhythm

8.2.9 Portuguese–English

The overlay of the L_1 consonant phonemes on the target English inventory results in the following:

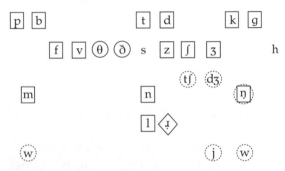

Other Portuguese phonemes: /ʎ, ɲ/

Missing target phonemes in L_1 include /θ, ð, tʃ, dʒ, ŋ/. Of these, the first two have the substitutes [t, d] respectively. The sounds [tʃ] and [dʒ] exist in Portuguese as the allophones of /t/ and /d/ respectively before /i/. Thus, we can expect problems when the target /t/ and /d/ occur before /i/, as in teacher, difficult, where the common renditions are [tʃ] and [dʒ], respectively, for the initial sounds. The sound [ŋ] is phonetically present before a velar stop.

Similar to other Romance languages, Portuguese voiceless stops are unaspirated and create problems for learners in dealing with English aspirated targets. In addition, no obstruent of Portuguese, except /s/, can occur in syllable/word-final position. Consequently, English words with such demands receive an epenthetic vowel.

Nasals do not occur in final position either. The result is the nasalization of the previous vowel in English targets (e.g. <u>from</u> [frã]).

Liquids present both phonetic and distributional challenges. The lateral, /l/, is phonetically not very different from that of English (i.e. it is 'dark'); in syllable-final position, however, it is very much vocalized and becomes a [w] (e.g. <u>Brazil</u> [braziw]). The target word from a brand name of an analgesic <u>Advil</u> puts together three pattern clashes between L_1 and L_2. The typical rendition of this word as [adʒiviw] is easily explainable: since /d/ is not allowed in syllable-final position, an epenthetic vowel [i] is inserted; now that /d/ is followed by an [i] it turns into the appropriate allophone [dʒ]; the final [w] is accounted for by the above-mentioned allophonic rule of the lateral.

The two r-sounds of Portuguese, alveolar tap [ɾ] and velar/uvular fricative [x/χ], are phonetically very different than that of English /ɹ/. Substitutions of English targets vary depending on the word position dictated by L_1 (i.e. [x/χ] in initial position, [ɾ] otherwise).

Glides /w, j/ create problems similar to those we observed in Greek–English mismatches; they are produced as high vowels /u/ and /i/ respectively, and give the impression of separate syllables.

The vowel mismatches between the two languages are shown below.

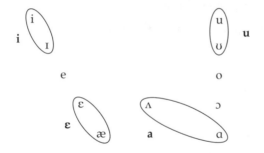

The syllable structure of Portuguese, which can be described as (C) (C) V (C), can match the English demands in a limited fashion. Final single coda is possible only if the consonant is /s/ or a liquid. Also, the double onsets can only have the following structure: C_1 = stop or /f/, C_2 = liquid. Any other English target onset predictably suffers a modification.

Portuguese stress tends to go on the 'penult', thus anything different demanded by English may prove difficult for learners.

Although Portuguese leans more towards the 'stress-timed' pattern (Brazilian Portuguese less than European Portuguese), it does not have the same vowel reductions as those of English. This, coupled with the different lexical stress, results in difficulties in target rhythmic patterns.

The following summarizes the major trouble spots:

- missing target phonemes
- different allophonic/distributional restrictions
- aspiration
- salient phonetic differences: non-lateral liquid
- insufficient separation of target vowel contrasts

- onset/coda clusters
- stress
- rhythm

8.2.10 Persian (Farsi)–English

The overlay of the L_1 consonant phonemes on the target English inventory results in the following:

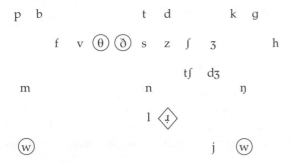

Missing target phonemes in L_1 include /θ, ð/, which are substituted by [t, d] respectively. Persian also lacks /w/; although several manuals suggest the rendition as [v], it actually is a frictionless approximant [ʋ].

The r-sound presents a salient phonetic difference, as it is an alveolar trill /r/ in Persian, with its allophones of a voiceless trill [r̥] in final position, and the tap [ɾ] intervocalically. The result is a clear foreign-accented English target /ɹ/.

Vowel mismatches creating under-differentiations are shown in the following:

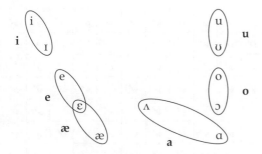

As in many other languages, the Persian vowels replacing the targets do not have the English distinctions of tense/lax; rather, the quality of the vowels is in between.

Syllable structure of Persian, which can be described as (C) V (C) (C), is responsible for the difficulties experienced with the target double and triple onsets of English. Epenthetic (prothetic in the case of s-clusters) vowels are used to break the impermissible clusters. Triple codas are problematic, as they do not exist in L_1. Also, although Persian allows double codas, the combinations are more limited than what is demanded by English, thus learners may experience difficulties with certain targets.

Since Persian stress is generally on the 'ult', there is considerable difficulty with English stress patterns. Combined with the difficulties in lexical stress, the syllable-timed characteristic of Persian, which does not allow any vowel reduction, may lead to a very different rhythmic pattern than that of English.

The following summarizes the major trouble spots:

- missing target phonemes: /θ, ð, w/
- salient phonetic differences: r-sounds
- insufficient separation of target vowel contrasts
- onset and coda clusters
- stress
- rhythm

The comparisons between English as L_2 and several languages as L_1 we have looked at repeatedly highlighted certain problematic areas for learners. Table 8.1 summarizes these important targets that create phonemic as well as some significant phonetic clashes (the 15 languages include the 10 we looked at and another 5).

Table 8.1 Significant phonemic and phonetic conflicts between English and several other languages

	Arabic	French	German	Greek	Hindi	Italian	Japanese	Korean	Mandarin	Persian	Russian	Portuguese	Spanish	Turkish	Vietnamese
θ ð → t d / s z	✔	✔	✔		✔	✔	✔	✔	✔	✔	✔	✔	✔	✔	✔
v → b					✔	✔	✔						✔		
w vs. v			✔	✔					✔	✔	✔		✔		
Onset/coda CC	✔			✔	✔	✔	✔	✔	✔	✔		✔	✔	✔	✔
Fin. C. Devoic.			✔	✔				✔	✔		✔			✔	✔
i vs. ɪ	✔	✔		✔		✔	✔	✔	✔	✔	✔	✔	✔	✔	✔
u vs. ʊ	✔	✔		✔		✔	✔	✔	✔	✔	✔	✔	✔	✔	✔
ɛ vs. æ	✔	✔	✔		✔	✔	✔	✔	✔	✔	✔	✔	✔	✔	✔
ʌ vs. ɑ	✔	✔	✔	✔	✔	✔	✔	✔	✔	✔	✔	✔	✔	✔	✔
Aspiration	✔	✔		✔		✔				✔	✔	✔			
ɹ	✔	✔	✔	✔	✔	✔	✔	✔	✔	✔	✔	✔	✔	✔	✔
Stress	✔	✔	✔	✔	✔	✔	✔	✔	✔	✔	✔	✔	✔	✔	✔
Rhythm	✔	✔		✔	✔	✔	✔	✔	✔	✔	✔	✔	✔	✔	✔

8.3 Differential Treatment of Mismatches

In the previous sections we observed, besides many phonetic mismatches, several examples of phonemic mismatches between a learner's L_1 and L_2. Although the difficulties resulting from these mismatches are real, there seem to be differences in quality among them, and consequently, degrees of difficulty created by different types of mismatches.

One type of phonemic mismatch between two systems was a result of a situation whereby the two sounds that were in contrast in L_2 were non-existent in L_1. This was exemplified by the /θ/ – /ð/ contrast of English (ether [iθɚ] vs. either [iðɚ]). As we saw above, many languages, including Arabic, French, German, Korean, Turkish, Persian, Portuguese, and Russian, lack these completely, and the likely substitutions created violations of target contrasts.

The second mismatch that resulted in phonemic violations occurred when two sounds that were in contrast in L_2 were present as the allophones of a single phoneme in L_1. As mentioned earlier, the English contrast between /t/ and /tʃ/ (e.g. tip [tɪp] vs. chip [tʃɪp]) is under-differentiated by learners whose L_1 is Portuguese, because the two sounds are allophones of the same phoneme in their L_1, as shown in the following:

Portuguese   **English**

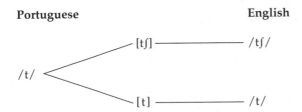

The first situation involves acquiring new phoneme(s), and the second type is a creation of a phonemic split from an existing allophonic variation in the native language. While one may be inclined to think that acquiring new phoneme(s) will be more difficult than rearranging the two existing sounds from allophones of the same phoneme to separate phonemes, research has proven otherwise. It has shown that learning becomes more difficult when the structures/sounds are similar between L_1 and L_2 than when they are dissimilar (Oller and Ziahosseyni 1970; Flege 1987, 1990; Major and Kim 1999).

8.3.1 Basic vs. derived context

The level of difficulty of going to a phonemic split for L_2 from an existing allophonic variation in L_1 has a correlation with various contexts. In a thorough examination of this issue, Eckman, Elreyes, and Iverson (2003) state that whenever there is a conflict between L_1 and L_2 in the above manner (i.e. two sounds are in contrast in L_2, but are the allophones of a single phoneme in L_1), the target language phonemic contrast will be acquired first in basic (tautomorphemic) contexts, then in derived (heteromorphemic) contexts. Going back to the Portuguese–English mismatch regarding the /t/ – /tʃ/ contrast of English, the expected rendition of target English words <u>tea</u> and <u>betting</u> in the earlier stages of learning will be [tʃi] and [bɛtʃɪŋ] respectively, which fails in regard to the target contrast. Eckman et al. describe this as 'stage I' ('no contrast') where the native language allophonic rule applies in both the basic context (i.e. tautomorphemic situation where the affected sound /t/ becoming [tʃ], and the relevant environment – following vowel /i/ – are in the same morpheme), and in a derived context (in heteromorphemic context). Eckman et al. predict the next stage (stage II) to show a partial contrast in the way the native rule applies only in the derived (heteromorphemic) context (i.e. the sound affected, /t/ becoming [tʃ] before high vowels taking place in <u>betting</u> realized as [bɛtʃɪŋ], while <u>tea</u> is realized as [ti] and not as *[tʃi]). The last stage (stage III) is the one where the target contrast is acquired in both the basic and the derived context (i.e. in both tautomorphemic and heteromorphemic contexts). Thus, the following implicational relationship holds: *if a target pattern is acquired in a heteromorphemic context, it implies that the same is acquired in a tautomorphemic context, but not vice versa.*

   This excludes a situation where the learner is successful in a derived context (e.g. <u>betting</u> pronounced as [bɛtɪŋ]), but will fail in the basic context where <u>tea</u> will be pronounced as [tʃi]. This hypothesis receives support from studies where the acquisition patterns reflect such an order (i.e. learning is earlier in basic contexts than in derived contexts).

8.3.2 Deflected contrast

Eckman et al. point out some situations where some phonemic mismatches between L₁ and L₂ result in an intersection of two interlanguage substitutions and that one of these substitutions is systematically blocked. The rendition of English interdentals /θ, ð/ by Portuguese speakers provides a good case for this. The typical substitution for the /θ/ target is [t] by the learners (e.g. <u>thank</u> realized as [tæŋk]). As we saw earlier, Portuguese also under-differentiates the English /t/ – /tʃ/ contrast. Since [t] and [tʃ] are the allophones of a single phoneme in Portuguese, learners pronounce the target <u>tip</u> and <u>chip</u> homophonously. While the learners realize the English target /t/ as [tʃ] before a high front vowel, they do not reveal the same tendency when the target word has /θ/ before a high front vowel. Thus, a word like <u>think</u> [θɪŋk] is not expected to be rendered as [tʃɪŋk], but rather as [tɪŋk]. In other words learners distinguish the fate of two different [t] sounds. While the native allophonic rule converts the /t/ into [tʃ] before high front vowels, the [t] sound which is the substitute for the target /θ/ does not follow the same path. In this way, learners distinguish the three target language phonemes /θ/, /t/, and /tʃ/, and prevent the neutralization of any contrast. Eckman et al. state that their studies with Korean and Japanese speakers also confirm this tendency by maintaining the target contrasts.

8.3.3 Hypercontrast

Language learners may also be found to have difficulties with a newly acquired contrast and substitute the wrong member of the phonemic pair. Eckman et al. call this phenomenon 'hypercontrast' and state that it results from overgeneralization or hypercorrection. It is suggested that hypercontrasts are motivated by speakers' awareness of past errors they have made via L_1 interference. For example, Spanish speakers have difficulties in acquiring the English /d/ vs. /ð/ contrast, as they are the allophones of a single phoneme in their L_1. Once they acquire the contrast, however, they may produce incorrect [d] for correct [ð] intervocalically. Another example would be the following: a newly learned item with a /d/ target in initial position, which is in accordance with the L_1 pattern, may be produced incorrectly as [ð].

8.4 Markedness

The different types of phonemic mismatches discussed above may be helpful in sorting out different degrees of difficulty that learners experience in the acquisition of L_2 phonology. They, however, are far from depicting the whole picture. The reason for this is the varying nature of structural elements with respect to their markedness. *Markedness* of a structure is derived from its common occurrence in languages. Simply stated, a structure (constraint) A is more marked than another structure B if cross-linguistically the presence of A in a language implies the presence of B, but not vice versa (Eckman 1977, 1985; Eckman and Iverson 1994). Accordingly, two structures A and B, where the first one is more marked than the second, will present different degrees of difficulty for L_2 learners. The classic example frequently discussed consists of the following identically characterized two situations provided by the mismatches of (a) German–English, and (b) English–French, with respect to voiced–voiceless contrast in obstruents. The voiced and voiceless stop series /b, d, g/ and /p, t, k/ are part of the inventory of both English and German. While both languages contrast the voiced and voiceless series in word-initial and word-medial positions, the final position contrast is available only in English (e.g. back – bag); German neutralizes the contrast in favor of the voiceless member, and does not allow the voiced member in this position. The mismatch created in this position can easily predict the difficulty that German speakers have in learning English final voiced stops, with the commonly observed substitutions such as cab [kæb] → [kæp], bed [bɛd] → [bɛt], and so on.

The second situation that can be described identically is a contrast existing in all word positions in L_2 but neutralized in one of the word positions in L_1. For this, we will consider the /ʃ/ vs. /ʒ/ contrast in English and in French. While both languages contrast the two sounds in medial and final positions, the initial contrast is available only in French. The prediction borne out from this discrepancy is that speakers of English learning French will have difficulties for the above-mentioned contrast in word-initial position similar to that of German speakers' difficulties for the final voiced stops of English.

		/ʒ/				Voiced stops		
	Init.	Med.	Final			Init.	Med.	Final
L₁ (English)	–	+	+	L₁ (German)		+	+	–
L₂ (French)	+	+	+	L₂ (English)		+	+	+

Both cases reveal descriptively identical situations in that L₂ has no restrictions of occurrence of the target in any word positions, while L₁ has a positional restriction (i.e. English does not have /ʒ/ in initial position, and German does not have voiced stops in final position). Professionals who have observed these two identically describable mismatches would quickly point out that the difficulties experienced in these two situations are very different, and the acquisition of the English final voiced stops by German speakers is a much greater challenge than acquisition of French initial /ʒ/ by speakers of English. Although both situations described deal with the voicing contrast in obstruents (/ʃ/ – /ʒ/ in fricatives, /p, t, k/ – /b, d, g/ in stops), acquiring the voicing contrast in final position is a more marked phenomenon than doing the same in initial situation. Cross-linguistically, voicing contrast in final position implies the contrast in initial position, but the reverse is not known to be true. Accordingly, the difficulty of acquiring the voiced stops is a result of the more marked nature of voicing contrast in final position. Thus, while simple contrastive analysis can make predictions on the basis of the mismatches between L₁ and L₂, it cannot go beyond that. It is only by referring to the relative markedness of the structures that we can account for the variable performance of the learners for the seemingly identical situations.

Digging further into the markedness relations, we can discover other factors that are relevant for remediation. For example, it has been observed that learners have greater difficulty in acquiring the voicing contrast with velars (i.e. /k/ vs. /g/) than with alveolars (/t/ vs. /d/); bilabials are the least difficult. That is, the tendency for neutralizing the contrast by devoicing is greater as the place of articulation moves further back. There is an aerodynamic explanation for such differences based on the place of articulation. The larger the supraglottal area for a stop, the better it can accommodate glottal flow for some time before oral pressure exceeds subglottal pressure and stops the vocal cord vibration. Since the cavity size gets increasingly smaller as we move from bilabial /b/ to alveolar /d/ and then to velar /g/, the velar has the least chance of maintaining the glottal flow and, thus, is more quickly devoiced.

It has also been suggested (Yavaş 1997) that the height of the vowel preceding the final voiced stop may be an important factor for final devoicing. Specifically, increasing the height (i.e. decreasing the sonority index) of the vowel creates a more favorable environment for the devoicing of the final voiced stop target. The reason offered for this is that high vowels (i.e. lower sonority vowels), by raising the tongue and creating more constriction than other vowels, cause higher supraglottal pressure and are more prone to devoicing (Jaeger 1978).

This vulnerability to devoicing seems to be carried over to the following final voiced stop. Thus, putting everything together, we might find a variable success rate, for example, for the following different combinations with different degrees of markedness:

pig [pɪg] (velar stop preceded by a high V)   most marked
bag [bæg] (velar stop preceded by a low V)
bib [bɪb] (bilabial stop preceded by a high V)
cab [kæb] (bilabial stop preceded by a low V)   least marked

Another example to show the insufficiency of simple contrastive analysis and the necessity of the markedness considerations comes from the coda consonants. While CV is a universally unmarked syllable structure in languages (i.e. no known language lacks CV syllables), any addition to it adds a degree of markedness. A CVC syllable, while not a highly marked structure, may be completely absent from a language, or alternatively, may have some restrictions regarding what class of consonants can occupy the coda position. For example, in a language such as Japanese, only /n/ is permitted as a single coda. A simple contrastive analysis will predict that any single coda other than a nasal (i.e. obstruent, liquid) in an English target word would be problematic for a Japanese speaker. While this prediction is accurate in a general sense, the degree of difficulty experienced by the learners between different classes of sounds is significantly different; for example, obstruent codas present much greater difficulties than liquid codas. This situation, while it will be inexplicable via contrastive analysis, is actually quite expected if we take into account the relative markedness of certain groups of sounds in coda position. Universally, obstruents are more marked (i.e. less expected) as singleton codas. In a language with CVC syllables, the coda position is most usually occupied by sonorants. There are two patterns that are observed in languages that allow CVC syllables: (1) obstruent and sonorant codas (e.g. English), (2) only sonorant codas (e.g. Japanese). There is no language that has obstruent codas but which lacks sonorant codas; this indicates that sonorants are more natural (unmarked) as codas than obstruents. Actual examples from L_2 learning situations support this view strongly. For example, for speakers of languages in which some obstruents and sonorants are permitted as codas, such as Korean, Japanese, and Cantonese (Eckman and Iverson 1994), and Portuguese (Baptista and daSilva Filho 1997), the difficulty encountered in learning single codas of English reflects the same hierarchy of difficulty, i.e. obstruents are more difficult than sonorants.

Patterns of acquisition of English liquids are also quite revealing with respect to markedness conditions. English makes a contrast between /l/ and /ɹ/ in all word positions. A language such as Mandarin restricts its contrasts between the liquids to the onset position; there are no syllabic liquids, and only /r/ is found in coda position. A simple contrastive analysis will predict that Mandarin speakers will be successful in onset position, and the liquid targets of English in other positions will be difficult. Paolillo (1995) examined the rendition of English liquids in five different environments: word-initial (e.g. rain, leaf), postconsonantal (e.g. play, free), intervocalic (e.g. around, polar), syllabic nucleus (e.g. razor, apple), and postvocalic (e.g. fall, cart), and found that there was a hierarchy of environments for successful rendition of the contrasts between the target English liquids. In descending order of favorable environments, it was word-initial, syllabic, intervocalic, postconsonantal, and postvocalic. If learners were not successful in one environment, it implied that they were not successful in the environment(s) that came after in the order. For example, if a learner had a problem in the intervocalic environment, s/he would have a problem in the postconsonantal and postvocalic environments. The explanation comes from the relative markedness of liquids in different environments, which relates to relative acoustic salience in each of these environments. Specifically, the relative salience is higher in initial or syllabic position than in other transitory positions or in clusters. This example shows that learners' difficulties cannot be explained by a simple contrastive analysis mismatch between L_1 and L_2, and the relative markedness of the targets in different environments should be considered.

For another example of the invaluable insights we can gain from markedness, we turn our attention to the aspirated vs. unaspirated stop mismatches between English and several other languages, which are a significant source of trouble. While English has aspirated stops in syllable-initial position, stops in languages such as Spanish, Portuguese, and so on are not aspirated. Thus, it is commonplace that speakers coming from these languages experience difficulties in their attempts to learn English; they replace the aspirated target stops [p^h, t^h, k^h] with their unaspirated versions [p, t, k]. While a contrastive analysis between L_1 and L_2 can predict that these mismatches would create difficulties, it cannot say anything about the varying degrees of difficulty among different targets. Several studies (Laeufer 1996; Port and Rotunno 1978; Thurnburg and Ryalls 1998; Major 1987; Yavaş 1996, 2002) found that learners experience less difficulty in acquiring the aspirated stops as we go from the bilabial to alveolar and to velar. In other words, we are dealing with the relative markedness among [p^h, t^h, k^h], the first being the most marked and the last being the least marked. The reason for the varying degrees of ease/difficulty (markedness) is related to the degree of abruptness of the pressure drop upon the release of a stop. The more sudden (abrupt) the pressure drop is, the sooner the voicing of the next segment (vowel or liquid) starts. In the case of different places of articulation, differences in the mobility between the articulators involved in occlusion are responsible for the different degrees of abruptness of the pressure drop. The tongue dorsum separates more slowly (i.e. less abruptly from the velum for the velar /k/ than the tongue tip from the alveolar ridge /t/, or the lips /p/). The slower, thus longer, release delays the proper pressure differential to begin voicing for the following segment, thus the longer lag (aspiration) for velars than for alveolars and labials.

It has also been suggested (Weismer 1979; Flege 1991; Klatt 1975; Yavaş 2002) that the sonority of the following segment may influence the degree of aspiration of the stop. An initial stop seems to have a longer lag before a segment that has a narrower opening (i.e. lower sonority index) such as a high vowel, than before another that has a more open articulation (i.e. high sonority index) such as a low vowel. The reason for this is that lower-sonority items (e.g. high vowels) have a more obstructed cavity than high-sonority items (e.g. low vowels). Since the high tongue position that is assumed during the stop closure in anticipation of a subsequent high vowel would result in a less abrupt pressure drop, a stop produced as such will have a longer lag than before a low vowel.

Putting all these together, we can show the relative markedness of the following:

Least marked:	kit	(velar with a high vowel)
	cat	(velar with a low vowel)
	tit	(alveolar with a high vowel)
	tat	(alveolar with a low vowel)
	pit	(bilabial with a high vowel)
Most marked:	pat	(bilabial with a low vowel)

Our final example with respect to markedness comes from a sequential relationship and looks at the English double onsets in which the first member is /s/. The possibilities can be described as (a) /s/ + stop (e.g. speak, stop, skip), (b) /s/ + nasal (e.g. small, snail), (c) /s/ + lateral (e.g. sleep), and (d) /s/ + glide (e.g. swim). Several languages that allow double onsets do not have the above combinations, and Spanish is one such language. Thus, it is expected that Spanish speakers will have difficulties with the initial sC (where C = consonant) targets in learning English and, indeed, they do. What is interesting, however, is that the difficulties experienced by the learners are not the same with respect to the different combinations of s-clusters (a), (b), (c), and (d) listed above. A decreasing degree of difficulty has been observed for (a) – (d) in the learning of English: '/s/ + stop' being the hardest, and /s + w/ being the least hard.

While a contrastive analysis between the two languages could predict that English initial sC clusters will be difficult for Spanish speakers (because Spanish does not have them), it will have no means of going beyond that to account for the different degrees of difficulty observed. Here, again, the explanation will come from the relative markedness of the targets. As mentioned in chapter 6, the relative naturalness of clusters is closely linked to the principle of sonority sequencing, which dictates that the sonority values should rise as we move from the margin of the syllable to the peak (nucleus). Among the targets in question, one of them, (a) '/s/ + stop', violates this principle, because the first member of the onset cluster, /s/, a voiceless fricative, has a higher sonority value, 3, than the second member, /p, t, k/, which has 1. Thus, as we move from C_1 to C_2, a 'fall', rather than the expected 'rise', in sonority takes place. Since this is a highly unexpected (marked) combination in universal terms, it is not surprising that it proves to be a very difficult target to acquire. The remaining targets, (b) '/s/ + nasal', (c) '/s/ + lateral', and (d) '/s + w/', all satisfy the sonority sequencing generalization, because there is a 'rise' in sonority as we move from C_1 to C_2 (/s/ + nasal: 3 to 5; /s/ + lateral: 3 to 6;

/s + w/: 3 to 8). As we noted earlier, there was a decreasing degree of difficulty among these three targets, and this also is explainable with reference to their relative naturalness. The fact that laterals are higher in sonority than nasals, and glides are higher than laterals, results in different degrees of sharpness in the sonority jumps between C_1 and C_2, and this seems to be responsible for the greater ease for /sw/ (sonority difference of 5) than /sl/ (sonority difference of 3). Similarly, /sl/ has a bigger difference than /s + nasal/ (sonority difference 2) and thus, expectedly, provides less difficulty.

It is also worth mentioning that speakers coming from languages that do not permit any onset clusters reveal different modification patterns with respect to different types of English clusters in contact situations. Error patterns of speakers of Egyptian Arabic, Sindhi, and Bengali (Broselow 1993) show that sonority sequencing-violating 's + stop' clusters are modified with a prothetic vowel, while the ones that do not violate the sonority sequencing receive an epenthetic vowel, which results in a speedier, native-like pattern:

Egyptian Arabic

| street | → [istirit] | sweater | → [siwetar] |
| study | → [istadi] | slide | → [silajd] |

Sindhi

| school | → [ɪskul] | please | → [piliz] |
| spelling | → [ɪspelɪŋg] | slipper | → [siliper] |

Bengali

| stamp | → [istamp] | glass | → [gelas] |
| school | → [iskul] | slate | → [selet] |

While, for reasons of space, we will not go on to other examples that demonstrate the importance of markedness, similar examples can easily be multiplied for many other phonological structures. The important message that comes out of all these is to alert remediators about the indispensable nature of such information. The more one can see the highly structured nature of events, the better remediator one can become.

All the above clearly demonstrates that interlanguage phonology is governed by the following three components: L_1, L_2, and universal principles (markedness). Although all these factors influence the productions of the learners, the role of each may be different at different stages of interlanguage development. The Ontogeny Phylogeny Model (hereafter OPM) proposed by Major (2001) deals with just that and states that in the earlier stages of L_2 acquisition L_1 interference is the dominant factor; the role of universals is minimal. Gradually, the influence of L_2 and universals increases, and the role of L_1 decreases. In later stages of acquisition, the only element on the rise is the influence of L_2 with concurrent decline of the role of L_1 and universals, as shown in figure 8.2.

Although this general account may be sufficient for the *normal phenomena*, Major carefully points out that the proportions of the three components will vary, depending on the phenomena under scrutiny. For example, in similar

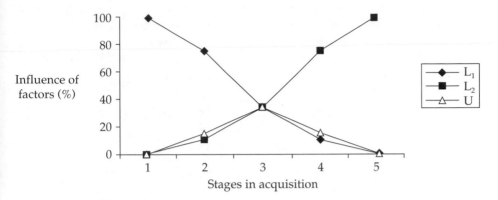

Figure 8.2 The Ontogeny Phylogeny Model: normal phenomena
(*Source*: from R. C. Major (2001) *Foreign Accent: The Ontogeny and Phylogeny of Second Language Phonology*. Reproduced by permission of Lawrence Erlbaum Associates.)

phenomena, L_2 increases in a slower fashion than above and the effects of L_1 also decrease slowly. Also, the increase and later decrease of universals are slower. To give an example for a similar phenomenon, we can think of the relationship between alveolar stops of English /t, d/ and their slightly fronted counterparts, dental stops in Spanish and Portuguese. Since such minimal distinctions are less likely to be noticed by the learner, a Spanish speaker would be likely to retain the L_1 interference longer here in his/her attempts at the target English alveolar stops than, let us say, for his/her substitutions of the alveolar trill for the English target retroflex approximant. Major's account of the similar phenomena is given in figure 8.3.

In the acquisition of the marked phenomena, earlier stages are again dominated by L_1 influence, and the acquisition of L_2 is again slower than for the normal phenomena. However, the effects of L_1 and universals are different in

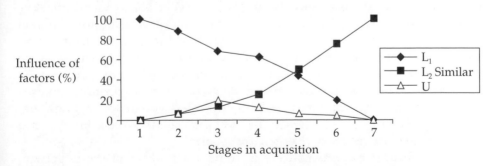

Figure 8.3 The Ontogeny Phylogeny Model: similar phenomena
(*Source*: from R. C. Major (2001) *Foreign Accent: The Ontogeny and Phylogeny of Second Language Phonology*. Reproduced by permission of Lawrence Erlbaum Associates.)

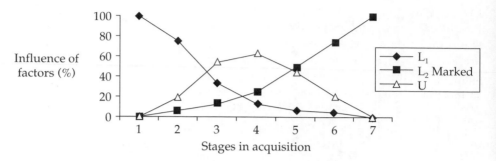

Figure 8.4   The Ontogeny Phylogeny Model: marked phenomena
(*Source*: from R. C. Major (2001) *Foreign Accent: The Ontogeny and Phylogeny of Second Language Phonology*. Reproduced by permission of Lawrence Erlbaum Associates.)

subsequent stages; the effects of L_1 decrease faster here and we see a rapid increase in the effects of universals. In later stages, the decrease in L_1 and universals are reminiscent of the similar phenomena, i.e. slow. Major shows this in figure 8.4.

Major also points out that his OPM model can account for the stylistic variation in interlanguage phonological production. Accordingly, as style becomes more formal, L_2 increases, L_1 decreases and universals increase then decrease. While it is stated this way, we are also reminded that, depending on the stage of the learner, the proportion of the different components can vary from speaker to speaker for the same style.

Summary

In this chapter we looked at several important variables that are influential in shaping the phonological productions of L_2 learners. We saw that contrastive phonological information can accurately pinpoint several difficulties that are encountered by learners of specific languages. Beyond the simple contrastive patterns, however, lie deeper principles which can account for different degrees of difficulty related to phonemic contrasts. Target contrasts are incorporated into the interlanguage phonology progressively; learners seem to have greater facility in creating a phonemic contrast of the target language in basic (tautomorphemic) contexts than in derived (heteromorphemic) contexts. Also observed is that whenever we have two intersecting interlanguage substitutions, one of these is systematically blocked (i.e. deflected contrast), and hypercontrasts are results of overgeneralization.

Native language patterns that are in conflict with those of the target language alone are not sufficient to account for all of the learners' difficulties; markedness of the L_2 structures also plays an important role in shaping the interlanguage phonology. Major's Ontogeny and Phylogeny Model, dealing with the three components of interlanguage phonology – L_1, L_2, and universals – has different predictions about the relative weight of these factors in the acquisition of different phenomena. Similar phenomena and marked phenomena are acquired more slowly than normal phenomena. In the earlier stages of acquisition, the patterns are basically governed by the effects of L_1 for all phenomena, the effects of universals are minimal, and the gradual decrease of L_1 influence is slower in similar phenomena than in others. In later stages, the influences of L_1 and universals decrease more slowly in similar and marked phenomena than in normal phenomena.

All the above are indicative of the fact that the learning of L_2 phonology is a highly structured process, and thus attempts in remediation should consider as many of these factors as possible. The capabilities of practices of remediators (language teachers, speech therapists) will definitely be enhanced by the inclusion of a greater number of linguistically based courses in their training.

EXERCISES

1. First, transcribe the following word-pairs, and then, with the contrastive
    information you had in this chapter, identify the languages whose
    native speakers would have problems related to these target English
    word-pairs.

    cheap – chip
    sieve – save
    age – edge
    bend – band
    band – bond
    fool – full
    backs – box
    look – Luke
    feast – fist
    wait – wet
    slept – slapped

2. Now, do the same for the following target pairs in contrast.

    glass – grass
    peach – beach
    pour – four
    went – vent
    feel – veal
    vowel – bowel
    dense – dens
    three – tree
    thick – sick
    those – doze
    leaf – leave
    rope – robe
    stow – stove
    curved – curbed
    math – mat
    forth – force
    soothe – sued
    clothed – closed
    sin – sing
    cart – card
    thin – chin
    lamp – ramp

sift – shift
sink – zinc
cheer – sheer
surge – search
dug – duck

3. Now, do the same for the following triplets.

huck – hock – hawk
panned – punned – pond
bag – bug – bog
bid – bead – bed
stack – stuck – stock

4. Although contrastive phonological information is indispensable for the prediction of learners' difficulties, it is not sufficient in many cases, because for certain phenomena, constraints based on universal markedness have been shown to be influential in explaining the degree of difficulty of targets. Order the following targets in terms of difficulty (from most difficult to least difficult), and state the rationale.

(a) single-coda consonants:
deal, deer, deem, beast, beach

(b) liquids:
/l/ full, elect, lamp, fly, belt
/ɹ/ green, boring, tire, room, card

(c) /s + C/ onsets:
slow, sticker, swing, small

(d) aspiration:
pig, keep, park, course, torn, tease

(e) final voiced stops:
lab, bid, rod, rag, rib, wig

5. Japanese lacks English target /θ/ and learners replace it with a [s] (e.g. thank [sæŋk]). Also, [ʃ] is an allophone of /s/ in Japanese before /i/. This results in renditions such as sip [ʃɪp]. While we have these

two patterns (/s/ as [ʃ] before /i/, and /θ/ as [s]) Japanese speakers' rendition of English <u>think</u> is [sɪŋk] and not [ʃɪŋk]. Does this support or counter-argue for the case made for deflected contrast in section 8.3.2. State your reasoning.

6. Transcribe the following. Citations on American English (*from* T. McArthur, *The English Languages* (Cambridge: Cambridge University Press, 1998, pp. 220–7).

    (a) The American I have heard up to the present is a tongue as distinct from English as Patagonian. (*Rudyard Kipling* 1889)

    ....

    ....

    (b) The rich have always liked to assume the costumes of the poor. Take the American language. It is more than a million words wide, and new terms are constantly added to its infinite variety. Yet, as the decade starts, the US vocabulary seems to have shrunk to child size. (*Stefan Kanfer*, 1980)

    ....

    ....

    ....

    ....

    ....

    (c) I mean that almost everyone who touches upon American speech assumes that it is inferior to British speech. Just as the Englishman, having endured for a time the society of his equals, goes on to bask in the sunshine of aristocracy, so the American, when he has used the American language for business or for familiar intercourse, may then, for higher or more serious purposes, go on to the aristocratic or royal language of Great Britain. (*Fred Newton Scott*, 1917)

    ....

    ....

    ....

    ....

    ....

    ....

    ....

nine

Spelling and Pronunciation

9.1 Irregularity of English Spelling

In chapter 2, we saw that the ideal alphabetic system should have a one-to-one relationship between the graphemes and the phonemes of a language. In other words, the ideal writing system should be phonemic in representation. As pointed out in chapter 1, however, this ideal one-to-one relationship is violated very frequently in English; the same phoneme can be represented by different letters (e.g. /i/ each, either, scene), the same letter may represent different phonemes (e.g. a in gate, any, father, above), and phonemes may be represented by a combination of letters (e.g. th for /θ/ or /ð/ as in thin and this respectively, gh for /f/ as in enough).

The reasons for such discrepancies, embedded in the history of English, are manifold. To start with, Christian missionaries used a 23-letter alphabet for the 35 or so phonemes of Old English, which forced the deviation from the one-to-one principle.

After the Norman Conquest of England in the eleventh century, the French scribes introduced several new spelling conventions. Accordingly, the following changes occurred. Old English cw was replaced by qu (e.g. quick), h was replaced by gh (e.g. might), c was replaced by ch (e.g. church), u was replaced by ou (e.g. house). Thus, by the beginning of the fifteenth century, the spelling of English had become a mixture of Old English and the changes made by French scribes.

Some of the discrepancies were due to changes in pronunciation that took place after the spelling system was established. For example, /l/ before a /d/ in 'modal verbs' such as would, could, and should, which was pronounced, but then disappeared from the pronunciation, is retained in other words (e.g. cold, hold). Velar stops, /k, g/, disappeared from the pronunciation before a nasal in syllable-initial position (e.g. knee, knife, gnat, gnaw); they are retained if the two sounds are in different syllables (e.g. acne [æk.ni], agnostic [æg.nɑstɪk]). Also noteworthy is the disappearance of /l/ before /f/, /k/, /m/ when simultaneously preceded by a which is standing for a low vowel /æ, ɑ, ɔ/: a __ /f/ (e.g. calf, half) but not in self; a __ /k/ (e.g. walk, talk) but not in silk, elk; a __ /m/ (e.g. calm, almond) but not in film, helm. Also, the deletion of final [ə] from Old English (OE) to Middle English (ME) gave us the so-called 'silent-e' as in nose, name, and so on.

The fricative system underwent significant changes; OE had only voiceless fricative phonemes /f, θ, s/ (and /x/, which was lost from OE to ME). The sounds [v, ð, z], which appeared as allophones of the voiceless ones became phonemic in ME. The sound /ʒ/ arose in the seventeenth century from the palatalization of the [zj] cluster (e.g. vision [vɪzjən] → [vɪʒən]). Mention also should be made of [ŋ], which was an allophone of /n/ before velars. Later in the sixteenth century /g/ was dropped after [ŋ] in certain positions and gave rise to the phonemic contrast between /n/ and /ŋ/ (e.g. sin [sɪn] – sing [sɪŋ]).

The Great Vowel Shift, which took place from the Middle English period through the eighteenth century, introduced a very significant reorganization of the vowel system by means of a series of modifications. Briefly stated, earlier long vowels were raised (geese [gɛːs] → [gis], and vowels already produced with high tongue position became diphthongs (e.g. tide [tid] → [taɪd], loud [lud] → [laʊd]). Since these changes occurred after the introduction of printing, no corresponding shift in spelling was made. Also, the fact that many printers came from the continent (for example, Dutch printers introduced the Dutch spelling of word-initial /g/ as gh, as in ghost), as well as any lack of standardization (there was no spelling authority) contributed to the problem.

Borrowings from French (e.g. bizarre, bouquet, beige, debris), Italian (e.g. motto, mezzanine, stucco, grotto), Spanish (e.g. junta, galleon, marijuana), German (e.g. schnapps, Gestalt, poltergeist), Portuguese (e.g. macaque, verandah), Russian (e.g. czar, intelligentsia), and Hungarian (e.g. goulash, czardas) retained their original spelling and created more irregularities. Not all borrowed items came with their original spelling. In some cases, they were introduced with 'transliteration' (e.g. items from Greek such as pneumonia, and mnemonic). Since these violate English phonotactic rules, they are pronounced without the first consonant.

In some cases, problems arose because of the zealotry of some academics to make the spelling reflect Latin and Greek etymology. For example, the words debt and doubt came to English from French dette and doute, respectively, without a b. The so-called 'silent b' was inserted to make the words resemble the original Latin debitum and dubitare, respectively.

Finally, for some words, confusion resulted because of sheer carelessness. For example, French coronelle, from which English colonel is derived, is adapted from Italian colonello. When the word entered the English vocabulary in the sixteenth century, it was spelled with an r. The confusion was resolved by the combination of Italian spelling and French pronunciation.

9.2 Phoneme–grapheme Correspondences in English

In dealing with the correspondences between graphemes and phonemes we start with the list of phonemes, and the graphemes used to represent them.

9.2.1 Consonants

Phoneme	Grapheme	Examples
/p/	p	*pull, leap*
	pp	*supper, apply*
/b/	b	*bed, lab*
	bb	*rubber, lobby*
/t/	t	*table, bet*
	tt	*attack, attend*
	th	*thyme, Thames*
	ed	*talked, walked*
/d/	d	*day, bed*
	dd	*ladder, addict*
	ed	*robbed, pulled*
/k/	c	*care, car*
	cc	*accord, acclaim*
	ck	*sack, back*
	ch	*character, chorus*
	cq	*acquire, acquaint*
	k	*keep, broker*
	qu	*liquor*
/g/	g	*give, bag*
	gg	*mugged, egg*
	gh	*ghost, ghetto*
	gu	*guard*
/f/	f	*fence, thief*
	ff	*offer*
	gh	*rough*
	ph	*phoneme*
/v/	v	*vowel*
	vv	*flivver*
	f	*of*
	ph	*Stephen*
/θ/	th	*thin*
/ð/	th	*they*
/s/	s	*sell*
	ss	*boss*
	sc	*scene*
	c	*cell*

/z/	z	*zero*
	zz	*puzzle*
	s	*is*
	ss	*scissors*
	x	*xerox*

/ʃ/	sh	*share*
	ce	*ocean*
	ch	*Chicago*
	ci	*special*
	s	*sure*
	sci	*conscience*
	sch	*schnapps*
	se	*nauseous*
	si	*tension*
	ss	*tissue*
	ti	*nation*

/ʒ/	g	*massage*
	s	*measure*
	si	*vision*
	z	*azure*

/tʃ/	ch	*chip*
	tch	*watch*
	t	*nature*
	ti	*question*

/dʒ/	j	*jail*
	d	*gradual*
	dg	*ridge*
	g	*magic*
	gg	*exaggerate*

/l/	l	*lake*
	ll	*sell*

/ɹ/	r	*rain*
	rr	*borrow*
	rh	*Rhode Island*

/m/	m	*mark*
	mm	*summer*

/n/	n	*name*
	nn	*tanner*

/ŋ/	ng	*king*
	n	*sink*

/w/	w	*week*
	u	*queen*

/j/	y	*year*
	i	*union*

/h/	h	*house*
	wh	*who*

If we look at the correspondences via reverse direction, that is, from grapheme to phoneme, the relationships are less diverse. First of all, several letters in the following list have regular phoneme correspondences. The ones given in bold type also have this regular correspondence in double letters.

Letter	Phoneme	Example
d/dd	/d/	*day, ladder*
f/ff	/f/	*fame, sufficient*
j	/dʒ/	*joy, jail* (Spanish borrowings are exceptions, *junta*)
m/mm	/m/	*moon, summer*
n/nn	/n/	*noon, innocent*
p/pp	/p/	*pay, appear*
r/rr	/ɹ/	*rain, carrot*
t/tt	/t/	*table, attack*
v	/v/	*vote, avid*
y	/j/	*yes, beyond*
z/zz	/z/	*zero, buzz*

Two letters, c and g, each have two corresponding phonemes:

c	/k/	*cat, cool*
	/s/	*cell, ceiling*
	(also, as /tʃ/ in some borrowings, e.g. *cello*)	
g	/g/	*get, bag*
	/dʒ/	*gem, rage*
	(also, as /ʒ/ in French borrowings, e.g. *prestige*)	

The letter s is the most prolific consonant, with the following correspondences:

s/ss	/s/	*sip, assist*
	/ʃ/	*tension, pressure*

It also has the following correspondences as a single letter:

s	/z/	*raise*
	/ʒ/	*vision*

The letter x is the only consonant that stands for a sequence of two phonemes; it represents /gz/ if the vowel following is in the tonic syllable (e.g. exact, exaggerate). If the stress falls on the vowel before 'x', then it corresponds to

/ks/ (e.g. <u>sex</u>, <u>excellent</u>, <u>execute</u>; a couple of words, <u>exit</u>, <u>exile</u>, may have either /ks/ or /gz/). Two double letters, gg and <u>cc</u>, have two corresponding values each:

gg	/g/	*egg*
	/dʒ/	*exaggerate*
cc	/k/	*account*
	/ks/	*accent*

The following five single letters have regular phoneme correspondence as well as being silent:

b	/b/	*book, rub*
	silent	*lamb, bomb*
h	/h/	*he, home*
	silent	*hour, honest* (words of Romance origin)
k	/k/	*kitchen, cake*
	silent	*knife, know*
l	/l/	*lake, ball*
	silent	*would, should*
w	/w/	*we, wake*
	silent	*answer, wrong*

Finally, we should mention that there are some isolated irregularities, as <u>m</u> is silent in <u>mnemonic</u>, <u>n</u> is silent in <u>autumn</u> (pronounced in <u>autumnal</u>), and <u>d</u> is silent in <u>handsome</u>, <u>sandwich</u>.

Besides the single and double occurrence of one letter, English spelling makes use of some combinations of consonant letters, with the following phoneme correspondences:

ck	/k/	*sick*
tch	/tʃ/	*watch*
ph	/f/	*phoneme* (/p/ + /h/ in successive syllables, *uphill*)
sh	/ʃ/	*shirt*

The following two-consonant letter combinations have two different values:

ch	/tʃ/	*change*
	/k/	*character*

in words and place names of French origin, it stands for /ʃ/ (*chef, Chicago*)

| gh | /f/ | enough |
| | silent | daughter |

in a few words, g<u>h</u> stands for /g/, as in *ghost, ghetto*

| ng | /ŋ/ | sing |
| | /ŋg/ | finger |

| th | /θ/ | thin |
| | /ð/ | this |

in a few words, it stands for /t/ (*Thomas, thyme*).

9.2.2 Vowels

The phoneme-to-grapheme correspondences for the vowels are as follows:

Phoneme	Grapheme	Example
/i/	e	be
	ea	meat
	ee	free
	y	silly
	ie	niece
	ei	deceive
	i	machine
	eo	people
	ey	key
	oe	amoeba
/ɪ/	i	miss
	y	mystic
	u	busy
	e	exam
	o	women
	ee	been
	ui	build
/e/	ay	say
	ai	wait
	a	name
	ei	weigh
	ea	great
	ey	they
	au	gauge
/ɛ/	e	set
	ea	heavy
	a	many
	ai	said

	ie	*friend*
	ue	*guess*
	ae	*aesthetic*
	eo	*leopard*
/æ/	a	*sat*
	au	*laugh*
/ʌ/	u	*bus*
	o	*son*
	ou	*couple*
	oo	*blood*
	oe	*does*
	a	*about*
	ai	*fountain*
	ia	*parliament*
/ɑ/	ea	*heart*
	o	*hot*
	a	*father*
	ow	*knowledge*
	e	*sergeant*
/ɔ/	a	*talk*
	o	*dog*
	aw	*saw*
	au	*cause*
	oa	*broad*
	ou	*ought*
/o/	ew	*sew*
	o	*no*
	oa	*soak*
	ou	*though*
	eau	*plateau*
	ow	*blow*
	eo	*yeoman*
/ʊ/	oo	*good*
	u	*put*
	ou	*should*
	o	*woman*
/u/	ui	*fruit*
	oo	*mood*
	ou	*soup*
	o	*who*
	oe	*shoe*
	eu	*neutral*
	au	*beautiful*
	ew	*grew*

/aɪ/	y	sky
	i	site
	ie	died
	uy	buy
	e	eye
	ai	aisle
	ei	height
/aʊ/	ow	vowel
	ou	about
/ɔɪ/	oy	boy
	oi	avoid

As in the case of the consonants, if we look at the grapheme-to-phoneme relationship of the vowels, we can find more regular correspondences. The five vowel letters and their sound values in monosyllabic words can be given as follows:

Letter	Phoneme	Example
a	(1) /e/	sale
	(2) /æ/	bad
e	(1) /i/	cede
	(2) /ɛ/	bet
i	(1) /aɪ/	dine
	(2) /ɪ/	sit
o	(1) /o/	nose
	(2) /a/	dot
u	(1) /ju/	mute
	(2) /ʌ/	but

If the 'vowel letter' in a monosyllabic word is followed by a consonant, which is followed by the letter e at the end of the word, the sound value for the vowel letter is the one given in (1) (the well-known 'silent e' rule taught in schools); otherwise, the sound value is the one given in (2).

The situation is more complicated in polysyllabic words. For example, how do we know the sound values of a in mutation and of u in reduction? Both in [mjuteʃən] and in [ɹədʌkʃən] the stress is on the syllable before the suffix. The rule is first to ignore the ending -ion, and then count the consonants that follow the vowel letter in question. In mutation, the vowel letter a is followed by a single consonant and thus the sound value will be the one given in (1), namely /e/ as in [mjuteʃən]. In reduction, the vowel u is followed by two consonants and thus the sound value is the one given in (2), namely /ʌ/ as in [ɹədʌkʃən]. Although this is quite workable, and indeed valid for any word with a suffix with the letter i if followed by a vowel, and then anything else (e.g. -ial, -ious, -iary), it is not problem-free. Specifically, there are problems with the letter i in the root. While in submission and addiction, the non-suffixal i is followed by two consonant letters and has the predicted value (2), namely /ɪ/, in revision and provision, it is followed by one consonant letter, but does not have the predicted sound value of (1), /aɪ/, as the pronunciations are [ɹəvɪʒən] and [pɹovɪʒən]. Unlike the examples discussed here, in some of the examples we looked at earlier, we saw the vowel letters represented the two possible sounds (i.e. long/short vowels) which cannot be accounted for by the number of following consonants. For example, in pairs such as grateful /e/ – gratitude /æ/, mine /aɪ/ – mineral /ɪ/, the first words have the bold-type focal vowel letter representing the long vowel/diphthong, which is in accordance with the expectations because the vowel letter is followed by a single consonant. The second words in these pairs, however, employ short vowels despite the fact that they are followed by a single consonant, and, according to the expectations, should employ long vowels.

Besides the single vowel letters, English uses several vowel-letter combinations for certain sound correspondences. The alphabet, which was borrowed from the Romans, provides five vowel letters, i, e, a, o, u, which were sufficient for Latin. However, English has many more vowels, and thus several vowel-letter combinations, called 'digraphs', are utilized to meet this demand. The values of the vowel-letter combinations do not change in stressed/unstressed syllables. (Most common values are given first, and then the secondary values are listed.)

Letter combination	Phoneme(s)
au	/ɔ/ cause; also /æ/ laugh
(rarely at the end of words)	
ea	/i/ meat; also /e/ great, and /ɛ/ heavy
(rarely at the end of words)	
eu	/ju/ or /u/ neutral
ie	/aɪ/ died, or /i/ niece; also /ɛ/ friend
(rarely at the beginning of words)	
oa	/o/ soak; also /ɔ/ broad
(rarely at the beginning of words)	
oi	/ɔɪ/ avoid
oo	/u/ mood; also /ʌ/ blood, and /ʊ/ good
ui	/ju/ or /u/ suit, fruit; also /ɪ/ build
ou	/aʊ/ about; also /ʌ/ couple, /ɔ/ ought, /o/ though, /u/ soup

We should also mention the letters y and w, which have sound correspondences related to consonants and vowels. As we discussed earlier, as syllable
onsets, as in yesterday and week, they stand for the glides /j/ and /w/, respectively. The letter y, after a vowel letter, as in ay, ey, uy, oy, stands for /e/ (e.g.
day), /i/ (e.g. *key*), /aɪ/ (e.g. *buy*), /ɔɪ/ (e.g. *boy*). The letter w, in the same position, represents /ɔ/ (e.g. *saw*), /o/ (e.g. *sew*), and /aʊ/ (e.g. *vowel*). The letter
y, occurring in final position after a consonant, represents /i/ (e.g. *happy, baby*),
or /aɪ/ (e.g. *fly, sky*), and usually changes to i when a suffix is added (e.g. *defy
– defiant; duty – dutiful; happy – happiness; lively – livelihood*). This change does
not apply with a suffix starting with i (to avoid two i's. Thus, we get *baby –
babyish, lobby – lobbyist, defy – defying*). Finally, when an -s suffix is added, y
turns into -ie (e.g. *deny – denies; fly – flies*). This rule has the following two exceptions: (a) y, which is part of an oy, ay, ey combination (e.g. *employ – employs;
obey – obeys*), and (b) -s cannot be the possessive suffix (e.g. *Tommy's, anybody's*).

9.3 Morphological Basis of English Spelling

Despite all these apparent variations and discrepancies, which violate one-to-
one phoneme–grapheme correspondences, English spelling reveals some useful lexical and morphophonemic information. For example, although prefixes
and suffixes often change their pronunciation from one word to another
depending on the phonological environment (allomorphy), their spelling is generally kept constant. For example, the -ed of the past tense is pronounced differently in tempted [tɛmptəd], sipped [sɪpt], and jogged [dʒɑgd]. Similarly, the
-s of the plural/possessive is realized differently in cats/cat's [kæts], and
dogs/dog's [dɔgz].

Roots and stems also maintain their spelling from word to word, despite their
differences in pronunciation due to full/reduced vowel alternations correlated
with stress, as in

telegraph [tɛləgɹæf]	–	telegraphy [təlɛgɹəfi]
agile [ædʒəl]	–	agility [ədʒɪləti]
senile [sinaɪl]	–	senility [sənɪləti]
plural [plʊɹəl]	–	plurality [pləɹæləti]

and in words in which vowels alternate in stressed syllables of morphologically related pairs, where the long vowel/diphthong is shortened when it
comes three syllables from the end of the word.

e – æ	sane [sen]	sanity [sænəti]
i – ɛ	meter [miDɚ]	metrical [mɛtɹəkəl]
aɪ – ɪ	mine [maɪn]	mineral [mɪnəɹəl]
o – ɑ	verbose [vɚbos]	verbosity [vɚbɑsəti]
u – ʌ	consume [kənsum]	consumption [kənsʌmpʃən]
aʊ – ʌ	pronounce [pɹənaʊns]	pronunciation [pɹənʌnsieʃən]

Prefixes borrowed from Latin behave differently than others in that their final consonant assimilates to the initial consonant of the stem. For example, the adjectival negative prefix in- changes to im- before p, b, m (consonant letters that represent bilabial consonants /p, b, m/) as in im-balanced, im-possible, im-mature, while remaining in- otherwise. There are other examples given in manuals, for example ad- "toward" is characterized as assimilated in ab-breviate, af-fect, al-lege, ap-point, ar-rive; the prefix con- "together" as in com-bat, col-lect, cor-rect; and the prefix sub- "under" (e.g. sub-merge) is considered assimilated in suf-fer, sug-gest, sup-port, and so on. While this way of looking at things may be accurate historically, I do not think one should put faith in its transparency in present-day usage, and such words should be treated as indivisible.

The morphological base of English orthography also surfaces in certain consonant letters' alternating behavior (silent/pronounced). For example, a postvocalic g before final nasals /n/ and /m/ is silent in sign, and paradigm ([saɪn], [pæɹədaɪm]), but is pronounced in derivatives of these words in signature, and paradigmatic. Similarly, word-final b after m is silent in bomb and limb, but is pronounced in related bombardment and limbic. Finally, word-final n after m is silent, as in damn and autumn, but is pronounced in related damnation and autumnal.

Morphology–orthography correspondence sometimes takes the form of 'same pronunciation but different spelling'. The suffix morpheme [əbl], which makes a root into an adjective, is orthographically represented as either -able or -ible. The orthographic representation is largely predictable on the basis of the sound value of presuffixal (root-final) consonant letters c and g; if these letters are pronounced as /k/ and /g/ respectively, then the ending is always -able (e.g. applicable, eradicable, navigable); if, on the other hand, they are pronounced as /s/ and /dʒ/ respectively, then the spelling of the suffix, commonly but not always, is -ible, as in eligible, invincible, reducible. (This is not applicable to cases in which there is a 'silent e' between c and the suffix; in these cases, the spelling of the suffix is -able, as in serviceable and changeable.)

An additional prediction can be made on the basis of whether the root takes the suffix -ation or -ion, -ition, -ive. If the former is the case (e.g. consider – consideration; apply – application; irritate – irritation, then the spelling of [əbl] is -able. If, on the other hand, the latter is the case (e.g. depress – depression, defense – defensive, digest – digestion – digestive) then the spelling of [əbl] mostly is -ible, as in depressible, defensible, and digestible (exceptions to this principle are found, as in support – supportive becomes supportable not *supportible, adopt – adoption – adoptable not *adoptible).

9.4 American English vs. British English

There are several differences in the spelling conventions used between American English and British English. The following illustrates some of the more noted ones.

(a) Nouns ending in or in AE are spelled as our in BE (e.g. armor, behavior, color, tumor, humor, favor, harbor, honor, labor, parlor, vapor, odor, rigor, rumor, splendor, vigor). The following nouns, however, are spelt the same way in the two varieties: error, collector, glamour, terror.

(b) In several words, there is a transposition of r and e between the two varieties. (the ending is -er in AE and -re in BE):

AE	BE
center	centre
fiber	fibre
somber	sombre
goiter	goitre
theater	theatre
meter	metre (unit of length), meter (instrument)

(c) Several words show -ize (AE) and -ise (BE) correspondence:

AE	BE
capitalize	capitalise
dramatize	
naturalize	
analyze	
realize	
organize	

(d) Sometimes the AE unstressed prefix -in (e.g. inquire, insure) has the corresponding -en in BE (enquire, ensure). This is not observed in all instances; both varieties agree, for example, in encamp, enchant, endorse, enclose, enable, endanger, enliven, enlist.

(e) Several words have the change of s (AE) to c (BE); thus, -ense of the following nouns such as defense, license, offense are realized -ence in BE.

(f) In several words a simple letter representation corresponds to digraphs (two-letter combinations) in BE:

AE	BE
anemia	anaemia
anesthetic	anaesthetic
archeology	archaeology
cesarian	caesarian
encyclopedia	encyclopaedia
ether	aether
leukemia	leukaemia
medieval	mediaeval
pediatrics	paediatrics
diarrhea	diarrhoea
maneuver	manoeuvre
fetus	foetus
estrogen	oestrogen

(g)   The ending -og of AE is -ogue in BE:

AE	BE
analog	analogue
catalog	catalogue
dialog	dialogue
epilog	epilogue
monolog	monologue
travelog	travelogue

(h)   While, on the one hand, we observe consonant doubling in AE at the end of verbs such as appall, enthrall, instill, fulfill, there is a correspondence of single versus double consonants in the other direction in the unstressed syllables (there is a drop of the redundant consonant letter in AE):

AE	BE
counselor	counsellor
kidnaper	kidnapper
traveler	traveller
worshiping	worshipping
jeweler	jeweller
panelist	panellist

(i)   There are several words of different types that are spelt differently in the two varieties:

AE	BE
airplane	aeroplane
check	cheque
draft	draught
curb	kerb
story	storey
mask	masque
mustache	moustache
plow	plough
skeptical	sceptical
sulfur	sulphur
blond	blonde
tidbit	titbit
tire	tyre
ax	axe
pajamas	pyjamas

(j)   The following creative spelling is noted especially in newspaper headlines and in advertising, in AE:

Xmas = Christmas
kool   = cool
Xing   = crossing
donut = doughnut
hi   = high
lo   = low
nite   = night
kwik   = quick
rite   = right
u   = you
thru   = through

SUMMARY

In this chapter, we looked at English spelling and its relationship with phonological patterns. Due to several historical factors, the present-day spelling of English possesses many discrepancies when measured by the ideal (one phoneme to one grapheme) alphabetic writing system. This, undoubtedly, makes the task of spellers difficult. However, it does not mean that we should judge the system totally defective, because its abstract lexical and morphological status serves as a useful tool for readers to create the connections.

1. The words in the following pairs are spelt differently; some pairs are pronounced the same (i.e. they are homophonous), and others are not. Identify each pair as either same (S) or different (D), and provide the phonetic transcription(s).

    Example: plain – plane (S)   [plen]
                    price – prize (D)   [praɪs] – [praɪz]

    (a)   key – quay
    (b)   gorilla – guerrilla
    (c)   person – parson
    (d)   profit – prophet
    (e)   rout – route
    (f)   draught – draft
    (g)   genes – jeans
    (h)   colonel – kernel
    (i)   raiser – razor
    (j)   patron – pattern
    (k)   temper – tamper
    (l)   cymbal – symbol
    (m) local – locale
    (n)   discreet – discrete
    (o)   review – revue
    (p)   critic – critique

2. Identify the vowel changes in the stressed syllables (spelt identically) of the following morphologically related words.

    Example: gradient – gradual   letter a [e] / [æ]

    derive – derivative
    provoke – provocative
    punitive – punishment
    harmonious – harmonic
    deduce – deduction
    satire – satiric
    serene – serenity
    major – majesty
    wild – wilderness

3. Find an appropriate morphologically related word for the similar vowel changes (represented by the same orthographic letter).

   Example: letter e̲   [i] / [ɛ]   austere – austerity

   (a) letter a̲ [e] / [æ]
       profane – _____   _____ – gratitude
       collate – _____   _____ – sanity

   (b) letter e̲ [i] / [ɛ]
       meter – _____   _____ – supremacy
       succeed – _____   _____ – discretion

   (c) letter i̲ [aɪ] / [ɪ]
       decide – _____   _____ – titular
       divine – _____   _____ – linear

   (d) letter o̲ [o] / [ɔ/ɑ]
       cone – _____   _____ – codify
       protest – _____   _____ – vocative

   (e) letter u̲ [u] / [ʌ]
       duke – _____   _____ – consumption
       resume – _____   _____ – assumption

4. Transcribe the following. Citations on American English (*from* T. McArthur, *The English Languages* (Cambridge: Cambridge University Press, 1998, pp. 220–7).

   (a) The foreign language which has most affected English in our own time is contemporary American. . . . The colloquial speech of the American is becoming, largely as a result of the foreign ingredients in the melting-pot, more and more remote from the spoken English of the educated Englishman, but, at the same time, the more slangy element in our language is being constantly reinforced by words and phrases taken from American, especially the type of American which is printed in the cinema caption. (*Ernest Weekley,* UK, 1928)

       ....
       ....
       ....
       ....
       ....

....

....

....

....

(b) It was the British empire, on which the sun never set, that originally spread English around the world, along with the tea breaks, cuffed trousers and the stiff upper lip. But when the imperial sun finally did set after World War II, the American language followed American power into the vacuum. (*Otto Friedrich* et al., US, 1986)

....

....

....

....

....

....

(c) Whose English language is it, anyway? From the tone of the new 'BBC News and Current Affairs Stylebook and Editorial Guide', you'd think the Brits invented it. With unmistakable disdain, the broadcastocrats in London call what we speak 'American'. As a user of Murkin English, I rise to the defense. (*William Safire*, US, 1993)

....

....

....

....

....

....

Recommended Readings

Topics covered in this book, with varying approaches and in varying depth, have been dealt with in several books and manuals. The following list is intended to help the reader gain further understanding of the issues discussed here.

Chapter 1: Phonetics

Clark and Yallop (1995), chapter 2
Ladefoged (2001a), chapter 1
Wolfram and Johnson (1982), chapter 1

Chapter 2: Phonology

Carr (1999), chapter 5
Katamba (1989), chapter 2
McMahon (2002), chapter 5
Wolfram and Johnson (1982), chapter 2

Chapter 3: English Consonants

Bowen (1975), chapters 3, 6, and 8
Celce-Murcia et al. (1996), chapter 3
Kreidler (2004), chapter 3
Ladefoged (2001a), chapter 3
Pennington (1996), chapter 2
Roach (1991), chapters 4, 6, and 7

CHAPTER 4: ENGLISH VOWELS

Bowen (1975), chapters 2, 4, and 8
Celce-Murcia et al. (1996), chapter 4
Davenport and Hannahs (1998), chapter 4
Giegerich (1992), chapter 3
Kreidler (2004), chapter 4
Pennington (1996), chapter 3

CHAPTER 5: ACOUSTICS OF VOWELS AND CONSONANTS

Kent and Read (1992), chapters 5–7
Ladefoged (2001a), chapter 8
Ladefoged (2001b), chapters 4–6
Lance and Howie (1994), pp. 267–344
Pickett (1980), chapters 5–9
Rogers (1991), chapter 9

CHAPTER 6: SYLLABLES

Carr (1999), chapter 7
Giegerich (1992), chapter 6
Hammond (1999), chapters 3 and 4
Kreidler (2004), chapter 6
Roach (1991), chapter 8
Yavaş (1998), chapter 9

CHAPTER 7: STRESS AND INTONATION

Bolinger (1989)
Carr (1999), chapter 8
Celce-Murcia et al. (1996), chapter 5
Hammond (1999), chapters 6 and 7
Kreidler (2004), chapters 9–11
Ladefoged (2001a), chapter 5

CHAPTER 8: STRUCTURAL FACTORS IN SECOND LANGUAGE PHONOLOGY

Avery and Ehrlich (1992), chapters 7 and 8
Kenworthy (1987), Part II
Major (2001), chapters 2–4
Scovel (1988), chapter 3

CHAPTER 9: SPELLING AND PRONUNCIATION

Carney (1997)
Celce-Murcia et al. (1996), chapter 9
Hall (1961), chapter 3
Kenworthy (1987), chapter 5
Pennington (1996), chapter 5
Wolfram and Johnson (1982), chapter 13

Glossary

affricate A consonant that is articulated via a complete oral closure followed by a slow release with a friction noise, as in the first and the last sounds of church.

alliteration The repeated use of the same initial consonant sound in a string of words.

allomorph Any of the forms that are the members of the same morpheme (with the same meaning). The forms [s], [z] and [əz] are the allomorphs of the plural morpheme (e.g. cats [kæts], dogs [dɔgz], and bushes [buʃəz]).

allophone Any of the phonetically similar sounds that are the realization of a single phoneme in varying contexts. For example, [pʰ] and [p] are the allophones of the phoneme /p/; the former occurs at the beginning of a stressed syllable (e.g. pay [pʰe]) and the other elsewhere (e.g. sport [spɔɹt]).

alveolar A consonant articulated in the region behind the upper front teeth (e.g. /t, s, n/).

ambisyllabic A consonant belonging to two syllables: /n/ in phoneme [fonim].

antepenult The third syllable from the end of the word (e.g. an.te.pe.nult).

approximant An articulation in which one articulator is close to another but not so close as to create a turbulent airstream (friction). In English, liquids, /l, ɹ/, and glides, /j, w/, are approximants.

aspiration A puff of air following the release of a voiceless stop at the beginning of a stressed syllable (e.g. pet [pʰɛt]).

assimilation A process whereby a speech sound is influenced by the surrounding sound(s) to make them more similar (e.g. voicing assimilation of the plural: cats [kæts], but dogs [dɔgz]).

bilabial A sound produced with both lips (e.g. /p, b, m/).

breathy voice (also **murmur**) A phonation type in which the vocal cords are only slightly apart.

cardinal vowels A system of conventional, arbitrarily chosen vowel qualities in terms of which actually occurring vowels may be identified.

citation form The form of a word when pronounced in isolation.

click A stop sound produced with a velaric ingressive airstream mechanism.

closed syllable A syllable that ends in one or more consonant sounds (i.e. a syllable with a coda (e.g. the first syllable of Atlanta, and the last syllable of geminate).

coda Whatever comes after the nucleus of the syllable (e.g. /t/ in cat).

consonant cluster Two or more adjacent tautosyllabic (in the same syllable) consonants (e.g. sprints has one three-consonant cluster at the beginning and one at the end).

content word   A word that contributes to the lexical meaning of an utterance; usually stressed (lexical morphemes such as nouns, verbs, adjectives, adverbs of time, manner, and place).

contraction   Deletion of the vocalic portion of auxiliary verbs and negations that creates the shortened forms (e.g. <u>I will</u> → <u>I'll</u>, <u>will not</u> → <u>won't</u>).

contrastive   Of a relation between two segments that can occur in the same environment to produce different meanings. From <u>pig</u> and <u>big</u>, we conclude that their initial sounds are contrastive.

creaky voice   (also **laryngealization**)   A type of phonation in which the arytenoid cartilages hold the posterior end of the vocal cords together so that they can vibrate only at the other end.

diphthong   A complex vowel sound in which the tongue moves from one position to another in the mouth (e.g. /aɪ/ in <u>buy</u>).

ejective   A stop sound produced with an egressive glottalic airstream.

elision   A process in which a consonant is left out in order to make the articulation easier (e.g. <u>fifth</u> is pronounced [fɪθ] instead of [fɪfθ]).

epenthesis   The insertion of one or more sounds in the middle of a word (e.g. <u>prince</u> is pronounced with an epenthetic [t], [pɹɪnts]).

formant   A concentration of acoustic energy within a particular frequency band.

frequency   The quantity representing the number of complete cycles performed by a given sound wave per unit time, commonly expressed in Hertz (Hz).

fricative   A consonant produced with a partial obstruction of the airstream in which the air is pushed through a narrow constriction, resulting in a friction noise (e.g. /f, s, θ/).

function word   A word that contributes little to the lexical meaning of an utterance; usually unstressed in a sentence (e.g. grammatical morphemes, such as prepositions, determiners, auxiliary verbs, and so on).

geminate   A sequence of two identical segments (e.g. geminate /n/ in Italian <u>nonno</u>). In English, it can occur only at morpheme boundaries (e.g. <u>unknown</u>).

glide (or **semi-vowel**)   A vowel-like speech sound which functions as a consonant (e.g. English /j, w/).

glottalic airstream mechanism   Upward/downward movement of pharynx air by the action of the glottis; stops produced this way are called **ejectives** (upward) and **implosives** (downward).

glottis   The space between the vocal cords.

heterosyllabic   Belonging to separate syllables (e.g. /b/ and /m/ are heterosyllabic in <u>submarine</u>).

homophones   Words that sound the same but are spelled differently (e.g. <u>right</u> – <u>write</u>, <u>scene</u> – <u>seen</u>).

homorganic   Of sounds, having the same place of articulation (e.g. the last two sounds of <u>limp</u> and <u>tent</u>).

implosive   A stop made with an ingressive glottalic airstream.

intonation   The pattern of pitch changes in a phrase or a sentence.

IPA   International Phonetics Association; also stands for the International Phonetic Alphabet.

labialization   The presence of some degree of lip rounding (e.g. English /ʃ, ʒ/).

labio-dental   An articulation involving the lower lip and the upper front teeth (e.g. /f, v/).

labio-velar   An articulation with the two lips approaching one another, and the back of the tongue raised toward the velum (e.g. /w/).

lateral   An articulation in which there is an obstruction in the midline but the airstream flows over the sides of the tongue (e.g. /l/).

lateral plosion   The release of a stop by lowering the sides of the tongue, as at the end of ladle.

liquids   Laterals and various kinds of r-sounds.

minimal pair   A set of two words that differ in one phoneme (e.g. chip – tip).

morpheme   The smallest meaningful unit in language. Cat has one morpheme, cats has two, unfaithful has three, and unfaithfulness has four morphemes.

murmur   See **breathy voice**.

nasal   A sound produced with a lowered velum so that, when the closure in the mouth is released, the air rushes out through the nose as well as through the mouth (e.g. the initial and final sounds of moon).

nasal plosion   The release of a stop by lowering the velum, so that the air escapes through the nose (e.g. the end of sudden).

nucleus   The most prominent part (peak) of a syllable; most often a vowel or a diphthong.

obstruent   A sound that is articulated with an obstruction in the vocal tract, which is enough to produce friction noise (e.g. stops, fricatives, and affricates).

onset   The components of a syllable preceding the rhyme (e.g. /bl/ of blue).

open syllable   A syllable with no consonant sound at the end (e.g. bee).

palato-alveolar   An articulation between the tongue blade and the back of the alveolar ridge (e.g. /ʃ, dʒ/).

penult   The next-to-last syllable in a word (e.g. pho.no.**lo.gy**).

phonetics   The study of speech sounds.

phonology   The description of patterns of sounds in a language.

phonotactics   A set of constraints of the possible sequences of phonemes within a syllable or a word.

pitch   The perceptual correlate of the frequency of a sound. The higher the frequency of vocal cord vibration, the higher the pitch.

prosody   See **suprasegmentals**.

pulmonic airstream mechanism   The movement of lung air by the respiratory muscles.

reduced vowel   A vowel that is pronounced with a centralized schwa ([ə]) quality (e.g. the first vowel of photography and the second vowel of photograph).

resonance   The way in which the body of air in the vocal tract will vibrate when set in motion.

retroflex   An articulation involving the tip of the tongue and the back of the alveolar ridge.

rhotic   Referring to a dialect in which /r/ is pronounced in any position of occurrence.

rhyme   The part of a syllable that follows the onset (e.g. /int/ in print).

segment   An individual sound, consonant or vowel.

semi-vowel   See **glide**.

sibilant   A fricative or an affricate that is produced with a high frequency energy, usually by means of a groove in the tongue (e.g. /s, z, ʃ, ʒ, tʃ, dʒ/).

sonorant   A sound that is not an obstruent (nasals, liquids, glides, vowels).

spectrogram   A picture of a sound showing how the component frequencies change with time.

stop   A consonant sound that is produced with a complete closure in some part of the vocal tract, followed by an abrupt release (e.g. /p, d, k/).

stress   Emphasis on a particular syllable established by loudness, greater duration, and higher pitch.

stress-timing   The rhythm in which stressed syllables occur at approximately equal intervals.

suprasegmentals   Phonetic features that apply to units greater than segments (i.e. syllables, phrases, sentences), such as stress, length, tone, and intonation.

syllabic consonant   A consonant which, in a particular case, functions as a syllabic nucleus (e.g. /n/ in button).

syllable-timing   The rhythm in which each syllable has equal weight and duration.

tautosyllabic   Refers to segments that belong to the same syllable. For example, /mp/ in temptation is tautosyllabic, but is not in complain.

tone   A particular pitch that affects the meaning of a word.

tonic syllable   The syllable that carries the major pitch change.

ult   The last syllable in a word (e.g. ra.di.o).

uvular   An articulation involving the back of the tongue and the uvula.

velar   An articulation involving the back of the tongue and the velum (e.g. /k, g, ŋ/).

velaric airstream mechanism   Movement of the mouth air by action of the tongue, as in clicks.

velarization   Raising the back of the tongue toward the velum, as in the dark /l/ (e.g. full).

voice bar   A dark area near the baseline in a spectrogram, indicating voicing in a consonant.

voiced   Refers to sounds made with the vocal cords vibrating (e.g. /b, d, m, w, z/).

voiceless   Refers to sounds made without vocal cord vibration (e.g. /p, s, k, ʃ, θ/).

voice onset time   The interval between the release of a stop and the start of voicing for the following segment.

weak form   The common, unstressed form of a function word (e.g. [ðət] for that).

References

Avery, P. and Ehrlich, S. (1992). *Teaching American English Pronunciation*. Oxford: Oxford University Press.

Bailey, C.-J. N. (1983). A concise but comprehensive approach to intonation for learners of English, *Arbeiten aus Anglistik und Amerikanistik* 8, 3: 3–27.

Ball, M. and Lowry, O. (2001). *Methods in Clinical Phonetics*. London: Whurr.

Baptista, B. and DaSilva Filho, J. (1997). The influence of markedness and syllable contact on the production of English final consonants by EFL learners. In J. Leather and A. James (eds.), *New Sounds 97: Proceedings of the Third International Symposium on the Acquisition of Second Language Speech* (pp. 26–34). Klagenfurt: University of Klagenfurt.

Beland, R., Caplan, D., and Nespoulous, J. L. (1990). The role of abstract phonological representation in word production: evidence from phonemic paraphasias, *Journal of Neurolinguistics* 5: 125–64.

Blumstein, S. (1978). Segment structure and the syllable in aphasia. In A. Bell and J. B. Hooper (eds.), *Syllables and Segments*. Amsterdam: North Holland.

Bolinger, D. (1989). *Intonation and its Uses*. Stanford, CA: Stanford University Press.

Bolinger, D. (1998). Intonation in American English. In D. Hirst and A. DiCristo (eds.), *Intonation Systems* (pp. 45–55). Cambridge: Cambridge University Press.

Bowen, J. D. (1975). *Patterns of English Pronunciation*. Rowley, MA: Newbury House.

Broselow, E. (1993). Transfer and universals in second language epenthesis. In S. Gass and L. Selinker (eds.), *Language Transfer in Language Learning* (pp. 71–86). Amsterdam: John Benjamins.

Broselow, E. and Finer, D. (1991). Parameter setting in second language phonology and syntax, *Second Language Research* 7: 35–59.

Camarata, S. and Gandour, J. (1984). On describing idiosyncratic phonologic systems, *Journal of Speech and Hearing Disorders* 49: 262–6.

Carney, E. (1994). *A Survey of English Spelling*. London: Routledge.

Carney, E. (1997). *English Spelling*. London: Routledge.

Carr, P. (1999). *English Phonetics and Phonology*. Oxford: Blackwell.

Catford, J. C. (1977). *Fundamental Problems in Phonetics*. Edinburgh: Edinburgh University Press.

Celce-Murcia, M., Brinton, D. M., and Goodwin, J. M. (1996). *Teaching Pronunciation*. Cambridge: Cambridge University Press.

Chin, S. (1996). The role of sonority hierarchy in delayed phonological systems. In T. W. Powell (ed.), *Pathologies of Speech and Language: Contributions of Clinical Phonetics and Linguistics* (pp. 109–17). New Orleans: International Clinical Phonetics and Linguistics Association.

Christman, S. S. (1992). Uncovering phonological regularity in neologisms: contributions of sonority theory, *Clinical Linguistics and Phonetics* 6: 219–47.

Clark, J. and Yallop, C. (1995). *An Introduction to Phonetics and Phonology*. Oxford: Blackwell.

Code, C. and Ball, M. J. (1982). Fricative production in Broca's aphasia: a spectrographic analysis, *Journal of Phonetics* 10: 325–31.

Crystal, T. H. and House, A. S. (1982). Segmental durations in connected speech signals: preliminary results, *Journal of the Acoustical Society of America* 72: 705–16.

Dauer, R. M. (1983). Stress-timing and syllable-timing re-analyzed, *Journal of Phonetics* 11: 51–62.

Davenport, M. and Hannahs, S. J. (1998). *Introducing Phonetics and Phonology*. London: Arnold.

Davis, S. (1988). *Topics in Syllable Geometry*. New York: Garland.

Eckman, F. (1977). Markedness and the contrastive analysis hypothesis, *Language Learning* 27: 315–30.

Eckman, F. (1985). Some theoretical and pedagogical implications of the markedness differential hypothesis, *Studies in Second Language Acquisition* 13: 23–41.

Eckman, F., Elreyes, A., and Iverson, G. (2003). Some principles of second language phonology, *Second Language Research* 19, 3: 169–208.

Eckman, F. and Iverson, G. (1994). Pronunciation difficulties in ESL: coda consonants in English interlanguage. In M. Yavaş (ed.), *First and Second Language Phonology* (pp. 251–65). San Diego, CA: Singular Publishing.

Ertmer, D. J. (2004). How well can children recognize speech features in spectrograms? Comparisons by age and hearing status, *Journal of Speech, Language and Hearing Research* 47: 484–95.

Ertmer, D. J. and Stark, R. E. (1995). Eliciting prespeech vocalization in a young child with profound hearing impairment: usefulness of real-time spectrographic displays, *American Journal of Speech-Language Pathology* 4: 22–38.

Ertmer, D. J., Stark, R. E., and Karlan, G. R. (1996). Real-time spectrographic displays in vowel production training with children who have profound hearing loss, *American Journal of Speech-Language Pathology* 5: 4–16.

Flege, J. E. (1987). The production of 'new' and 'similar' phones in a foreign language: evidence for the effect of equivalence classification, *Journal of Phonetics* 15: 47–65.

Flege, J. E. (1990). English vowel production by Dutch talkers: more evidence for the 'similar' vs. 'new' distinction. In J. Leather and A. James (eds.), *New Sounds 90: Proceedings of the Amsterdam Symposium on the Acquisition of Second Language Speech* (pp. 255–93). Amsterdam: University of Amsterdam.

Flege, J. E. (1991). Age of learning affects the authenticity of voice-onset time (VOT) in stop consonants produced in second language learning, *Journal of the Acoustical Society of America* 89: 395–411.

Fromkin, V. A. (1973). *Speech Errors as Linguistic Evidence*. Berlin: Walter de Gruyter.

Fry, D. B. (1955). Duration and intensity as physical correlates of linguistic stress, *Journal of the Acoustical Society of America* 27: 765–8.

Fry, D. B. (1979). *The Physics of Speech*. Cambridge: Cambridge University Press.

Giegerich, H. (1992). *English Phonology*. Boston, MA: Cambridge University Press.

Hall, R. A. (1961). *Sounds and Spelling in English*. New York: Chilton Books.

Hammond, M. (1999). *The Phonology of English*. Oxford: Oxford University Press.

Hansen, J. (2001). Linguistic constraints on the acquisition of English syllable codas by native speakers of Mandarin Chinese, *Applied Linguistics* 22: 338–65.

Hogg, R. and McCully, C. (1987). *Metrical Phonology: A Coursebook*. Cambridge: Cambridge University Press.

Jaeger, J. J. (1978). Speech aerodynamics and phonological universals, *Proceedings of the Berkeley Linguistics Society* 4: 311–29.

Jenkins, J. (2002). *World Englishes*. London: Routledge.

Katamba, F. (1989). *An Introduction to Phonology*. London: Longman.

Kent, R. D. and Read, C. (1992). *The Acoustic Analysis of Speech*. San Diego, CA: Singular Publishing.

Kenworthy, J. (1987). *Teaching English Pronunciation*. London: Longman.

Klatt, D. (1975). Voice onset time, frication and aspiration in word-initial consonant clusters, *Journal of Speech and Hearing Research* 18: 686–706.

Kreidler, C. (2004). *The Pronunciation of English* (2nd edn.). Oxford: Blackwell.

Ladefoged, P. (2001a). *A Course in Phonetics* (4th edn.). Boston, MA: Heinle & Heinle.

Ladefoged, P. (2001b). *Vowels and Consonants*. Oxford: Blackwell.

Laeufer, C. (1996). The acquisition of complex phonological contrast: voice timing patterns of English initial stops by French native speakers, *Phonetica* 53: 86–110.

Lance, D. M. and Howie, S. M. (1994). Spectrographic analysis of English phonemes and allophones. In J. K. Kenyon, *American Pronunciation*. Ann Arbor, MI: Whurr.

McArthur, T. (1998). *The English Languages*. Cambridge: Cambridge University Press.

McMahon, A. (2002). *An Introduction to English Phonology*. Oxford: Oxford University Press.

Maddieson, I. (1984). *Patterns of Sounds*. Cambridge: Cambridge University Press.

Major, R. C. (1987). English voiceless stop production by speakers of Brazilian Portuguese, *Journal of Phonetics* 15: 197–202.

Major, R. C. (2001). *Foreign Accent: The Ontogeny and Phylogeny of Second Language Phonology*. Mahwah, NJ: Lawrence Erlbaum Associates.

Major, R. C. and Kim, E. (1999). The similarity differential rate hypothesis, *Language Learning* 46: 465–96.

Maki, J. E. (1980). Visual feedback as an aid to speech therapy. In J. Subtelney (ed.), *Speech Assessment and Speech Improvement for the Hearing-Impaired* (pp. 167–76). Washington, DC: A. G. Bell Associates.

Maki, J. E. (1983). Application of the speech spectrographic display in developing articulatory skills in hearing-impaired adults. In I. Hochberg, H. Levitt, and M. J. Osberger (eds.), *Speech of the Hearing-Impaired: Research, Training, and Personnel Preparation* (pp. 297–312). Baltimore: University Park Press.

Maki, J. E., Streff-Gustafson, M. S., Conklin, J. M., and Humphrey-Whitehead, B. K. (1981). The speech spectrographic display: interpretation of visual patterns by hearing-impaired adults, *Journal of Speech and Hearing Disorders* 46: 379–87.

Ohala, D. K. (1999). The influence of sonority on children's cluster reductions, *Journal of Communication Disorders* 32: 397–422.

Oller, J. W. and Ziahosseyni, S. M. (1970). The contrastive analysis hypothesis and spelling errors, *Language Learning* 20: 183–9.

Paolillo, J. (1995). Markedness in the acquisition of English /r/ and /l/. In F. Eckman, D. Highland, P. Lee, J. Mileham, and R. Weber (eds.), *Second Language Acquisition Theory and Pedagogy* (pp. 275–91). Mahwah, NJ: Lawrence Erlbaum.

Pennington, M. C. (1996). *Phonology in English Language Teaching*. London: Longman.

Peterson, G. E. and Barney, H. E. (1952). Control methods used in a study of vowels, *Journal of the Acoustical Society of America* 24: 175–84.

Pickett, J. M. (1980). *The Sounds of Speech Communication: A Primer of Acoustic Phonetics and Speech Perception*. Boston, MA: Allyn & Bacon.

Port, R. F. and Rotunno, R. (1978). The relation between voice-onset time and vowel duration, *Journal of the Acoustical Society of America* 66: 654–62.

Roach, P. (1991). *English Phonetics and Phonology*. Cambridge: Cambridge University Press.

Rogers, H. (1991). *Theoretical and Practical Phonetics*. Toronto: Copp Clark Pitman.

Romani, C. and Calabrese, A. (1998). Syllabic constraints in the phonological errors of an aphasic patient, *Brain and Language* 64: 83–121.

Scovel, T. (1988). *A Time to Speak: A Psycholinguistic Inquiry into Critical Period for Human Speech*. New York: Harper & Row.

Selkirk, E. (1984). On major class features and syllable theory. In M. Aranoff and R. T. Oehrle (eds.), *Language and Sound Structure: Studies in Phonology Presented to Morris Halle by his Teacher and Students* (pp. 107–36). Cambridge, MA: MIT Press.

Thurnburg, D. and Ryalls, J. (1998). Voice onset time in Spanish–English bilinguals: early versus late learners of English, *Journal of Communication Disorders* 31: 215–29.

Trudgill, P. and Hannah, J. (2002). *International English* (4th edn.). London: Edward Arnold.

Weismer, G. (1979). Sensitivity of voice-onset time (VOT) to certain segmental features in speech production, *Journal of Phonetics* 7: 197–204.

Wells, J. C. (1982). *Accents of English*. Cambridge: Cambridge University Press.

Wolfram, W. and Johnson, R. (1982). *Phonological Analysis: Focus on American English*. Englewood Cliffs, NJ: Prentice Hall.

Yavaş, M. (1996). Differences in voice onset time in early and later Spanish–English bilinguals. In J. Jensen and A. Roca (eds.), *Spanish in Contact: Issues in Bilingualism* (pp. 151–61). Somerville, MA: Cascadilla Press.

Yavaş, M. (1997). The effects of vowel height and place of articulation in interlanguage final stop devoicing, *International Review of Applied Linguistics* 35: 115–25.

Yavaş, M. (1998). *Phonology: Development and Disorders*. San Diego, CA: Singular Publishing.

Yavaş, M. (2002). Voice onset time in bilingual phonological development. In F. Windsor, M. L. Kelly, and N. Hewlett (eds.), *Investigations in Clinical Phonetics and Linguistics* (pp. 341–50). Mahwah, NJ: Lawrence Erlbaum.

Yavaş, M. and Someillan, M. (in press). Patterns of acquisition of /s/-clusters in Spanish–English bilinguals, *Journal of Multilingual Communication Disorders*.

Index

The index lists the technical terms and names in the book, together with the number of section(s) in which they are introduced/discussed.